Celtic Dimensions

of the

British Civil Wars

Celtic Dimensions of the British Civil Wars

Proceedings of the
Second Conference of the
Research Centre in Scottish History
University of Strathclyde

Edited by

JOHN R YOUNG

Lecturer in History
University of Strathclyde

JOHN DONALD PUBLISHERS LTD
EDINBURGH

ISBN 0 85976 452 4

British Library Cataloguing in Publication Data.

A catalogue record for this book is available
from the British Library.

Front Cover: Charles I, with Edinburgh in
the background. By Cornelius van Dalen.

PostScript Typesetting & Origination by Brinnoven, Livingston.
Printed & bound in Great Britain by Bell & Bain Ltd, Glasgow.

Acknowledgements

This collection of essays is based on the proceedings of the Second Conference of the Research Centre in Scottish History, University of Strathclyde, held on 5 April 1995. The overall aim of the conference was to bring together a new generation of younger historians working in Scottish and Irish aspects of the British Civil Wars. The conference itself was highly successful and attracted an international audience of scholars from Scotland, Ireland (north and south), and England, undergraduate students, and interested members of the public. The success and organisation of the conference was greatly enhanced by the contributions of various individuals at the University of Strathclyde. Professor Tom Devine, Professor of Scottish History, Director of the Research Centre in Scottish History, and Deputy Principal of the University Strathclyde is greatly thanked for his continuous academic encouragement and support for the whole idea of the conference from day one, as well as institutional backing as a senior officer of the university. Dr Richard Finlay, Associate Director of the Research Centre, is likewise thanked not only for his strong academic backing, but also his personal help in the minutiae of organising a successful conference. Professor Jim McMillan, Professor of European History and the former Head of Department, was similarly very helpful in the release of departmental funds to support the travel of several of the younger historians from Ireland. Dr Simon Adams, a recognised international authority in early modern British History, is thanked for his academic encouragement and his overall support to strengthen the early modern historical base at Strathclyde. In terms of the conference itself, Dr John Morrill, Professor Allan Macinnes, Professor Ted Cowan, and Professor Aidan Clarke are thanked for their professional expertise in chairing the conference sessions. Last but not least, I owe a personal debt of gratitude to Neil Rafeek and David Forsyth, two of our Strathclyde postgraduate students, for their efficient organisational skills on the day of the conference itself. Their professionalism and commitment ensured that the conference ran smoothly. Many thanks likewise go to Russell Walker and the staff of John Donald for their full support for this new venture from a very early stage.

John R Young, Glasgow 1996

Abbreviations and Conventions

AHR   *American Historical Review*

APS   *Acts of the Parliaments of Scotland*, T Thomson & C Innes (eds), volumes v-vii (Edinburgh, 1814–1872)

BAV   Biblioteca Apostolica Vaticana

BL   British Library

CSPD   *Calendar of State Papers Domestic* (1637-1661), seventeen volumes, W D Hamilton & M A Everett Green (eds), (London, 1869-1886)

EHR   *English Historical Review*

EUL   Edinburgh University Library

HJ   *The Historical Journal*

HMC   Historical Manuscripts Commission

NLI   National Library of Ireland

NLS   National Library of Scotland

PRO   Public Records Office

RPCS   *Records of the Privy Council of Scotland*

RSCHS   *Records of the Scottish Church History Society*

SHR   *The Scottish Historical Review*

SHS   Scottish History Society

SRO   Scottish Records Office

TCD   Trinity College Dublin

TRHS   *Transactions of the Royal Historical Society*

Contents

Notes on Contributors

Sharon Adams is a postgraduate student in the Department of Scottish History at the University of Edinburgh. She is completing a doctoral thesis on religion, politics, and society in south-west Scotland in the reigns of James VI and Charles I.

Éamonn ó Ciardha is a graduate student at Clare Hall, University of Cambridge. He is currently completing a doctoral thesis on Jacobitism in Ireland and among Irish exiles in the eighteenth century. His Master's thesis at University College Dublin was entitled 'Woodkerne, Tories, and Rapparees in Ulster and north Connaught in seventeenth-century Ireland'.

Dr John Coffey is a Junior Research Fellow at Churchill College, University of Cambridge. His book on Samuel Rutherford is due to be published by Cambridge University Press in 1997.

Dr Tadhg ó hAnnracháin completed a PhD at the European University Institute in 1995. He is a College Lecturer at University College Dublin and is currently completing a book on the role of the Papal Nuncio in Ireland during the 1640s.

Clare Jackson is a postgraduate student at the University of Cambridge, researching a doctorate on the intellectual history of Restoration Scotland. For her Master's degree she undertook an analysis of the political thought of Sir George Mackenzie.

Dr William Kelly recently completed his doctoral thesis, 'The Early Career of James Butler, twelfth Earl and first Duke of Ormond, (1610–88), 1610–43' at the University of Cambridge in 1995. Dr Kelly lectures for the Workers' Educational Association (WEA) in Londonderry.

Dr Ronnie Lee has recently completed his PhD thesis in the Department of Scottish History at the University of Glasgow. His doctoral thesis was entitled 'Government and Politics in Scotland, 1661–1681' (1995).

Dr Pádraig Lenihan teaches at the University of Limerick. His doctoral thesis at University College Galway dealt with the war effort of the Confederate Catholics in Ireland, 1642–49 and he has published a number of articles on early modern Irish history and on military history.

Dr John Morrill is a Fellow and Vice-Master and Reader in Early Modern History at Selwyn College, University of Cambridge. He has recently been elected as a Fellow of the British Academy and he has been at the forefront of the recent debates on the British Civil War(s).

Dr John Scally is a Curator in the Department of Printed Books in the National Library of Scotland. He completed his PhD on 'The Political Career of James, third Marquis and first Duke of Hamilton (1606–1649) to 1643' at Cambridge University and he is researching a full biography of Hamilton.

Dr John Young is a Lecturer in History at the University of Strathclyde and a member of the Research Centre in Scottish History there. He undertook his PhD research in the Department of Scottish History at the University of Glasgow. He has recently published *The Scottish Parliament 1639–1661: A Political and Constitutional Analysis* (1996).

CHAPTER 1

Historical Introduction and Overview: The Un-English Civil War

John Morrill

Sir William Brereton was the firebrand Puritan MP for Cheshire in the Long Parliament and the Roundhead commander-in-chief in the West Midlands in the English Civil War of 1642–46. Only twice in his life — as far as we know — did he leave England. In 1634 he went to the Netherlands to further his knowledge of agriculture and horticulture and to visit as many churches of as many Protestant denominations as he could. And in 1635 he went on a more extended tour of Scotland and Ireland. He went to Scotland to escape the fetid air of Laudian England and to breathe in the ozone-laden breezes of Calvinist discipline. He went to Ireland to see whether the displacement of papist landowners by Protestant planters was as good an investment opportunity as it was a godly imperative. In the event he decided against, and bought lands instead on the Charles River in Massachusetts Bay.[1]

Brereton was not untypical of seventeenth-century Englishmen in his condescending attitudes to the Scots and his warily exploitative attitudes to the Irish. Twentieth-century historians — especially those like myself born so close to Brereton's birthplace — must be wary of falling into the same traps.

The recent explosion of interest in the War(s) of the Three Kingdoms or the British Civil Wars has been largely initiated by English or Anglocentric historians and can all too easily appear as a new form of cultural imperialism. Keith Brown recognizes that 'the politics and religion of seventeenth-century Britain does demand some weaving together of the different national histories of the three kingdoms' but he also finds that too often English historians indulge in a form of 'tokenism' and in English history writ large, or at least that for them 'the emergence of the British state looks like a reincarnation of the English state.'[2] And Nicholas Canny, addressing me directly, pleads for the merits of a comparative but not an integrationist or holistic account of the affairs of the three kingdoms.[3]

Whatever else this splendid collection of essays represents, it represents an antidote to such hazards. Here are six Scots and four Irish

1

scholars (and I defy anyone to determine from their writing which five took or are taking their doctorates in Cambridge!) writing about a scattered selection of topics united by being about non-English aspects of the crisis of Triple Monarchy in the mid-seventeenth century. The emphasis is very much not on how events in Scotland and Ireland contribute to the outcome of events in England but on the internal dynamics of the Scottish and Irish rebellions against Stuart mis-government. And yet it is a book which in sum teaches us much about the ways in which historians of Ireland and Scotland (and England) can learn from one another. In a sense, we have until recently had a situation in which English, Irish, and Scottish historians have had conversations about the same sort of things, but each group has been in separate if adjacent rooms. They have thus occasionally caught snatches of conversation through the walls, and have been tempted into shouting comments which have sometimes been heard and sometimes not. More recently, the English have been holding parties calling everyone together and demanding that all join in the discussion they have initiated. This book represents a meeting from which the English were excluded (or told they would only be admitted if they promised to stay silent) and in which the Irish and the Scots carry on conversations amongst themselves, one group occasionally addressing comments directly at the other. Nonetheless, these are conversations members of each group find themselves drawn to eavesdrop on, conversations which feed into their own internal debate.

It would be idle to pretend that there was much more coherence to this book than that. It represents the happy conjunction of a group of ten young scholars — at the time of the conference five had recently gained doctorates and five were completing — coming together to report what they had discovered. There is an occasionally raw but always vital, engaged, fresh feel to these essays. The subjects vary greatly and there is no great congruity or coherence thematically or methodologically. What binds the volume together is a very loose sense of the need to examine the non-English aspects of British civil wars. What is striking, however, is the ways pairs of essays, more often than not by happenstance rather than design, *chime* with one another. This is true of the essays by Scally and Kelly, of Adams and ó hAnnracháin, of Lenihan and ó Ciardha, of Coffey and Jackson; Young, and Lee; Lee and Jackson, and more. In the process, the essays pour floods of light on the origins, nature, course, intellectual and social contexts, and consequences of the conflicts within Ireland and Scotland, between Ireland and Scotland, and (willy-nilly and not by intention) between

Scotland, Ireland and England. Thus the smile of the Cheshire cat remains ever-present, seeking to avoid condescension.

Origins

The early chapters all remind us that there is one transcendent cause of the war(s) of the three kingdoms[4] — Charles I himself. John Scally lays bare the monarch's incomprehending mismanagement of the Scottish crisis of 1638–40 (an 'uncounsellable king'[5] as he puts it). His careful analysis is a devastating indictment of a king who would not be told the truth, and could not recognize reality even when it stared him in the face. Scally shows how a shrewd and knowing Marquis of Hamilton was unable to tell the king 'that what he wanted was ridiculous or unfeasible. He could only illustrate the impossibility of the king's demand by telling him what would be required to effect it.' Twice, Scally suggests, Hamilton showed the king how a disagreeable damage-limitation exercise could end the current crisis:

> in June 1638 Hamilton advised Charles to sacrifice the
> Canons, Prayer Book and Perth Articles, and to accept the
> explanation of the Covenant in order to gather a Royalist
> party and save Episcopacy in a reduced form. [The
> following year] it was to sacrifice Episcopacy to save
> his civil authority,[6]

As early as June 1638 Hamilton was far-sighted enough to tell Charles that 'itt shall never by my advyse if your Matti can clearlie sea hou ye can effeckt your end uithout the haserdding of your 3 crounes.'[7]

Billy Kelly's essay is no less impressive in its analysis of the paralyzing assertiveness of Charles I's policy in Ireland. Spurning the advice of Wentworth on the limits of the possible in using troops from Ireland to resolve the Scottish crisis, Charles demanded the unleashing of the Catholic Irish on the Western Highlands. If anything were to hazard Charles's position in the three kingdoms it was this provocation and this escalation. But Kelly goes on to show that even when Wentworth got his way and Charles fell back on the Protestants of Ireland as his helpmeets, he was seriously overreaching himself. Where Hamilton practiced a soft-shoe shuffle to avoid the public odium for being the instrument of a doomed policy in Scotland, the 24 year old Earl of Ormond, Lieutenant General of the Protestant Army in Ireland and (in Wentworth's absence trying to talk sense into Charles) its commander-in-chief, adopted a less sophisticated but equally effective policy of pleading his wife's sickliness as an excuse for immuring himself at Kilkenny so as to avoid personal responsibility for the crumbling of Charles's fantastical three-kingdom attempt to bully his Scottish subjects into submission. Ormond's behaviour demonstrates

> a fundamental unease at the irrevocable drift to war and
> [at] the ultimate aim of royal policy. [It represents] a
> shrewd politician's assessment of the risks his own
> prominent role might entail.[8]

Ormond's yearning for office and advancement was controlled by a precocious sense of self-preservation. Charles's paranoia was driven by the unreasonable demands he placed on those he at once trusted and distrusted.

When Charles appointed men capable of giving him sound advice, he was incapable of listening to them. Increasingly he turned to men who had as little sense of the limits of the king's enforceable will as the king himself. Two of the essays in this book — those by Sharon Adams and John Coffey — draw attention to one such man, Thomas Sydserff, who stands as representative of Charles attempts to introduce ecclesiastical *intendants* into Scotland. What is striking is the very evident counter-productive zeal of what Adams calls the 'new-deal episcopate.'[9]

Each of these case studies, then helps us to see that it is not enough to say, as some have done, that Charles I had an English problem because he had a Scottish and Irish problem. If we want to understand the fall of the Stuart monarchies it is better to begin by recognizing that Scotland, Ireland, and England all had a Charles I problem. Beyond this, however, the essays in this book demonstrate what Conrad Russell has called the 'billiard-ball effect' of events in one kingdom in events in the others,[10] and the ways in which one kingdom provides a yardstick against which to gauge events elsewhere.

Thus I could not help being struck by the irony of Billy Kelly's discussion of Wentworth's remarks to Secretary Windebank that the arming of the O's and the Macs, sons of habituated rebels, would affright the whole council:

> what might become of the English in Ireland, the Lord
> Deputy asked, if Antrim's native Irish troops were to
> fall suddenly on them, armed, of all things, with weapon
> supplied by the government in Dublin.[11]

It was for his alleged offer to let the English of Ireland, armed by the government of Dublin, fall upon the English of England that Wentworth was to lose his head on Tower Hill just two years later.

More substantial are the reminders we find in these essays that the events in each kingdom do impinge on events in the others. Kelly again reminds us that

> Wentworth's primary concern in the early stages of the
> Scottish crisis was how it would affect Ireland, even if
> all minds at court were preoccupied with Scotland.[12]

And Tadhg ó hAnnracháin is unambiguous in showing how the
Scottish National Covenant inspired the oath of the Catholic
Confederation as its members strove to legitimate their political
structures in 1642. As his essay unfolds, the likely fruitfulness of an
extended comparison of and contrast between the role of the clergy in
Scotland and Ireland across the 1640s becomes apparent. The
intellectual congruence is made the more credible by John Coffey's
demonstration of the ease with which a radical Calvinist could draw
on the writings of Spanish neo-Thomists. Is it too fanciful to claim that
in societies like Catholic Ireland and Lowland Scotland where the
secular instruments of law and arbitration were so much less visible
(and actual) than in England, and where social welfare and much moral
policing remained with the church rather than (as in England) in the
civil officers of a civil parish, the Presbyterian minister and Catholic
priest retained an authority that was vanishing in England. Sharon
Adams's account of the role of the minister in south-west Scotland
certainly bears this out. This would make the development of growing
powerful clericisms in the 1640s in Scotland and Ireland more
comprehensible. There are important contrasts, of course, but also a
crucial contrast with the way clerical power in England went back-
wards. When Cromwell invaded Ireland in 1649–50 he was confronted
by the Irish clergy gathered in conclave at Clonmacnoise. When he
invaded Scotland, he was confronted by the Scottish clergy in conclave
at Edinburgh. When was he ever confronted by the English clergy
gathered together as a self-appointed conclave?

The Nature of the Conflict

To ask whether the conflicts within the 'Atlantic archipelago'[13] add up
to one big conflict or a series of separate conflicts which keep on
getting muddled together is to ask a very familiar question. There is a
helpful parallel, of course, with the Thirty Years War (1618–48), a
complex series of interlocking wars. The Kings of Spain and France
no doubt saw it as a single entity and planned strategically when and
in which theatres to intervene. As Holy Roman Emperor, Ferdinand II
(1619–1637) probably had a slightly narrower perspective. It is
unlikely that he saw English attempts to come to help of the Huguenots
at La Rochelle as part of his attempt to reassert his dynastic rights
throughout the Habsburg lands and Imperial power within the Holy

Roman Empire. A similar narrowed view prevailed in Amsterdam, Copenhagen and Stockholm; and it would have been narrower again in Poland or Transylvania. And at the level of the peasant farmer, the local war was quite enough to know about. So, at one level, the nature of war looked very different from the perspective of Charles I, Ormond or Hamilton than from the perspective of a farmer in Suffolk, Dingwall, or the island of Mull. The fact that it was a single conflict in different theatres for those who moved tens of thousands of men around between the kingdoms makes it more obviously a single war. In the course of 1643 and 1644, for example, there were significant numbers of Irish soldiers in England and Scotland, Scottish soldiers in England and Ireland, and English soldiers in Ireland but not Scotland.

But then again armies behaved differently depending not on where they came from, but where they found themselves. The brute fact is that there were a set of rules and conventions of warfare — such as the conduct of sieges and the taking and care of prisoners — which acted as a kind of set of Geneva Conventions *avant la lettre* and which operated in England and which all armies fighting in England observed for the greater part.[14] None of these conventions applied to the same extent in Scotland and Ireland and many did not apply at all. This is specifically true of English or Scottish armies in Ireland.[15] The 'British' had no way of keeping prisoners and the English practice of inviting captured soldiers to change sides just did not apply. Officers could be ransomed and common soldiers were best killed. And then there was an element of reprisal and deliberate *in terrorem* menace. Cromwell's behaviour at Drogheda and Wexford reflected the Irish-theatre codes of military conduct. He had adapted quickly.

The essays in this volume add considerably to our understanding of this issue. Pádraig Lenihan's main purpose is to explain how the Confederates lost the war in Ireland, but in the process he lays the ghost that the war in Ireland saw an uneven contest between 'modern' English and Scottish armies and 'Celtic warfare' heroically but disastrously committed to the 'Highland charge'. The armies of the Confederation were trained in Spanish rather than Swedish ways and that put them at a disadvantage, but it was shortage of cavalry rather than outmoded weapons and tactics that tipped the balance against them in the large open engagements. In Scotland, Montrose's Irish Redshanks could still revert to traditional clan warfare and win. This reinforces the view that the part of the war(s) that fits least satisfactorily into a 'one-war in three theatres model' is the renewal of bloodfeud in the Western and Northern Highlands. It distracted the

Campbells but not the Lowland nobility and lairds who controlled the Covenanting Movement in Edinburgh. It gave false hope to Charles I, but it was a pyrotechnic sideshow. So it is not how they fought, but under what rules of engagement, that distinguishes the various theatres of the war.

Éamonn ó Ciardha's essay offers a rather different but complementary perspective. He looks at what happened when the Confederate armies disintegrated and the Cromwellian armies allowed political control to pass to the English Commonwealth. He too challenges two false assumptions: the first that all the defeated Confederate soldiers took up the invitation to flee to the Continent to fill the mercenary forces of the Catholic kings; and the second that the Woodkerne, 'Tories', and Rapparees were 'mere bandits' whose preying on the countryside was graced by no political or religious vision. Ó Ciardha draws on a particularly impressive range of sources — not least in his sensitive handling of Gaelic poetry — to show that much 'Tory' activity was in fact the disciplined and purposeful work of deregimented but not undisciplined Confederates conducting a guerrila war against the English army and settlers. I thought his recovery of the excommunication issued by the Catholic clergy in December 1649 which differentiated between confederate stealths and 'Tories and such plunderers not in colours'[16] was particularly revealing. Discovering that there are bandits and then there are stealths reminds me of the difference between pirates and privateers.

In two other respects, ó Ciardha tantalizes. He offers us some suggestive parallels between his Irish Tories and the Moss-troopers of the Highlands, and I wish he had had space to develop his ideas about the 'notable comparison between the dwindling fortunes of the Scottish Cavalier Middleton and his Confederate counterpart Sir Phelim O'Neill.'[17] The three-kingdom dimension of Charles II's attempts to recover his crowns in the 1650s has yet to be written. And more could be said about the development of reprisals policies in Interregnum Scotland and Ireland which were different from one another but which resembled one another in that they existed for Scotland and Ireland but not for England. Summary execution and transportation for living in a place where attacks on the Commonwealth's soldiers took place is further evidence that war changed its visage as it left England and Wales.

The Nature of the War(s)

John Pocock has recently helpfully attempted to make sense of the patterns of conflict within three kingdoms by adapting a Roman model for internal conflict within the Empire, the distinction between a *bellum civile* and a *bellum sociale*, a war *inter cives*, amongst citizens for control of the state and a war *inter socios*, polities associated in a system comprising a multiplicity of states — as when various Italian *socii* sought to attain the status of *cives Romani*. Pocock argues that the English experienced a classic *bellum civile*, Scotland and Ireland something much more a *bellum sociale*.[18] This would explain the uneasiness with which the affairs of the three kingdoms interact without ever quite mulching down into a single conflict. Indeed, I am so enthusiastic for Pocock's model that I have urged that it be taken much further than he does himself: that we add a third type of internal conflict within any state system, a war of secession or independence (for example, the Jewish Revolt of AD69–70), and that then we see that England had a classic *bellum civile* (though with aspects of the others), Scotland both a *bellum civile* and a *bellum sociale* and Ireland aspects of all three.[19]

The essays in this volume address this issue, but rather obliquely. Peeping over the horizon in Pádraig Lenihan's essay — and explicit in the thesis from which it is drawn — is the view that the Catholics formed an embryonic commonwealth in the 1640s and that there were elements in the leadership who were edging towards the creation of a state independent of the English Crown. This takes a little further the conclusions of Jane Ohlmeyer in another recent essay; and together they present the best case yet made for seeing secession as *one* of the elements in the political thinking of some of the leading Confederates.[20]

But for the most part the essays in this book counsels against overstating the significance of the struggle for constitutional rearrangements within the archipelago in the minds of those who shaped its progress. John Young is primarily involved in his essay with the social redistribution of power at the heart of the Covenanting Revolution, and we will return to that subject shortly, but what also struck me about his essay was how he could construct an account of a decade of constitutional dynamism around an exclusively Scottish agenda. Successive Scottish Parliaments were faced by an unfolding series of problems peculiar to the political process set rolling by the National Covenant and then by the achievement of self-determination in the Treaty of London (1641). Even in 1650, as Cromwell prepared for the invasion and conquest of Scotland, the issue most central to the Scottish Parliament was whether or not to reverse the Act of Classes and to restore the former Engagers so as to create a movement of national unity. It is striking that there is no overlap at all with the essay I have recently published suggesting that at the heart of Scottish politics in the 1640s there is a constantly evolving sense of the shape of any post-war settlement in terms of a redefined relationship of the three kingdoms.[21]

In just the same way, Tadhg ó hAnnracháin's essay shows that there was much more to the internal strains within the Irish Confederation than disagreement about the extent to which the security of Irish Catholicism rested upon a willingness to help Charles I win the wars in Britain. Ó hAnnracháin points out that there was an agenda here which owed more to the Council of Trent than to the priorities of the king at Oxford or of Ormond in Dublin Castle. It was the creation of a properly resourced and properly housed Catholic clerical estate that lay even more at the centre of the vision of GianBattista Rinuccini and other ultramontane leaders of the Confederacy. Readers of Éamonn ó Ciardha's chapter will need no reminding of how great was the moral authority of the Irish Bishops in the 1640s or how potent was their weapon of excommunication. There may well be a British dimension to Scottish and Irish politics in the 1640s, but there was a uniquely Scottish dimension to Scottish politics and a uniquely Irish dimension to Irish politics. A 'British' dimension might help to resolve some problems insoluble within an exclusively Scottish or Irish or English history of the mid-seventeenth century. It does not supplant those histories.

Intellectual Contexts of the Revolution

In a similar fashion, the essays of John Coffey and Clare Jackson demonstrate that there is a great gulf fixed between the English mind and the Scottish mind in the seventeenth century. Ideas carry no passports and respect no frontiers and so it is not surprising to find Scotsmen and Englishmen reading one another and even learning from one another, but essentially the intellectuals of the two countries were men divided by two common languages — English and Latin.

Coffey has provided us with a rich contextualization of the thought of Samuel Rutherford and especially of *Lex, Rex* (1644). (Can any political tract of the period be so well known and so little read?). It is not the fact that the work is suffused with the natural law theorist of the Spanish Thomists which surprises in this context, but the peculiar intensity of his covenant theology, linked as he shows it to have been to a millenarianism which was not so much Scottish or universal as *British*. What glued the English people together as a people, John Pocock has suggested, was first and foremost an intense legalism and ancient constitutionalism.[22] Such a culture had never permeated down through Scottish society. Scotland was a society bound together by stronger ties of kinship and by oaths and bonds.[23] The spiritualization of such bonds had begun in the 1580s and it reached its apogee in the 1640s,[24] and Rutherford was the most powerful of the many legitimizers of Covenanting political theology. Rutherford's British apocolyptism ('who knows but this great work which is begun in Scotland now when it is going into England and is tane some footing there, but the Lord he will make it go over the sea?' or his dream of 'Britaines Israel and Judah, England and Scotland comming together, weeping and asking the way to Zion') is in lineal descent from the late sixteenth-century British apocolypticism so powerfully laid bare for us by Roger Mason and Arthur Williamson.[25]

Sir George Mackenzie was a man who owed little to the mental world of Samuel Rutherford. But he too was quintessentially Scottish and his contribution to the creation of a self-assured legal culture in Scotland is challenged only by that of Stair. On another occasion, I hope Clare Jackson will explore the equally assured and distinctive features of Mackenzie's absolutist theory, but here she unravels his *Aretina*, with its elaborate analogical account of the War of the Three Kingdoms. The most striking aspect of this precocious work by an uppity young graduate is its strikingly un-neurotic rejection of zeal — its *politique* quality, as Clare Jackson expresses it — with its assurance of Scottish cultural superiority over the English. Scotland after all was seen as the Athens of Britain to England's Sparta. Mention England to the Scots and they thought not of Shakespeare, Byrd, and Sir Edward Coke, but of Flodden, Pinkie, and Dunbar. Mackenzie represents a generation of Scots freed from the itch to render the English safe by converting them to Scottish Protestant virtue, a generation willing to work out a clear identity for themselves in a composite monarchy with one king and three separate kingdoms. Few of the arguments would have resonated in England.

Social Contexts of the Revolution

Whatever the merits of a holistic approach to the history of the Atlantic archipelago, they seem least to manifest themselves when we turn to look at social history. One can certainly look at the way Anglo-Norman patterns of landholding and inheritance were extended throughout the archipelago in the sixteenth and seventeenth century (to take the very simplest example, the principle of primogeniture prevailed in 1500 in perhaps 70% of the area of England, 40% of Scotland and Wales, and 30% of Ireland. By 1700 it was ubiquitous except where Anglo-Irish laws strove to subvert it in the case of the Catholic Irish so as to divide and destroy Irish Catholic landowning).[26] But otherwise the social histories of the three kingdoms remain unassimilable. Scotland and Ireland are fundamentally aristocratic societies with weak gentries and very different proportions of freehold and dependent farming communities. Urban development is also distinctive. Some of the political and intellectual consequences have already been seen. What this book does then, is offer some suggestive comparisons and rather more warnings about the hazards of collating the experiences of the three kingdoms.

Sharon Adams portrays a deeply aristocratic society in south-west Scotland (the area, she graphically describes as bordered by the A74, the M8, and the sea!). She enters a field already much studied by Jenny Wormald, Keith Brown, Allan Macinnes, Walter Makey, and others and both the disparities in wealth and power,[27] and in which there have been sharp exchanges about the lineaments of crisis and recovery. Adams does not resolve these difficulties, although her revelation that in 1639 Charles I released the tenants of 'rebels' from paying rents and offered them long leases if they moved to crown estates is certainly suggestive. Nothing of the kind was envisaged or would have been meaningful in an English context by that year. Equally suggestive is the reminder that in Scotland there was something much closer to the *noblesse d'épeel noblesse de robe* tension so characteristic of early modern France but not of early modern England. Her description of the two 'spheres of religious networks'[28] with strong links between nobility and radical ministers needs fuller correlation with the extraordinary fervour of the Holy Fairs of the region, but again it is the distinctiveness of the Scottish situation that stands out.

Aristocratic domination of the internal politics of Scotland is a sub-text in the essays by Scally, Lee, and Jackson, but Young sets out to suggest that at the heart of the covenanting revolution of the 1640s was a readjustment of power within the Scottish Parliament towards the representatives of the shires and burghs. His claims are based on a massive and thorough quantitative analysis of participation rates in the Scottish Parliaments and Conventions of the period 1639–51. It is open to the counter that the Covenanting leaders were too busy waging war to spend day after day in the Parliament and so left it to the shire (and to a lesser extent) the burgh representatives who were their dependents and spokespersons. At the conference of which this volume is the proceedings, there was a hugely entertaining, good-natured, and vigorous debate between Drs Young and Scally on the significance of the former's argument, and the issues raised seem to me to be still wide open ones. A similar debate — conducted in public and private with more venom — has of course possessed the historians of England in this period. How truly bicameral was the Long Parliament and was control of the House of Commons still effectively with the clients and collaborators of peers rather than with anti-aristocratic and 'pure country' MPs? Young tells us who did what and certainly establishes that the nature of parliamentary activity changed. Less certain is how far these men were free agents and how far the clients and collaborators of those Covenanting nobles busy waging war. Given the anti-war sentiment amongst the less well organized 'Royalist' nobility, it would have been natural for the Covenanting leaders to drive home their policies through their dependents and spokespersons. Yet there are clear signs that the 'gentry' and burgesses had their own sectional interests and were pursuing them. Only more work on this aspect of this subject, and more prosopography of the members will settle the matter. Meanwhile, Young offers us a powerful thesis to ponder and be challenged by.

I will end with a mischievous thought. Each of the kingdoms had its own Parliament. Each was very different in its structure, procedure, and political role. But it is an unconsidered possibility that the Parliaments learnt from one another in the course of the seventeenth century and that kings learnt from their techniques of control in one kingdom how to control the Parliaments of the others. Danby's techniques of parliamentary management in the 1670s are a case in point — it is quite possible he had the Crown's successes in Scotland in mind. James II's plans for a packed and managed English Parliament in 1687–88 may have owed something to earlier Crown experience in Ireland. So, when Sir George Mackenzie, as quoted by Clare Jackson, defended non-union of the kingdoms on the ground that 'whilst the kingdoms stood divided, his Majesty had two Parliaments whereof the one might always be exemplary to the other,'[29] he may have been saying more than we have realized. Where did the Scots of the 1640s get their ideas for institutional development of the Parliament from?

Consequences

We have already seen that Sir George Mackenzie represents a strong Scottish renunciation of everything Samuel Rutherford stood for. Mackenzie stood for the divine right of the king and of the aristocracy but not of the Presbyter. Mackenzie stood for a Stuart Scotland developing alongside a Stuart England. He seems to have believed in neither constitutional convergence not constitutional divergence. Ronnie Lee's account of Scotland's retreat from revolution suggests that Mackenzie was entirely typical of the political mood of 1661. One consequence of the Covenanting Revolution was to weaken Scottish attachment to federal unionism and it was never to reappear. Another was to establish the tradition that what happened in England took more extreme forms (and usually happened first) in Scotland: absolutist theory; religious persecution; religiously-inspired insurrection and violence (up to and including political assassination). As a history of British state formation, this represents the low point in the early modern period. As far as the history of political and religious echo-effects goes, it represents an apogee.

The Celtic Dimension of the British Civil Wars

Whatever else this book is about, it is not about the Celtic dimensions of the British Civil Wars. It is about the non-English dimensions and that is a very different matter. What is happening over the sixteenth and seventeenth centuries is, in John Pocock's words, that the component parts of the 'British Isles interacted so as to change the conditions of one another's existence',[30] and that 'British history denotes the historiography of no single nation but of a problematic and uncompleted experiment in the creation and interaction of several nations.'[31] I agree with him and in several articles I have tried to gloss those mission statements in various ways.[32] I have come to stress that we need to separate out two processes: the development of a British 'state system' which in many ways parallels and in general falls not far short of what was happening in 'France', 'Spain' or 'Austria'; and the transformation of senses of nationhood in each of England, Ireland, Scotland and Wales.

There was nothing very Celtic about Welsh, Scottish, or Irish identities by 1660 or 1700. In each country, the English language, English (or in the case of Scotland Anglo-Norman/ Humanist) codes and process of law, English or Anglo-Norman social institutions had come to predominate. In Ireland and in the Western Highlands, the sense of Gaelic and of sept or clan identity retreated as a sense of inhabitant-of-Ireland and inhabitant-of-Scotland identity strengthened. Allan Macinnes has elsewhere explored the growing divergence of the Gaeldoms.[33]

Gaeldom survived, but it was marginalized. The authors of these essays — with the exception of Éamonn ó Ciardha are not writing about a Celtic world. The mental world of Hamilton and Ormond was a Briticized if not an anglicized one. Samuel Rutherford or George Mackenzie on the one side, and the bishops discussed by Tadhg ó hAnnachráin on the other, were not promoting a Celtic christianity but reforming faiths steeped in the learning and experience of continental Europe by-passing the English experience. The Parliament of Scotland discussed by John Young and Ronnie Lee was not a Celtic institution. The forces radicalizing south-west Scotland in the 1640s were not Celtic ones. These were all un-English if not always anti-English phenomena. A seventeenth century 'British History' must recognize the uncomfortable fact that it must contain 'the increasing dominance of England as a political and cultural entity.'[34] But it is not a story of effective assimilation. Instead ethnic identity was refashioned and re-rooted. In Ireland it was Catholicism that became the badge of Irish nationhood. In Scotland a complex blend of kirk and legalism. (It was a paradoxical consequence both of the systematization and codification of Scottish law and of the magnitude of the Presbyterian triumph of 1689 and subsequent purges of the kirk, that made the Scottish élite able to relax into a hedged incorporative union in 1707).

A book on the Celtic dimensions of the Wars of the Three Kingdoms would enter the mental world described by Éamonn ó Ciardha. It is a world defined in negativities, perhaps, looking for a new groundedness. It was a world marginalized and splintered. What was to give a new centricity to this world, however, was not a yearning for Celtic homelands and free Gaelic commonwealths but for the Stuarts of the second exile (after 1691). Gaeldom was to rediscover itself as a Jacobite cause, and until the Gaelic sources for Gaelic Jacobitism have been properly studied (and this is ó Ciardha's current enterprise), its full significance will not be grasped.

Conclusion

This is an important set of essays by an engaged, lively and challenging young generation of scholars. In themselves and in their interactions, these essays teach us much about the un-English if not about the Gaelic dimensions of the British Civil Wars. Its publication will make it harder in the future for historians to treat British history as an aspect of English historiographical imperialism. Good.

NOTES

1. *The Journal of Sir William Brereton*, E Hawkins (ed), (Chetham Society, 1st series, volume one, 1842), passim; R N Dore, 'The Early Life of Sir William Brereton', *Transactions of the Lancashire and Chesire Antiquarian Society*, 63, (1953), 1–26.

2. K Brown, 'British History: a sceptical comment', in R Asch (ed), *Three Nations: a common history?* (Bochum, 1990), 117, 124–125.

3. N Canny, 'Responses to Centralization c. 1530–c. 1640, in A Grant and K Stringer (eds), *Uniting the Kingdom? The making of British History* (London, 1995), 147–169.

4. J G A Pocock, 'The Atlantic Archipelago and the War of the Three Kingdoms', in B Bradshaw and J Morrill (eds), *The British Problem 1534–1707: State Formation in the Atlantic Archipelago* (London, 1996), 183–184. Pocock discusses the tension between the singular and plural forms of the war(s) at these pages. The rest of his chapter seeks to resolve that tension.

5. This is a conscious modification of Peter Donald's description of Charles I as an 'uncounselled king'. See P Donald, *An Uncounselled King. Charles I and the Scottish Troubles 1637–1641* (Cambridge, 1990). Scally explores this ambiguity in his review of Donald's monograph which appeared in *Parliamentary History*, 12, (1993), 96–97. This apart, their interpretations agree about far more than they differ about.

6. See J Scally, 'Counsel in Crisis: James, third Marquis of Hamilton and the Bishops' Wars, 1638–1640', 26–27.

7. Ibid.

8. W Kelly, 'James Butler, Earl of Ormond, the Irish Government and the Bishops' Wars, 1638–1640', 46.

9. S Adams, 'The Making of the Radical South West: Charles I and his Scottish Kingdom, 1625–1649', 64.

10. C Russell, *Unrevolutionary England* (London, 1990), 231–252, especially at 244.

11. Kelly, 'James Butler, Earl of Ormond', 36–37.

12. Ibid.

13. This is John Pocock's term and is to be preferred to 'The British Isles' because of the latter's proprietorial assumption with respect to the island of Ireland.

14. B Donagan, 'Codes and conduct in the English Civil War', *Past and Present*, 118, (1988), 65–95; B Donagan, 'Atrocity, War Crime, and Treason in the English Civil War', *AHR*, 104, (1994), 1137–1166.

15. P Lenihan, 'The Catholic Confederacy 1642–9: and the Irish State at War', (National University or Ireland, PhD thesis, 1995), 318–332, 350–351, 378–379,

396–400, 430–440; D Stevenson, *Scottish Covenanters and Irish Confederates* (Belfast, 1980), 106–110 and passim.

16. É ó Ciardha, 'Tories and Moss–Troopers in Scotland and Ireland in the Interregnum: A Political Dimension', 142.

17. Ibid, 149–150.

18. Pocock, 'The Atlantic Archipelago and the War of the Three Kingdoms', especially 183–190.

19. J S Morrill, 'Three Kingdoms and one Commonwealth? The enigma of mid-seventeenth century Britain and Ireland', in Grant and Stringer (eds), *Uniting the Kingdom?*, especially 188–190.

20. Lenihan, 'The Catholic Confederacy 1642–9', 1–19; J. Ohlmeyer (ed), *Ireland From Independence to Occupation, 1641–1660* (Cambridge, 1995), chapter five.

21. Morrill, 'Three Kingdoms and one Commonwealth?', 173–190.

22. J G A Pocock, 'Two kingdoms and three histories? Political Thought in British Contexts', in R Mason (ed), *Scots and Britons. Scottish political thought and the union of 1603* (Cambridge, 1994), 293–312

23. See especially J Wormald, *Lords and Men: Bonds of Manrent 1442–1603* (Edinburgh, 1985), especially chapters five to seven; K Brown, *Bloodfeud in Scotland 1573–1625* (Edinburgh, 1986), especially chapter two.

24. For the background to this, see J Ford, 'The lawful bonds of Scottish society', *HJ*, 37, (1994), 45–64.

25. R Mason, 'Scotching the Brut: politics, history and national myth in sixteenth-century Britain', in R Mason (ed), *Scotland and Britain 1286–1815* (Edinburgh, 1987), 60–84; A Williamson, *Scottish National Consciousness in the age of James VI* (Edinburgh, 1979).

26. I am referring to the act of 1704 by which Catholics could not buy land (except for leases up to 31 years), could not bequeath land by will, and were subject to partible inheritance unless the eldest son conformed to the Protestant Church. See J C Beckett, *The Making of Modern Ireland 1603–1923* (second edition, 1981), 157–158.

27. A Macinnes, *Charles I and the Making of the Covenanting Movement 1625–1641* (Edinburgh, 1991); K Brown, 'Aristocratic finances and the Origins of the Scottish Revolution', *EHR*, 54, (1989), 46–87; K Brown, 'Noble indebtedness in Scotland between the Reformation and the Revolution', *Historical Research*, 62, (1989), 260–275; W Makey, *The Church of the Covenant 1637–1651* (Edinburgh, 1979).

28. Adams, 'The Making of the Radical South West', 67–68.

29. C Jackson, 'The Paradoxical Virtue of the Historical Romance: Sir George Mackenzie's *Aretina* (1660) and the Civil Wars', 124.

30. J G A Pocock, 'The Limits and Divisions of British History', *AHR*, 87, (1982), 317.

31. Ibid, 318.

32. J S Morrill, *The Nature of the English Revolution* (London, 1993), 91–117, 252–272; J S Morrill, 'The Britishness of the English Revolution', in Asch (ed), *Three Nations: a common history*, 83–116; J S Morrill, 'The fashioning of Britain', in S G Ellis and S Barber, *Conquest and Union: Fashioning a British State, 1485–1725* (London, 1995), 8–39; J S Morrill, 'The British Problem', in Bradshaw and Morrill (eds), *The British Problem 1534–1707*, 1–38; Morrill, 'Three Kingdoms and one Commonwealth?', 170–190.

33. A I Macinnes, 'Gaelic culture in the seventeenth century: polarization and assimilation', in Ellis and Barber (eds), *Conquest and Union. Fashioning a British State,* 162–194.

34. J G A Pocock, 'British History; a plea for a new subject, *Journal of Modern History*, 47, (1975), 619.

CHAPTER 2

Counsel in Crisis: James, third Marquis of Hamilton and the Bishops' Wars, 1638–1640

John Scally

Although the Covenanting Revolution and the Wars of the Three Kingdoms that grew out of it has been well served by historians in recent years, one of the major gaps has been the study of prominent individuals involved in the course of events.[1] In this respect, Scotland perhaps fares worst of all three kingdoms. However, it may be a sign of changing times that a number of contributors to this volume discuss leading figures, which should go some way to filling this gap. What I will argue here is that to focus on one individual, especially one with an enormous manuscript archive, can throw new light on the period. In this case it takes us to the heart of the relationship between the king and his chief Scottish Counsellor, James, third Marquis of Hamilton, and the difficulties experienced by Hamilton in providing counsel to Charles I. To demonstrate this, I intend to look at Hamilton's period of negotiation in Scotland in 1638 as Royal Commissioner to settle the Scottish troubles, and the First and Second Bishops' Wars of 1639–40 that followed the collapse of the 1638 talks.

As a preliminary, however, I would like to offer some background shots to dispel a few myths about the subject of this paper: James, third Marquis of Hamilton, was Master of the Horse to Charles I, Privy Councillor in Scotland and England, the king's lay adviser on Scottish affairs, and from 1638 Royal Commissioner to settle the Scottish troubles, and from 1639 General of the King's forces in Scotland. First, Hamilton was not a political lightweight nor 'a man of straw'.[2] Neither was he a selfless servant to the king — a knee-jerk Royalist, unthinkingly carrying out the royal will.[3] Hamilton's career prior to the Scottish troubles indicates that he was committed to an active foreign policy in Europe, a policy at odds with the king; that he was unhappy with certain aspects of the Personal Rule in England (a regime that he regularly tried to reform from within); and that he was anti-Episcopal, particularly in the promotion of bishops into civil places in Scotland. Furthermore, although Hamilton was the king's chief counsellor on Scottish affairs at Court, he had nothing to do with the Canons and

Prayer Book of 1636–37 or any aspect of religious policy in Scotland. In all of these areas, Hamilton went against the orthodox policy of the 1630s as promoted by Charles, Lord Treasurer Portland, Archbishop Laud, Lord Deputy Wentworth, and the Bishops of Ross and Brechin. This explains why Hamilton was extremely reluctant to become embroiled in the troubles in Scotland: not because he was timorous, or weak, but because he was not involved in what was, on the surface and at least in the beginning, a dispute occasioned by the application of religious policy. It was neither his problem, nor indeed was it of his making, and in the end Charles had to command Hamilton to take the Commissionership to settle the Scottish troubles in April 1638.[4]

In common with much of Hamilton's historical reputation, the backdrop to this paper, The Bishops' Wars, is misleading since it produced very little war and a lot of negotiation — a lot of talk and no fighting. Most of the time was spent negotiating in a backdrop of armed military build-up on both sides. They were all much more keen to talk than to fight — at least until the drastic change of policy at Berwick in the summer of 1639, which brought Thomas, Lord Wentworth, the Lord Deputy of Ireland, into the contest.[5] Nothing was inevitable, and from the outbreak of the Scottish troubles in July 1637, to the assembly of the English Parliament in November 1640, the natural impulse on most sides was to secure settlement without recourse to arms.

The strong urge to find settlement is nowhere more evident than in the manuscript correspondence between the king and his commissioner during the latter's period of negotiation in Scotland between June to December 1638.[6] What this shows is that Hamilton consistently told Charles I that what he wanted — mainly the surrender of the Covenants, before the demand for a free General Assembly and Parliament could be considered — was unrealistic and could only be done by force, perhaps even by outright conquest of Scotland. But Hamilton never advised force — he advised the king to reconsider, to give some ground, and to make a settlement with the Covenanters. Hamilton advised this because the king's position in his other two kingdoms was so poor that he could not rely on support from England and Ireland to hammer the Scots. This was not what Charles wanted to hear, and it brings us to another important point.

The survival of the Hamilton/Charles correspondence of 1638 and 1639 is deeply significant, since it is perhaps the only time the king had to be advised from afar, and so it offers a window into the dilemmas of counsel right at the start of the crisis.[7] What it shows is that a counsellor could not tell a king, especially a king like Charles I, that what he wanted was ridiculous or unfeasible. He could only illustrate the impossibility of the king's demand, as Hamilton did, by telling him what would be required to achieve it.[8] In 1638, it grew very quickly from force to conquest of Scotland and, by June of that year, to the hazarding of the king's rule in his three kingdoms.

A central plank of my argument is that a settlement may have been made in June 1638, had the king taken Hamilton's advice. But Charles chose to ignore his commissioner's counsel, and the warning of June 1638 was to become a worryingly accurate prophecy. In fact, the problem of providing counsel, especially when it was hamstrung by the courtly protocol in which the Commissioner was immersed, and, more importantly, when it was met by royal intransigence, combined to provide a singular factor which led to the deepening of the crisis.

The period following Hamilton's departure from Scotland in December 1638 down to the Scottish invasion of the north of England in August 1640, is equally revealing when viewed in the same way. It shows the shambolic nature of the attempt to mobilise a de-militarised England, as well as exposing Hamilton's deep reservations about the success of the project. The focus on Hamilton will also show that the king's decision to make peace in the First Bishops' War was partly determined by his belief that he had been betrayed by those around him. Equally, Hamilton's decision at Berwick to adopt a lower profile in the troubles was a sign not only that Charles was losing the confidence of his moderate Protestant ministers, but that the attempt, albeit on the surface, to use Scotsmen to deal with a Scottish problem had failed.

I

By the time Hamilton was appointed Royal Commissioner to settle the Scottish troubles in April 1638, and even more by the time he arrived in Scotland at the beginning of June, both sides were asking for much more than the other would give. The Covenanters, whose demands had been slowly increasing, wanted a free General Assembly and Parliament, and, more importantly, as Hamilton's brother-in-law John, 10th Lord Lindsay had told him at Berwick, the Scottish episcopate reduced to the 'baire title'.[9] Charles, on the other hand, wanted everything returned to normal and the Covenants surrendered before the request for an Assembly and Parliament would be considered.[10] It was a classic political power-play with crowds in the streets, the Covenanters beginning to arm, and the king doing the same in England and Ireland. Now strictly speaking, Hamilton's job as Commissioner was to carry out his constrained remit, but he also tried to find a way forward, and that is why at Berwick on 4 June 1638 he wrote to the King:

> If the informatione which I have reseved heire be trew,
> ther[e] is no hoope to effeckt anie thing, (bot by foors)
> that can give your Mattie satisfactioun...[11]

Statements like this could be misinterpreted and cited as evidence that the Hamilton caved in as soon as he arrived in Scotland and told the king to invade.[12] What Hamilton was actually telling the king was that his demands were unrealistic and should be reconsidered — and this becomes clearer when the correspondence is read as a whole.[13] However, in the same letter, Hamilton also advised Charles on more aggressive courses, which was part of his remit as Royal Commissioner.[14] These three themes of despair, compromise, and conquest figure again and again in Hamilton's letters to Charles. The dilemma was how to phrase advice that did not overtly suggest concession, but made it the only prudent way forward, while simultaneously puffing the future military solution favoured by the king. Once we penetrate that conundrum, then Hamilton's behaviour can be viewed in a different light.

Yet what is most revealing about Hamilton's Commissionership in 1638, is that he was able to hold the Covenanters within legal limits for so long. He managed to fob them off on 16 June, when they presented a petition demanding a free General Assembly and Parliament; they allowed him to return to Court twice, once in July, and again in September, to persuade the king to relax his demands, accept the explanation of the National Covenant, and allow an Assembly and Parliament, and it was not until 28 November 1638 that the Covenanters refused, after some hesitation, to obey the royal will dissolving the Glasgow Assembly.[15] In the summer of 1638, the Covenanters were not all recalcitrant hard-liners with a set agenda intent on abolishing Episcopacy, reforming Parliament and completely re-interpreting the relationship between Crown and State, Crown and Church.[16] Yes they had plans, some far-reaching and which put pressure on Covenanter unity, such as the fate of Episcopacy and the extent to which the royal will could be resisted.[17] Even then, however, because there were different plans around in the summer of 1638, whether on the Covenanters' side or indeed the king's, does not mean that their application was a foregone conclusion, especially during the Commissioner's first month in Edinburgh. Many of those who had signed the National Covenant in February were in June still unsure about the means to resolve the deepening crisis.[18]

If we accept this description of the situation in Scotland in the first half of June, then Hamilton's letter of advice to the king on 20 June becomes highly significant. The first part of the letter builds upon what Hamilton had said previously about force being the only option which would give Charles 'satisfaction' without conceding ground, and Hamilton was perfectly aware that the king was in no position to mobilise and coerce the Covenanters at this stage[19]:

> I doue nou assure your Matti the difficultie is greatt to
> keipe them from the indictking of ane assemblie, and
> loong they uill not be keipped from itt, bot if your
> Matties preparatiounes Can not be quickly redie your
> Matti must inlarge your derectiouns to me, or otheruayes
> they uill uerie quicklie have a formed bodie of ane armie
> to gidder.[20]

What Hamilton was telling Charles, was that if he persisted in his hard line, he initially risked not only losing his right to call a General Assembly, but, also open, armed rebellion. The second part of the letter is even more important, for it focuses on the king's refusal to accept the National Covenant, that elegantly posed statement which had galvanised the protest movement by a mixture of appeals to historical precedent and avoiding some of the more controversial issues.[21] For Hamilton, and for many others, Charles's refusal to accept the National Covenant was a crucial barrier to winning over a large part of those who had signed it, and thereby gathering a party able to support a compromise settlement. If Charles could be brought to understand that the National Covenant was not incompatible with royal authority, then everything else might still fall into place. Indeed, there is a constant refrain through-out Hamilton's correspondence in 1638, in which the National Covenant is dressed up in different ways to make it acceptable to the king.[22]

Hamilton's attempt to bring Charles round to this way of thinking in his letter of 20 June is one of the best examples of this line of policy. The Commissioner told Charles that all of those who had signed the National Covenant would never be brought to renounce it; that the majority of the Privy Council and Court of Session believed the Covenant stood with the laws of the country, if an explanation was provided of the part which tied them 'mutuallie in defens one of ane other'[23]; and that the majority of the opinion in Scotland — including Charles's moderate ministers — believed that the king should give way. In a highly significant final sentence, Hamilton concluded 'bot itt shall never be my advyse if your Matti can clearlie sea hou ye can effectk your end uith out the haserdding of your 3 Crounes'.[24]

With this advice, Hamilton brought Charles, King of Scotland, face to face with the Scottish Privy Council and Session, face to face with the Scottish people, and face to face with the Scottish National Covenant. Not only that, Hamilton also predicted the long term hazard to Charles's rule in his three kingdoms, if he refused to accept what was deemed legal in Scotland.[25] To strengthen the argument, he warned Charles that his other kingdoms could not be relied upon to assist against the Scots. England, he told the king,

> uill not be so fourduart in this as they ooght, nay thatt
> [there] ar so manie malitious spereites amongst them
> thatt no sounner uill your bake be turned, bot they uill
> be redie to dou as ue have doun heire.

As for Charles's third kingdom, Hamilton pointed out, 'Iyrland uantes not itt is oune discontents, and I feire much help they can not give'. Neither could Charles rely on help from abroad. In fact the king could depend on France and Spain fanning the Covenanter flames, given Britain's recent foreign policy position.[26]

On 20 June 1638, Hamilton told Charles I to make a u-turn: accept the explanation of the National Covenant and settle the religious issues through a General Assembly and Parliament. Otherwise, the fire would spread to his other kingdoms. There was also an implicit observation that Charles's rule in his three kingdoms had not been a success prior to the troubles, and therefore the king was in no position to dictate. Given the problems of counsel already alluded to, this was plain, unambiguous, advice which offered a realistic route out of the situation.

There are two lists side by side in the Hamilton Papers which were probably drawn up at this time.[27] The first list is in Hamilton's hand and contains the names of 25 of the leading Covenanters, divided into five classes: nobles, barons, burgesses, ministers, and advocates. The class for nobles includes the names of the Earls of Rothes, Lothian, and Weymes, Lords Eglington, Lindsay, and Balmerino. The class for barons includes the names of Auldbar, Keir, and Durie; that for the ministers Andrew Cant, Alexander Henderson, and Samuel Rutherford; and finally for the advocates, Archibald Johnston of Wariston 'and as mani more as can be all most named'.[28] There are no real surprises here. The second list consists of nobles who might be supporters of the Crown, or, perhaps more accurately, Royalists, waverers, and neutrals. This second list amounts to 46 nobles and includes the obvious Royalists such as the Duke of Lennox, Marquis of Huntly, and Earl of Traquair, and Catholics such as the Marquis of Douglas and Earl of Abercorn. But it also contains a trunk of waverers, amongst them the Earls of Southesk, Lauderdale, Dunfermline, Glencairn, Haddington, Tullibardine and Lord Almont, many of whom were of the same pragmatic stamp as the Commissioner. It is difficult to be absolutely sure about why these lists were drawn up, nevertheless, I would suggest that if we line them up with Hamilton's advice to the king on 20 June, they might be evidence that the Commissioner was playing with numbers in the knowledge that a compromise settlement might just have been possible, if the king gave the go-ahead. Yet all too predictably, Charles refused to budge. His mind was set on mobilisation and he refused to accept any 'explanation of their damnable Covenant'.[29] As with most unpalatable counsel, the king chose either to ignore it or to reject it with a few pithy comments.

Next to the signing of the National Covenant itself, the king's rejection of Hamilton's counsel of 20 June was the single most important event in 1638, not only because of the timing, but because what was conceded later was too little, too late. June 1638 was the point at which the Scottish troubles could have been defused. It was the point where the Covenanting Movement could have been split, and a negotiated settlement forced through in a General Assembly and later in a Parliament. From then on, Crown policy consistently fell short of what was required to wrest the initiative away from the Covenanters.[30]

II

Of course the failure of Hamilton's mission to Scotland in 1638 cleared the way for the open hostilities of the Bishops' Wars. Professor Fissell has recently argued that the failure of the English mobilisation in the First Bishops' War of 1638/9, and the Second Bishops' War of 1639/40, was less to do with the inherent weakness of the English militia and Ordnance Office, and more to do with the impractical and naive demands put on them by the king.[31] Yet that does not explain why, of the 5,000 soldiers drawn from four English counties that made made up Hamilton's naval expeditionary force, which sailed up the Forth at the beginning of May, only 200 had ever held a musket, or why most of the muskets were defective.[32]

In practice, therefore, the resort to arms in 1639 had as many holes in it as the attempt at settlement the previous year. This helps explain why channels of communication were kept open to try and effect a settlement, and in the end both sides agreed to peace talks before a battle rather than after one.[33] Not surprisingly, Hamilton played a large part in continuing the dialogue. He was almost in daily contact with the Covenanters during May; whilst sailing in the Forth with his untrained Englishmen and broken muskets; he had regular visits from the Covenanters in Edinburgh and even had his taxation records brought on board on 17 May.[34] More seriously, it was Hamilton who brought the king round to considering 'patching it up', as he called it in a letter in early May.[35]

It never came to a battle, and neither the military logistics of how the Scottish Commander General Alexander Leslie outmanoeuvred the English army on the Borders in early June,[36] nor as Conrad Russell has argued, the king's sudden realisation of 'the weaknesses of the system behind him,'[37] are as important factors in explaining why the king opted to make peace at Berwick, than Charles's suspicion that he had been betrayed by those around him. The evidence for this can be recovered in a letter from Sir Henry Vane, Comptroller of the Household, summoning Hamilton to the king's camp on the Borders:

> His ma[jes]ty doth now clearly see and is fully satisfied
> in his owne judgment that what passed in the Gallerie
> betwixt his ma[jes]ty yr lords[hip] and my selfe hath
> been but too much verified on this occasion; and therfore
> his ma[jes]ty would not have you to beginn [fighting]
> w[i]th them.[38]

What Hamilton had told Charles in the Gallery at Whitehall was the same thing that he had told him on 20 June 1638: that the English would reluctantly follow the king into an offensive war against the Scots.[39] The conversation in the Gallery had also turned on the appointment of officers for the army, given the lack of will of some in England for the contest.[40] And so Charles's statement a few weeks earlier, that he trusted only Vane, Hamilton, and Arundel, becomes clearer.[41] So too does Hamilton's deep suspicion of the Covenanters' appeals to the Protestant English noblemen in the king's army — particularly the Earls of Holland and Essex — in the weeks before Leslie's encampment on Duns Law.[42] And, when hearing of these approaches, Hamilton warned the king to 'remember Saye and Brooke', namely William Fiennes, First Viscount Saye and Sele and Robert Greville, Second Lord Brooke, the two most prominent English objectors to the king's war with his Protestant Scottish subjects.[43] Indeed, rumours were rife in the king's camp at the beginning of June 1639 that General Leslie had 'communication' with individuals around the king, since Leslie appeared to anticipate all of the English army's manoeuvres.[44]

III

It is in this light that the Peace Negotiations at Berwick must be viewed, with their atmosphere of mutual distrust and suspicion. In fact this also explains another historical conundrum: why the king unexpectedly sat in on the peace talks between the Scottish and English delegates.[45] On the one side sat the Earls of Rothes and Dunfermline, Lord Loudoun, Archibald Johnston of Wariston, Sir William Douglas of Cavers (Sheriff of Teviotdale) and Alexander Henderson; and on the other side, the Earls of Arundel, Essex, Holland, Salisbury, Berkshire, Sir Henry Vane, Sir John Coke, and Hamilton.[46] Given Charles's deep suspicion of the motives of his subjects on both sides of the table, it is less than surprising that he arrived unannounced at the first meeting on Tuesday 11 June, and thereafter dominated the discussions.[47] However, it is more important for our purposes to examine how Hamilton reacted to the deteriorating situation at Berwick, since it marked an enormous shift in his political profile. The evidence lies in two papers that he submitted to the king on 5 and 8 July and a subsequent agreement made between the king and Hamilton on 17 of that month. Taken together, these two papers constitute not only a brilliant manoeuvre to avoid being sent back to Edinburgh with an impossible brief, but also a means to retain the king's confidence whilst simultaneously courting the goodwill of the Covenanters.

The first was an advice paper which posed the question of whether or not the General Assembly and Parliament allowed in the peace articles should convene.[48] After exploring the various policies available to the king, in particular pointing out that Charles risked losing his negative voice in Parliament if he used it to try and save Episcopacy, Hamilton boiled the options down to:

> uhidder to permitt the abolasing of Episs[copacy], the
> lesning of kingly pouer in exclesiastick eaffares, the
> estabelising of Civill authorati in such maner as the
> iniquity of the tymes uill suffer...or to call a
> parll[iament] in ingland and leive the event ther of to
> hasard and ther discretiouns, and in the interime,
> Scott[land] to the government of the covenanters.[49]

This was good counsel, much like the counsel in June 1638. It was realistic. It was telling the king what was within reach. It was the same counsel that Hamilton had proffered the year before but with different parameters. In June 1638 Hamilton had advised Charles to sacrifice the Canons, Prayer Book, and Perth Articles, and to accept the explanation of the National Covenant in order to gather a Royalist party and save

Episcopacy in a reduced form. Now, it was to sacrifice Episcopacy to save civil authority, and to retain some ecclesiastical influence. In both cases, Charles was advised to concede ground immediately or lose more later. By this advice, Hamilton remained consistent to his policy of damage limitation to the Scottish Crown tempered by the Marquis's own sense of the politics of the possible. Charles's answer to this advice has not survived — but characteristically he took a bit from both options, allowing Episcopacy to be abolished in Scotland and also calling a Parliament in England, which is not what Hamilton had intended, since calling a Parliament in England meant a second war.

The second paper delivered three days later on 8 July probably provides us with Hamilton's reaction to the king's response to his first paper.[50] In sum it contained a compelling set of reasons why Hamilton should not be sent to Edinburgh as Royal Commissioner to the forthcoming Parliament agreed in the Berwick Peace. It was also a subtle critique of the king's policy since Hamilton had been made Commissioner in April 1638, highlighting how the executors of the king's policy, rather than the king himself, were placed in an invidious position. Hamilton was now hated by his nation; he was also discredited as a Commissioner since what he had 'so often suoorne and said your Matti uoold never condeschend to uill nou be granted'.[51] In short, the eight points outlined in the paper followed the Covenanters' description of an Incendiary, and pre-dated the English Long Parliament's description of an evil counsellor. At present, Hamilton was both. Despite the courtly melodrama of these addresses, they were the views of a politician who had reached a cross-roads, and Hamilton, like the good politician that he was, had opted for self-preservation. Less tangible, though no less important, was the suggestion that Charles could no longer protect his servants either from his political opponents or the baying crowds in Edinburgh.[52] This was a lesson that the Lord Deputy of Ireland and the Archbishop of Canterbury would learn too late.

The final piece in the jigsaw was a secret agreement, ostensibly a licence for deceit, between Hamilton and the king. This agreement stated that Hamilton was to speak the language of the Covenanters, and to try to find out what their plans were for replacing bishops in Parliament, and what the further intentions of the Covenanters were.[53] By this remarkable contract Hamilton was able not only to bolt himself closer to the king, but with royal approval was allowed to confer with the Covenanters as a sympathiser.[54] It is perhaps a less objectionable agreement if we consider that Charles, and indeed Hamilton, probably believed that the atmosphere of deception had been introduced by others. What it also shows is that the politics of deceit — and possibly in the king's mind, betrayal — occasioned by real or imaginary Anglo-Scottish contacts, was not a product of the harsher political world of the Second Bishops' War of 1640, as Dr Donald and Professor Russell have argued, but began instead in the summer of 1639 in the circumstances surrounding the king's decision to sue for peace at Berwick.[55]

On a more personal level, Hamilton had skilfully wriggled out of being sent back to Edinburgh, and John Stewart, 1st Earl of Traquair, the Lord Treasurer and Hamilton's close collaborator in 1638, was sent instead.[56] Traquair's reaction to his appointment has not survived, though the fact that he collected a series of incriminating statements allegedly made by Hamilton at Berwick, suggests that he believed that the Marquis had passed him a poisoned chalice. One of these statements recorded a warning that Hamilton had apparently given a 'noble man' at Berwick:

> that the Scotes had reasone to stick close togither: for
> if the king got his will, he would prove the most bloodie
> man that ever was knowne.[57]

IV

Although Hamilton was involved in the preparations for the Second Bishops' War, his high public profile of the First was prudently reduced, the reasons for which he summarised to his friend, the Earl of Lauderdale; 'heirefter I intend to meddill les in affaires of thatt kingdom as having smarted for thatt sufficient alreder'.[58] Over seventeen months of groping towards a settlement had led nowhere — the negotiation phase of Hamilton's Commissionership between May and December 1638 had been as unsuccessful as the subsequent military phase between January and June 1639. The pivotal expectation in both years of an indigenous Scottish party supporting the king had been disappointed, mainly due to the king's refusal to accept his Commissioner's advice, especially that of 20 June. The fractious settlement at Berwick was little more than an armistice until the following spring.

The central role of the king in the shaping of all this is beyond doubt. The quality of Hamilton's advice suggests an *Uncounsellable King*, rather than an *Uncounselled King*.[59] The reconstruction of the political situation in Edinburgh in June 1638 questions the inevitability of events in that year, and suggests that there was a considerable body of waverers and Crown supporters who might have been willing to get behind a compromise settlement, had the king accepted the explanation of the National Covenant. Such a hypothesis has implications not only for our understanding of the political profile of Scotland in 1638, but also for the way we look at the politics of the 1640s under the Covenanters. The waverers were either absorbed into the broad church of the Covenanting polity in the decade 1638-1648, or temporarily drifted out of politics, only to cluster around Hamilton or Argyll in 1643-44, and in 1646-48.[60] Using Hamilton as our compass has also shown us that Charles, even in 1639, was beginning to alienate his moderate ministers, forcing them to look to Charles's opponents as more likely to bring a lasting constitutional settlement. Hamilton's correspondence with the king also casts new light on the strict protocol that hampered the provision of counsel, which often led to a situation where the king was cushioned from the reality of the crisis. The transmission of counsel, albeit haphazard and often wrapped in extremely diplomatic language, was further complicated by the king's predilection to take opposition as a personal insult rather than as opposition to a particular policy at a particular time. The king's suspicion of the motives of those around him complicated further the route to settlement.

And so by degrees royal policy turned to outright conquest of Scotland, and the exponent of that approach arrived at Court from Ireland at the end of September 1639.[61] It would be difficult to imagine two such contrasting figures as Wentworth and Hamilton, each with a hand on the tiller of state. Quite apart from their famous enmity towards each other, Hamilton had never fully endorsed the ideological implications of Wentworth's policy — English hegemony in Scotland — and he had started to step aside at Berwick to make way for the Lord Deputy. Amongst other things, it was the exchange of policy leadership from Hamilton, a Scotsman, to Wentworth, an Englishman, which effectively signalled the end of conciliation and the phoney war of 1639. It was this change that helped persuade the Covenanters that in the Second Bishops' War it would perhaps be more prudent to act first.

NOTES

1. For example, see B Fitzpatrick, *Seventeenth Century Ireland* (Dublin, 1988); J H Ohlmeyer, *Civil War and Restoration in the Three Stuart Kingdoms: the Career of Randall MacDonell, Marquis of Antrim, 1609–1683* (Cambridge, 1993); J H Ohlmeyer, *Ireland from Independence to Occupation, 1641–1660* (Cambridge, 1995); M Perceval-Maxwell, *The Outbreak of the Irish Rebellion of 1641* (Dublin, 1994); A I Macinnes, *Charles I and the Making of the Covenanting Movement 1625–1641* (Edinburgh, 1991); P Donald, *An Uncounselled King. Charles I and the Scottish troubles, 1637–1641* (Cambridge, 1990); J Morrill, *The Nature of the English Revolution* (London, 1993); C Russell, *The Causes of the English Civil War* (Oxford, 1990); C Russell, *The Fall of the British Monarchies 1637–1642* (Oxford, 1991); J Morrill (ed), *The Scottish National Covenant in its British Context 1638–51* (Edinburgh, 1990); K M Brown, *Kingdom or Province? Scotland and the Regal Union, 1603–1715* (London, 1992); K M Brown, 'Aristocratic finances and the origins of the Scottish Revolution', *EHR*, 54, (1989), 46–87; D Stevenson (ed), *The Government of Scotland Under the Covenanters, 1637–51* (SHS, Edinburgh, 1982); M Lee, jr, *The Road to Revolution: Scotland Under Charles I, 1625–1637* (Urbana & Chicago, 1985). The notable Scottish exception is E J Cowan, *Montrose: For Covenant and King* (London, 1977).

2. For example, see S R Gardiner, *History of England, 1603–42* (12 volumes, London, 1883–1884), VII, 297, VIII, 339–341, IX, 17, 20; D Stevenson, *The Scottish Revolution 1637–1644. The Triumph of the Covenanters* (Newton Abbot, 1973), 94, 270. Hamilton also tended to polarise the opinions of contemporaries and his political reputation was harmed rather than recovered by Bishop Gilbert Burnet's Restoration apologia, *The Memoirs of the Lives and Actions of James and William Dukes of Hamilton* (Oxford, 1673). See also, [Marchamont Nedham], *Digitus Dei, or God's justice upon treachery and treason exemplified in the life and death of the late James, Duke of Hamilton, being an exact relation of his traitorous practices since the year 1630* (London, 1649); P Gordon, *A Short Abridgement of Britane's Distemper, 1639–1645*, J Dunn (ed), (Spalding Club, Aberdeen, 1844), 59–60, 207–208; R Baillie, *Letters and Journals, 1637–1662*, D. Laing (ed), three volumes, (Bannatyne Club, Edinburgh, 1841–42), I, 74–75, 92, 220; *The Diplomatic Correspondence of Jean de Montereul and the Brothers De Bellievre, French Ambassadors in England and Scotland, 1645–1648*, J G Fotheringham (ed), two volumes, (SHS, Edinburgh, 1898), volume one, 236, volume two, 51, 71, 175, 183, 189, 242.

3. cf Burnet, *Memoirs of the Lives, passim*.

4. SRO Hamilton Papers, GD 406/M9/42; Baillie, *Letters and Journals*, I, 74–75; I am currently working towards a full biography of Hamilton, but in the meantime, see John J Scally, 'The Political Career of James, third Marquis and first Duke of Hamilton (1606–1649) to 1643', (University of Cambridge, PhD thesis, 1992).

5. C V Wedgwood, *Thomas Wentworth First Earl of Strafford 1593–1641:* A Revaluation (London, 1964), 258–259, 265.

6. A large part of the correspondence between Hamilton and Charles I has survived intact (see SRO Hamilton Papers, GD 406). Some of the archive has been printed in *HMC Hamilton, HMC Hamilton Supplementary,* S R Gardiner (ed), *The Hamilton Papers* (Camden Society, 1880).

7. There was also a considerable amount of paper counsel in 1646 while Charles was at Newcastle. See Russell, *Causes of the English Civil War,* 190.

8. See Scally, 'The Political Career of James, third Marquis and First Duke of Hamilton', 233–262. See also Russell, *The Fall of the British Monarchies,* 43–60.

9. SRO Hamilton Papers, GD 406/1/552.

10. SRO GD 406 Hamilton Red Books, I, 64, 65.

11. SRO Hamilton Papers, GD 406/1/325. Hamilton's justification of his counsel to Charles written six months later (SRO GD 406/1/10510, printed in Gardiner, *The Hamilton Papers,* 42–46) clarifies the meaning of the above statement:

    your Matt may be pleased to remember thatt I Have oft
    tould you I had lytill hoope of uoorking of thatt by
    treatie uhich uoold be exseptabill to you: and thatt my
    aduyce uas you should gooe another uay to uoork with them

12. For this tendency, see Gardiner, *History of England,* IX, 339–341; G. Donaldson, Scotland, *James V–James VII* (Edinburgh, 1965), 317.

13. Scally, 'The Political Career of James, third Marquis and First Duke of Hamilton', 214–262.

14. SRO GD 406 Hamilton Red Books, I, 64, 65.

15. Scally, 'The Political Career of James, third Marquis and First Duke of Hamilton', 214–262; Baillie, *Letters and Journals,* I, 137, 142, 144–145, 146–147.

16. Macinnes, *Charles I and the Making of the Covenanting Movement,* 158–192; A I Macinnes, 'The Scottish Constitution, 1638–1651. The Rise and Fall of Oligarchic Centralism', in Morrill (ed), *The Scottish National Covenant in its British Context,* 106–134; E J Cowan, 'The Making of the National Covenant', in Morrill (ed), *The Scottish National Covenant in its British Context,* 68–89; J R Young, 'The Scottish Parliament, 1639–1661: A Political and Constitutional Analysis', (University of Glasgow, PhD thesis, three volumes, 1993), volume one, 1–18, 526–536.

17. J Leslie, Earl of Rothes, *A Relation of Proceedings Concerning the Affairs of the Kirk of Scotland, from August 1637 to July 1638,* J Nairne (ed), (Bannatyne Club, Edinburgh, 1830), 10, 73–74, 76–79. See also the Covenanters' obsessive desire to compose regular historical accounts of their proceedings (ibid, 52, 55–56, 81). The proclamation of 8 December 1638,

following the Glasgow Assembly, suggests that the Covenanters planned the rebellion from the outset, a charge which they denied; see [W Balcanqual], *A large Declaration concerning the late tumults in Scotland (London, 1639), 366–374 and passim;* [William Kerr, Earl of Lothian], *A True Representation of the proceedings of the kingdom of Scotland since the late pacification* ([Edinburgh] 1640), 3–7 and *passim;* NLS MS 2263, Salt and Coal: Events, 1635–1662, ff 49–52, 88–91.

18. Robert Baillie is the classic example; Baillie, *Letters and Journals*, I, 48–53, 137, 142, 144–145, 146–147, but see previous note. See also, Donald, *An Uncounselled King,* 42, 79–80, 116; Russell, *The Fall of the British Monarchies*, 172, 198.

19. On the strategic problems, see M C Fissel, *The Bishops' Wars. Charles I's campaigns against Scotland 1638–1640* (Cambridge, 1994), 1–61, 287–299, and *passim.* See also Scally, 'The Political Career of James, third Marquis and first Duke of Hamilton', 264–271.

20. SRO Hamilton Papers, GD 406/1/327/1.

21. The text of the National Covenant is printed in W C Dickinson and G Donaldson (eds), *A Source Book of Scottish History*, three volumes, (second edition, Edinburgh, 1961), volume I, 32–35, 95–104.

22. The promotion of an alternative Covenant to that of February 1638, the so-called King's Covenant, in September 1638 was another attempt to reconcile Charles to the idea of Covenanting.

23. SRO Hamilton Papers, GD 406/1/327/1. A considerable amount of Charles's fury at the National Covenant was based on the part of the band attached to the Confession of Faith, which bound the signatories in

> mutual defence and assistance, every one of us of another
> in the same cause of maintaining the true Religion and
> his Majesty's Authority, with our best counsel, our
> bodies, meanes, and whole power, against all sorts of
> persons whatsover.

See the text of the National Covenant printed in Dickinson and Donaldson, *A Source Book of Scottish History*, I, 32–35, 95–104, especially 102.

24. The conjunction 'if' in the last sentence is highly significant.

25. See also SRO Hamilton Papers, GD 406/1/10525, also printed in Gardiner, *The Hamilton Papers*, 62–64.

26. Hamilton reminded Charles that the French had not forgotten the Isle de Rhe or La Rochelle and that the French probably had their own intelligence agents in Scotland. The Spanish agent's recent insult to Charles was well known in Edinburgh (SRO Hamilton Papers, GD 406/1/327/2).

27. SRO Hamilton Papers, GD 406/2/M9/88/6–7. There is also a joint list of Royalists and Covenanters in the Bodleian Library, University of Oxford,

MS Dep.c.172, folio 11. See J. Morrill, 'The National Covenant in its British Context', in Morrill (ed), *The Scottish National Covenant in its British Context*, 15, 27, n.68.

28. The scathing comment on the legal fraternity's support for the Covenanting Movement recalls Hamilton's frustration at the lawyers' united assertion that the National Covenant was legal, and at the prominent role of Wariston and, to a lesser degree, Sir Thomas Hope of Craighall, Lord Advocate.

29. Burnet, *The Memoirs of the Dukes of Hamilton*, 75–77; SRO Hamilton Papers, GD 406/1/10492. Charles's furious rejection 'of there damnable Covenant' 'with or without an explanation' was a rejular feature in his letters.

30. For the attempts at a settlement after June 1638, see Scally, 'The Political Career of James, third Marquis and first Duke of Hamilton', 25–262; Donald, *An Uncounselled King*, 87–118.

31. Fissell, *The Bishops' Wars*, 287–299, 1–61 and *passim*.

32. SRO Hamilton Papers, GD 406/1/10541, GD 406/1/938/1; Gardiner, *The Hamilton Papers*, 74.

33. For a detailed narrative, see Donald, *An Uncounselled King*, 141–152. Conrad Russell has suggested that Charles, with his army still in pay on the Borders, was in a better position to fight the Scots in 1639 than he was in 1640 following the failure of the Short Parliament to back the war (*The Fall of the British Monarchies*, 89–90).

34. Hamilton MSS (His Grace the Duke of Hamilton, Lennoxlove, East Lothian), TD 91/109/M3/1.

35. SRO Hamilton Papers, GD 406/1/10548. This is printed with some differences in Gardiner, *The Hamilton Papers*, 78–80.

36. Gardiner's description of the military manoeuvres has never been bettered. See S.R. Gardiner, *History of England*, IX, 20–57.

37. Russell, *The Fall of the British Monarchies*, 78.

38. SRO Hamilton Papers, GD 406/1/1179. In a postscript Charles wrote,

Having no tyme my selfe to wryte so much, I was forced to use his Pen, therfor I shall onlie say that what is heere written, I have directed, seene, & approved, CR.'

39. See above; Burnet, *The Memoirs of the Dukes of Hamilton*, 175–176.

40. SRO Hamilton Papers, GD 406/1/1188/1–2.

41. SRO Hamilton Papers, GD 406/1/10543.

42. Baillie, *Letters and Journals*, I, 203–204; *Fragment of the Diary of Sir Archibald Johnston, 1639*, G M Paul (ed), (SHS, Edinburgh, 1896), 36–37.

43. Gardiner, *The Hamilton Papers*, 80–83; Baillie, *Letters and Journals*, I, 203–204.

44. SRO Hamilton Papers, GD 406/1/844/1.

45. SRO Hamilton Papers, GD 406/M1/90; *CSPD*, 1639, 304; P. Yorke, Earl of Hardwicke (ed), *Miscellaneous State Papers 1501–1726* (two volumes, London), II, 130–141.

46. The negotiations commenced on 11 June, but Wariston, Henderson, and Hamilton did not attend until the second meeting on 13 June (*CSPD*, 1639, 312).

47. *Fragment of the Diary of Sir Archibald Johnston of Wariston*, 71; Hardwicke, *Miscellaneous State Papers*, II, 130–141.

48. SRO Hamilton Papers, GD 406/1/M1/60.

49. Ibid. For another paper by Hamilton with assent to the abolition of Episcopacy as a means to wrest the initiative away from the Covenanters, see SRO Hamilton Papers, GD 406/M9/88/4.

50. SRO Hamilton Papers, GD 406/1/948.

51. Ibid.

52. Hamilton's trip to Edinburgh on 22 June to repossess the castle, during which time he was shouted down in the streets and exhorted to 'stand by Jesus Christ', had a strong impact on his behavioue when he returned to Berwick (*CSPD, 1639*, 355; Burnet, *The Memoirs of the Dukes of Hamilton*, 181).

53. SRO Hamilton Papers, GD 406/1/809.

54. It is also striking that the document has survived since it incriminates not only Hamilton, but also Charles. It underlines once more the untrustworthy nature of the king.

55. Donald, *An Uncounselled King*, 245–255.

56. SRO Hamilton Papers, GD 406/1/865.

57. Traquair MSS, (Maxwell-Stewart, Traquair House, Innerlethen), 28/i/13.

58. SRO GD 406/1/936.

59. Donald, *An Uncounselled King*, especially 320–327.

60. For a discussion of Scottish parliamentary politics in the 1640s, see J. Scally, 'Constitutional Revolution, Party and Faction in the Scottish Parliaments of Charles I', in *The Scots and Parliament*, *Parliamentary History* special volume, volume 15 part one, 1996) 54–74.

61. Wedgewood, *Thomas Wentworth*, 259, 265–267. It is interesting to note that Charles's letter written at Berwick, recalling Wentworth from Ireland, was dated 23 July 1639, two years to the day since the Prayer Book riots in Edinburgh.

CHAPTER 3

James Butler, twelfth Earl of Ormond, the Irish Government, and the Bishops' Wars, 1638–40

William Kelly

In July 1640 the Lord President of Munster, Sir William St Leger, was billeted with the Irish army at Carrickfergus in north-east Ulster preparing an invasion of Scotland to suppress the Covenanters' revolt. From this vantage point he assured his commanding officer, the Earl of Ormond, Lieutenant General of the army, that he now had at his disposal a force of 'such brave gallant fellows such as a man would choose if a crown were at stake.'[1] Even if we disregard St Leger's hyperbole about an army which he took pride in having personally transformed from 'poor stinking rascally freaks'[2] into soldiers, the importance of this evidence is that it reveals the awareness among contemporaries of the great height to which the troubles in Scotland had grown in the short time since the subscription of the National Covenant in 1638. The stakes were indeed high. Three crowns, rather than merely one, were at stake. By the summer of 1640 Ormond also had no illusions as to what fortunes and careers might eventually be at risk were the venture to fail and the Scots, perhaps in alliance with the opposition in the English Parliament, emerge as the victorious party.

With that background in mind, this paper will examine the impact of the Bishops' Wars on the government of Ireland in general. More particularly it will analyse, by means of a short case-study, how the Earl of Ormond reacted to the political crisis which the Scottish wars engendered. I will suggest that there is evidence of a marked reluctance to unhesitatingly obey the orders of their king even on the part of those, like the Earl of Ormond, whom posterity has identified as stalwart Royalists. As the crisis of the three kingdoms accelerated and the potentially disastrous implications became more balefully apparent the reluctance to become too closely identified with a policy that seemed to some not only misguided but doomed to failure grew commensurately.

Firstly, however, an understanding of the context of Irish events is a necessary prelude to any analysis of the impact of these wars in that kingdom. Some recent historical debate has centred on whether or not the 1641 Rebellion in Ireland came as an unexpected explosion in an otherwise prosperous and generally peaceful kingdom. While it is not possible at this stage to come to any firm conclusions on this issue, it is at least clear that if the Irish government failed to foresee the scale of the violence which overtook the kingdom in October 1641 it was nevertheless constantly aware that it governed a country in which low-level unrest was endemic. Indeed, one of the factors which modulated policy in Ireland was the assumption that rebellion could and would break out at the first opportunity. In putting the events of the Bishops' Wars in an Irish context here, we should perhaps remind ourselves that historians have largely accepted that one of the consequences of Charles I's difficulties in Scotland, and the means by which he sought to resolve them, was to provide that opportunity.

Specific Irish problems therefore conditioned Lord Deputy Thomas Wentworth's initial reaction to the king's demands that his Irish kingdom should provide assistance against his Scottish subjects. Wentworth's primary concern in the early stages of the Scottish crisis was how it would affect Ireland, even if all minds at Court were preoccupied with Scotland.[3] Wentworth's anxieties about the probable consequences in Ireland helps to explain his initially cool reception to the king's plans to resolve his difficulties in Scotland by force of arms. It is also true, of course, that his policy was influenced in part by his animosity towards the Randall MacDonnell, 2nd Earl of Antrim, whom Charles I had authorised to lead an assault on Argyll's lands in the Western Isles. But personal antipathy apart, Wentworth had justifiable grounds for condemning any plan to use Antrim. For one thing, Antrim's adventure could be counter-productive and might very well result in a pre-emptive invasion of Ulster by the Scots.[4] For a man who had expended much time and energy during his tenure of office denying the Scots, especially Antrim's patron James, 3rd Marquis of Hamilton, access to Irish lands, such a development would have been doubly unwelcome.[5] Wentworth doubted that the small Irish army of 2,000 foot and less than half that number of horse could contain such an incursion since the Covenanters would obviously derive widespread support in Ulster from their notoriously recalcitrant Presbyterian brethren in the province.[6]

Antrim was also a Catholic. In a well known report on an interview with the Earl regarding his plans, Wentworth remarked that he had informed him of his intention to arm as his Confederates in the enterprise as many O's and Mac's, sons of habituated rebels, as would affright an entire council.[7] What might become of the English in

Ireland, the Lord Deputy asked, if Antrim's native Irish troops were to suddenly fall on them, armed, of all things, with weapons supplied by the government in Dublin.[8]

The king had also requested troops from the Irish army to help garrison his Scottish strongholds.[9] Again Wentworth demurred although he sent 500 men under Sir Francis Willoughby to occupy Carlisle.[10] Drawing troops from Ireland was a risky business at any time but all the more so now, he protested. Without his army 'the chief control we have over this great people' he could not guarantee law and order in the 'unsettled' provinces of Connaught or Munster, bedevilled by lawlessness as a direct consequence of those plantations relentlessly pursued by Wentworth.[11] Nor could he take adequate meaures to suppress banditry in Donegal or to control 'the wicked course of burning Englishmen's houses' as near to home as Wexford and Wicklow.[12] An already unsettled Ireland could very quickly collapse into rebellion.

But Wentworth was not opposed to a military resolution of the crisis. He disagreed with the strategy. Suggesting that Fabius rather than Marcellus should be the example to follow, he recommended an alternative.[13] Time should be spent preparing a professional force firmly under the control of the government, (that is, under Wentworth's command) unlike Antrim's potentially rebellious ragbag of Redshanks and Gaelic Irish. Wentworth argued to Sir John Coke that to go off at half-cock with 'an imperfectly disciplined and knowing army', was worse than doing nothing.[14] If the Covenanters were to be crushed they must be demonstrably and utterly crushed. Moreover, at the first indications of trouble in Scotland Wentworth had moved to increase the army in Ireland and to make contingency plans in the event of any trouble from the Ulster Scots. As a result of these precautions the Earl of Ormond was promoted to Lieutenant-General of Horse.[15]

In 1638 command of the tiny cavalry force assigned to the Irish army may not have appeared a mark of any great distinction or approbation. However, Ormond's appointment must be viewed in the light of the plans to expand the Irish forces with the specific object of training the army for service against the Covenanters in Ulster or even in Scotland. Ormond's appointment at this time therefore reflects the trust reposed in him by the Lord Deputy. As commander of the cavalry in any expeditionary force the Ormond would in effect have been Wentworth's second-in-command. The young Earl embraced his promotion enthusiastically. Some months later his troop of carabins was replaced, at his request, by one of cuirassiers.[16] In explanation of this decision to the King, Wentworth typically emphasised, a little optimistically, that Ormond had the financial wherewithal to maintain a troop of the more heavily armed cuirassiers at his own cost.[17] Furthermore, Wentworth stressed his high opinion of the young Earl's assistance hitherto,

> being a person by much the most considerable of the
> Irish; of Affections and Parts, as I conceive, which
> deserve encouragement and fit for the service of a
> Crown.[18]

Two months later, in October 1638, the Lord Deputy proffered the further assurance that Ormond, 'by his Cheerful and Right Affections to Your Majesty's service, will approve the opinion I have of him'.[19] However, Wentworth also made it clear that it was Ormond's political utility rather than any military talent which had persuaded him to promote him in so high a degree. The sum of the young Earl's military training had been gained with his troop of carabins on the parade ground under Wentworth's supervision during the army reforms. Both men were novices in military affairs and usually deputised military manoeuvres to their more experienced subordinates.[20] One month before Ormond's promotion the Lord Deputy had expressly requested that he be sent a military adviser to assist in preparing the army.[21] By October 1638 contingency plans were well advanced for using the troops in Scotland in an effort to overawe the Covenanters. On 17 October Wentworth earnestly requested Ormond to attend a Council of War at Dublin Castle on 21 November presumably to work out the details of an invasion, and swore him to secrecy until that time.[22] Ormond's troopers were to be rearmed on the same day with new weapons ordered from Holland.[23] The details of the plan are clear from a memorandum to the king in which it was confidently envisaged that a total of nine troops of horse and almost 9,000 foot would land on the west coast of Scotland, temporarily occupy Leith, and thereby terrify the Covenanters into 'turning their coats.'[24] Although no date was set for the enterprise it would most probably have taken place at the beginning of the next campaigning season.

As a short-term alternative, while the army was being prepared, Wentworth suggested in May 1639 that he station soldiers in the north of Ireland to distract the Covenanters, Argyll in particular, by threatening their flank while simultaneously bringing the Presbyterians in Ulster to heel.[25] At the same time he imposed an oath of allegiance there, the notorious Black Oath, which even the presence of 1,500 troops could not fully enforce.[26] But in June 1639 Wentworth's warnings about striking too soon were fully justified when the Scots humiliated the king on the border, demonstrating beyond doubt their determination and superior organisation. One consequence was that the necessity of deriving support from Ireland was now all the more important. During the breathing space provided by the Treaty of Berwick in June 1639 Wentworth was summoned to Court to plan a new attack scheduled for the following summer, in which he and Ireland were expected to play as full a role as he had earlier advised.[27] That Ormond was viewed by contemporaries as the Lord Deputy's right-hand man is evidenced by the significant, if mistaken intelligence relayed by Lionel Cranfield, Earl of Middlesex, to the Marquis of Hamilton at Court that the Lord Deputy had returned to England 'and with him the Earl of Ormond.'[28] Raised to the peerage as Earl of Strafford in January 1640, Wentworth set about over the winter of 1639–40 organizing the recruitment and arming of a new Irish army of 8,000 foot and 1,000 horse.[29]

During his absence he needed to delegate authority and responsibility to trusted adherents. His cousin, the Master of the Rolls, Sir Christopher Wandesford, was to be Lord Deputy but he turned to Ormond to oversee military affairs.[30] This is unsurprising given the fact that Ormond was already counted amongst that group of trusted adherents who now managed Ireland on the absent Deputy's behalf. He was also a natural choice as commander of the army.

Although his only military experience had been as an aide to the Deputy in reforming the Irish army, Ormond had many attractive qualities which probably convinced the Lord-Lieutenant of his suitability for the post. It was not an insignificant consideration that Ormond was a close personal friend, and Strafford needed friends, now addressed in intimate terms since Wentworth's enoblement.[31] He had already amply demonstrated his willingness to serve the Crown and his patron and was a valued member of the administration. Ormond's own authority and network of local connections was an obvious asset in the recruitment of troops. As a commander of horse he had already demonstrated his administrative skills. Moreover, in his person Ormond was possessed of additional attributes which made him, at this time especially, an inspired choice as commander of the Irish army. Above all, he was well acquainted with the officers and men of the standing army from which it was envisaged the officer corps of the enlarged army would be drawn.[32] These men were to form a nucleus of experienced soldiers who would train and officer the new levies of largely Irish Roman Catholic, and by definition, potentially unreliable troops. The officer corps of the new army was therefore to be almost exclusively Protestant;[33] officers who would have found service under a Roman Catholic commander against their conscience. However, there were no doubts about Ormond's religious sympathies. Nevertheless, some of the officers were Old English Catholics and although Ormond's religion distanced him from them in this respect, it did not disqualify him from exercising the authority conferred by his earldom. As prime nobleman of the kingdom, Ormond's prestige and standing commanded the respect of New English, Old English, and Gaelic Irish alike, while in his capacity as His Majesty's Lieutenant-General he commanded their allegiance in the king's name. Ormond was ideally placed to unite under his command an army riven by sectarian and political faction.

More to the point, as far as Strafford was concerned, Ormond's political credentials as a supporter of the government were impeccable. Since he had arrived in Ireland as Lord Deputy in 1634, the two men had worked closely together in the government of the kingdom. Ormond had collaborated in the management of elections to the Irish Parliament.[34] It was only with the Ormond's assistance that Wentworth had been able to implement plantations in Munster, a central plank of his policy in Ireland.[35] The alliance was mutually beneficial in that Ormond was rewarded for his assistance in grants of offices and financial renumeration. He became a Privy Councillor aged only twenty-four in 1635, and Lieutenant-General of Horse in the army three years later.[36] But, for Ormond, the alliance brought obligations as well as benefits. In fact he was now being called on to serve in the front rank against the king's enemies. For a cautious politician, and Ormond was ever cautious, the deepening crisis in the three kingdoms revealed the potentially perilous course on which his king and his patron appeared irrevocably set; a course in which Ormond was expected to play a leading part. Ormond's central role was attested by Strafford in April 1640 when he told the king that he had decided

> to leave the Execution of all we have resolved in that
> Great Affair to the care of my Lord of Ormond, the Master
> of the Ordnance, and Lord President of Munster, who I am
> very confident will be so awake, as nothing shall be
> neglected in my absence.[37]

Prime responsibilty rested with Ormond. He was now to be Lieutenant-General of the Irish army and Commander-in-Chief during the Lord Lieutenant's time at Court, charged with raising the troops and ensuring that they mustered on schedule at Carrickfergus.[38] In addition he was now given the colonelcy of a regiment of cavalry.[39]

For the Irish administration this was a considerable task. The new army had to be recruited, trained, maintained, and mustered in Ulster by May for service in Scotland by late June.[40] On 9 February 1640 Strafford wrote to Ormond delegating in full his authority in military matters and giving him, in effect, a licence to act in his name.[41] Since it had been resolved that the necessary finance should be provided in Ireland, a new session of Parliament was called and in March 1640 the Lord-Lieutenant hurried back to Dublin to ensure a successful outcome.[42] As it turned out the parliamentary assembly was enthusiastic to assist the king. Old English collaboration gave the government an easy passage and Parliament voted four subsidies and even passed a laudatory preamble to the act in thanksgiving for Strafford's good government of the kingdom.[43]

As we might expect, given his prominent role in the administration, Ormond was very active during the parliamentary session. He escorted Strafford at the formal opening on 20 March and attended the House on almost every sitting thereafter.[44] On 28 March he was appointed to a committee of twelve lords to meet the Commons to discuss the draft declaration concerning the subsidies.[45] Ormond was also instrumental in persuading the Lords to accept a declaration assuring Charles I of their resolve 'not to stay here at these four subsidies' should the king require further assistance.[46] Ormond's support for Strafford and his policies was even more in evidence on the last day of the session when he was the prime mover in having the Bishop of Killala removed from the House of Lords as a favourer of the Scottish National Covenant.[47]

Outside Parliament, during February and March 1640, Ormond had again used his influence on behalf of the administration to return government supporters to the Commons. One of the areas in which Old English Catholic representation was reduced over this period was Kilkenny, where Ormond's influence was, if not paramount, impossible to ignore. In Kilkenny the Old English held eleven out of twelve seats available.[48] After Ormond's intervention government nominees accounted for six of these same seats.[49] The members returned reflect the strongly pro-government ethos of the young Earl. Two were close relations of Wandesford, and one a particular friend of the Lord-Lieutenant, Sir Thomas Wharton.[50] A similar pattern emerged in Tipperary, another sphere of Ormond's interest. Strafford's secretary, Sir Thomas Little, was again returned for Cashel.[51]

Parliament came to a successful conclusion and the Lord-Lieutenant returned to England immediately afterwards to superintend what he over-confidently expected would be a similarly favourable outcome in the impending Parliament there.[52] The Irish Parliament would not meet again until June 1640 and had, in any case, displayed so accommodating an attitude that any worries about what transpire during his absence were largely dispelled. Moreover, Strafford could feel confident that his own supporters dominated the government. On his return to England he felt satisfied that he had taken all possible precautions to ensure sound management of the political situation in Ireland until he could return to take personal command of the army in the summer.[53]

In the meantime, Ormond moved swiftly to carry out his orders, holding daily Councils of War, and within a matter of weeks most of the required men had been recruited.[54] But soon after Strafford's departure things began to go badly awry in Ireland. When Parliament reassembled in June the Commons were no longer in so accommodating a frame of mind. Given the benificent mood of the previous session, Wandesford had little reason to assume that the House would behave any differently in the new session. But the situation had altered drastically since the Lord-Lieutenant had made his triumphant return to England with lavish promises of support from Ireland in his pocket. For one thing, Black Tom Tyrant, as Strafford was unflatteringly known in Ireland, was not on hand to manage, overawe or intimidate opposition. Secondly, and more significantly, the Short Parliament in England, called on his advice, had manifestly failed to follow the Irish example. In fact, matters turned out exactly opposite to what Strafford had expected and predicted. The Irish Parliament took its cue from the English rather than *vice versa*. The English had refused to grant subsidies without redress of grievance, incidentally exposing the king's weakness and providing a subversive model for their Irish counterparts. During the vacation the Irish Commons' committee had not been inactive either and, it has been pointed out, it was probably during the deliberations of this body that an identity of interest between the Old English and New English emerged.[55]

The Irish opposition now seized the opportunity to reverse the political balance. Traditionally, the second session of Parliament allowed for the redress of grievances on the subject's part, the government's requirements having been satisfied in the first session. But the somewhat incongruous alliance of the administration and the Old English which had facilitated the smooth passage of the subsidy bills in the first session broke down in the second session when these same MPs used the window of opportunity presented by the government's financial discomfiture to form an equally contradictory but opportune alliance with New English opponents of the regime. The alliance was based on a number of disparate grievances, all of which coalesced, however, in antipathy for Strafford's administration.[56] The compliant Parliament of some months previously had now become a vociferous and recalcitrant body of opposition which chose to demonstrate its disaffection by repudiating legislation including, crucially, the subsidy bill to provide funds for the new army.[57] Even in the House of Lords, where the government could generally expect support, the situation had altered in favour of the opposition.[58] In the course of just over a fortnight, Wandesford was left with no other option than to prorogue the session of 17 June.[59] The defection of the Old English, and Wandesford lamented, 'those of our own party' erased the government majority and, it rapidly appeared, with it the confidence of some, like the Earl of Ormond, who had previously been stalwarts in their support for the Lord-Lieutenant and his administration.[60]

Ormond's lack of confidence, his doubts about the course of policy and its conseqences, not only for himself but for the kingdom of Ireland, are evident in his actions over the late spring and summer of 1640. He left Dublin soon after Strafford's departure for England and in late April or early May he retired to his seat at Kilkenny.[61] Remarkably, given his position as effective commander of the army, Ormond remained there throughout the summer of 1640. Initially, he gave as his reason for going his wife's impending confinement and her ill-health, but the available evidence points to a conclusion that he retired to Kilkenny to await events and contemplate the implications of his present position. Most suggestive of all is his absence from Parliament, especially since it is difficult to believe that with his network of family and clients, some of whom played leading roles in the parliamentary oppostion, that the Earl of Ormond remained unaware of the subversion brewing between the sessions and the probable outcome when Parliament reassembled. Indeed, at Kilkenny Ormond was as much concerned with Strafford's health as he was about that of the Countess. During his time there he wrote concerned letters to Wandesford anxiously enquiring after his friend's condition.[62] He was also kept reliably abreast of events in England by George Carr and Sir George Radcliffe at Leicester House.[63] What Ormond feared, with many others, was that the ailing Lord Lieutenant might not survive his illness to return to Ireland. Even if he did his political position in Ireland and England was already being called into serious question. While the almost distraught Lord Deputy presided over what has been described as the disintegration of the Irish government, Ormond, the most powerful nobleman in the kingdom, remained in Kilkenny, apparently powerless to intervene.[64]

In early May Ormond had informed Wandesford that he could not attend the forthcoming parliamentary session and he formally requested leave of absence late in the same month.[65] Wandesford had little choice but to comply with the Earl's initial request but his disappointment is evident in his confession to Ormond that 'your presence here would be of great benefit to the King's service.'[66] At the beginning of June Wandesford wrote to Ormond urging him to return to Dublin:

> the sooner and your occasions permitting it, the sooner
> you come the better that we may have your assistance here
> upon the setting forth of this army.[67]

Ormond suggested instead that he should go to the army in Ulster to rendezvous with the foot but Wandesford reminded him of Strafford's orders that St Leger should take charge of their training there.[68] Evidently the Lord Lieutenant's intention was that Ormond should assist in Parliament. At the end of the month Wandesford complained to Ormond that his absence from the Lords had been unfortunate, that he had had

> a pretty time of Ease and advantage, we have no small
> trouble here and our hands have been full of difficulties
> both with the Parliament and the Army and had not my
> Lady's great belly required your coming your Lordship
> should have been desrired to take your share with us
> here.[69]

It is clear from Wandesford's correspondence with Ormond that Strafford had insisted his subordinate delegate command of the troops for the very reason that his presence in Dublin was of far greater benefit politically than any military contribution he could make at Carrickfergus. In any case, the Lord Lieutenant intended to take personal command of the army by the late summer. At the end of June, Lady Elizabeth Butler gave birth to a daughter. Her husband's initial reasons for delaying at Kilkenny were removed but Ormond nevertheless chose to remain there for over two months more, again on the pretext that her health was still at risk.[70]

However, political concerns apart, it is also evident that Ormond, even at this stage, had grave doubts about the chances of military victory over the Scots. He had every reason to be sceptical given the failure of the Marquis of Hamilton to provide the necessary shipping, the inability of the Irish administration to provide funds, and the lateness of the season.[71] The local musters had been postponed until the start of June and then put off for almost another three weeks on account of the lack of finance and transportation for the artillery and baggage.[72] Ormond had also learned in May of a serious reverse inflicted on the king's naval forces by Argyll near the proposed landing ground, an area which his correspondent informed him the entire population 'were ready upon any Occasion in Arms to withstand assault upon them' and had forced the royal ships to withdraw to the Irish coast.[73] Ormond's anxieties about the chances of military defeat by the well-armed and organised Scots are also evident from his notes on a map of the proposed landing ground which clearly shows how Argyll had managed to dominate the area by fortifying Dumbarton.[74] It is clear that Ormond's gloomy assessment of the military situation reinforced his doubts about the political wisdom of his patron's belligerent policies.

Indeed, Ormond's lack of enthusiasm became even more apparent in the months which followed and was reinforced by events in England and Scotland. Shortly before the Scots ignominiously routed the royal army at the Battle of Newburn in August 1640 Ormond had been ordered to join his troops and proceed with the invasion.[75] Ormond's doubts about the possibilty of defeat were reinforced by his superior's instructions to build two large flat bottomed craft, 'in the manner of ferri-boates,' to assist with the landing of troops and to provide covering fire since Strafford thought it all too likely the men would have to disembark 'in difficult places.'[76] More problematically for Ormond, after Newburn Strafford's return to Ireland to take command and responsibility in person was now out of the question and he transferred his plenary powers as Captain-General to the Ormond.[77] Ormond's misgivings at this turn of events are apparent a number of queries he set down on receiving these instructions.[78]

Primarily, Ormond was not convinced that Strafford could delegate authority in

> these high matters...without a particular licence from
> the King under the Great Seal...wherein a particular
> person is to be named.[79]

Even if he could, was it legally certain, Ormond anxiously pondered,

> Whether a deputy whose deputation is not a record under
> the Great Seal can invoke and use the great powers
> aforesaid?[80]

With an astute eye to the possible consequences of the Scots victory at Newburn Ormond wondered what would be the legal standing of that deputy should 'the king and Parliament of England...upon a full peace make an act to warrant the Scottish actions?'[81] That the commission did not include any provision for the absolution of the deputy was therefore a cause for greater concern because, as he put it,

> Whether the words, (for the safety of the King and state)
> do limit all parts of the letters Patent that if (in the
> event of misconstruction) the contrary should happen to
> be taken; in what danger is the Deputy being a Deputy
> without the great seale?[82]

In fact Ormond was not at all certain, 'Whether it be safe for the Deputy to take the charge upon him without clear satisfaction in these particulars,' and concluded that the only option which could guarantee protection was to 'get a commission under the great seal...to do and execute in the absence of my Lord Lieutenant.'[83]

These queries do not, of course, suggest that Ormond had any intention of not carrying out his orders even if his fears were not allayed by a commission under the Great Seal. But at some stage here he requested just such a commission and a full clarification of his warrant.[84] What his queries do reveal, however, is a fundamental unease at the apparently irrevocable drift to war and the ultimate aim of royal policy. These queries were a shrewd politician's assessment of the risks his own prominent role might entail. For even so staunch a Royalist as the Earl of Ormond there was an awareness that the king's policies were not by definition the only policies never mind the most sensible. One can conclude here that Ormond returned to Kilkenny in 1640 in an effort to sit out the crisis. His wife's pregnancy was a convenient excuse but Ormond's reasons for remaining at his seat had more to do with the political and physical health of Lord Lieutenant Strafford and the wisdom or otherwise of his policies than solicitude for his wife's condition. Although Ormond was very closely allied to Strafford's faction he was also only too well aware that Lord Deputies, and Lord Lieutenants, come and go. By the late summer of 1640 it was evident to even the most uninformed that Strafford may have had his day. In Ireland this would mean a readjustment of the factional balance in the Irish government and those who had put as much distance as possible from the worst excesses of the policies of Black Tom Tyrant would be in the best position to capitalise on the new situation.

Moreover, although this paper has focused on the Earl of Ormond's reaction to the Scottish crisis he was by no means alone in attempting to withdraw from involvement in a policy which he deemed not only unwise but dangerous. By December one of his officers with the army at Carrickfergus, the renowned and indomitable Sir Charles Coote, came to the same conclusions soon after his superior. Less astute than Ormond and further from the centre of power, Sir Charles did not grasp the implications of the king's policy as readily as Ormond, but when he did his reaction was the same, even if more impetuous. Soon after he had made contact on his own initiative with some Covenanters in Ulster Coote wrote to Ormond informing him that he had suddenly been 'visited with such affliction and perplexity of mind, oppressed with melancholy and unsettled thoughts,' and asked permission to leave the army and go to his son's house.[85] Sir Charles's was perhaps motivated by fears for his own personal safety and his illness was convenient but his sudden affliction is indicative of the resolve of some prominent figures to detach themselves from their king's policies. In conclusion here it must be said in fairness to Ormond that his anxieties about the drift of policy went beyond the merely personal. One consequence of Charles I's adventurism in Scotland was the destabilisation of an already unsettled Ireland which resulted in the rebellion of October 1641. Ormond's fears in this regard were tragically borne out in October 1641 when the country collapsed into a civil war, the horrors of which Thomas Burke predicted in 1642 would, and sadly did, make another Germany of the kingdom.[86]

NOTES

1. Sir William St Leger to Ormond, 21 July 1640, Bodleian Library, Oxford, Carte MSS, i, ff 214–215.

2. Ibid.

3. A Clarke, 'The Earl of Antrim and the First Bishops' war,' in *Irish Sword*, vi, (1963), 108–115,112. For a fuller account of these events, see M Perceval-Maxwell *The Outbreak of the Irish Rebellion of 1641* (Dublin, 1994).

4. W Knowler, (ed), *The earl of Strafforde's letters and despatches with an essay towards his life by Sir George Radcliffe...*, (two volumes, London, 1739), volume. ii, 285–290, 289, 325–328. Wentworth believed that Argyll was 'the likelier of the two to begin the sport with our Earl on this side, than my lord of Antrim's going over to him.' See also, Lord Deputy to the King, 10 February 1639, Knowler (ed), *Strafforde's letters*, ii, 277–279, 278; Wentworth to Vane, 30 May 1639, *HMC Cowper MSS*, ii, 229–230, 230. For Antrim's role in these events see J. H. Ohlmeyer, *Civil War and Restoration in the three Stuart Kingdoms. The Career of Randal McDonnell, Marquis of Antrim 1609–1683*, (Cambridge 1993).

5. D Stevenson, D., *Scottish Covenanters and Irish Confederates: Scottish-Irish relations in the mid-seventeenth century*, (Belfast, 1981), 14.

6. Wentworth to Vane, 30 May 1639, HMC, 12th Report, Appendix Part II, *The Manuscripts of the Earl Cowper, Preserved at Melbourne Hall, Derbyshire*, volume II, 229–230, 230.

7. Knowler (ed), *Strafforde's letters*, ii, 300, 300–305.

8. Ibid, 292–298, 297; H F Kearney, *Strafford in Ireland 1633–41. A study in absolutism* (second edition, Cambridge, 1989), 188.

9. Knowler, (ed), *Strafforde's letters*, ii, 228.

10. Sheffield Central Library, Wentworth Woodhouse Muniments, Strafford MSS, xi, part 1, f 218 (Wentworth to Windebank, 15 April 1639).

11. *HMC Cowper MSS*, II, 229–230, 230.

12. Ibid.

13. Ibid, 229.

14. Ibid, 227.

15. Bodleian Library, Oxford, Carte MSS, i, f 169; Knowler, (ed), *Strafforde's letters*, ii, 225–226; Strafford MSS, iii, ff 340–342. There is no record of the exact date of Ormond's promotion but Wentworth's recommendation of 11 August refers to the Earl as 'being already Lieutenant-General of Horse.' However, it was certainly before the end of June 1638. See Christopher Wandesford to Sir George Radcliffe, 30 June 1638: 'My Lord hath appointed since you went these new officers: the Earl of Ormond, Lieutenant-General of Horse,' T D Whitaker, *Life and original letters of Sir George Radcliffe*, (London, 1810), two volumes, ii, 248.

16. Knowler (ed), *Strafforde's letters*, ii, 225–226.

17. Wentworth's estimation of Ormond's financial situation was greatly in error. In fact, the Earl's perennially perilous finances were even further strained by this additional burden. Indeed, he appears to have used his military allowances as security for loans and he defaulted much of his pay over the coming months. He explained to his tailor, William Perkins of Fleet St, London, that he 'could not pay for the buff coat(s) at this time because the charges of [his] troop have been too heavy.' The unfortunate Perkins was still trying to recover much of this bill almost ten years later. See Ormond's receipts from Vice-Treasurer Loftus, February–September 1639, Carte MSS, clxxvi, ff 79, 81, 87, 90, 92, 93, 95; Ormond to William Perkins, 16 July 1639, Carte MSS, i, 171; J C Beckett, *The Cavalier Duke. A Life of James Butler first Duke of Ormond, 1610–1688* (Belfast, 1990), 42.

18. Strafford MSS, iii, part 1, ff 340–342.

19. Strafford MSS, iii, part 2, f 3.

20. This inexperience did not prevent Wentworth penning a military manual, a copy of which Ormond kept in his library at Kilkenny castle. The Lord Deputy's martial pretentiousness made him the butt of some unflattering jokes in the

ranks. His inspection of the troops wearing his new armour seems to have been the cause of much hilarity. See Inventories of Ormond's furniture, pictures, tapestry, plate and books, HMC *Calendar of the Manuscripts of the Marquess of Ormonde, K.P. Preserved at Kilkenny Castle*, New Series, eight volumes, (London, 1902–1920), vii, 497–527; C V Wedgwood, *Thomas Wentworth First Earl of Strafford 1593–1641, A Revaluation* (London 1955), 133.

21. Strafford MSS, iii, part 1, ff 336–9, f 339.

22. Carte MSS, i, 169.

23. Ibid.

24. *CSPD, 1638–9*, 63.

25. For a more detailed discussion of this policy see, Stevenson, *Scottish Covenanters and Irish Confederates*, 18–19, 21–22, 32; M Perceval-Maxwell, 'Strafford, the Ulster Scots and the Covenanters,' *Irish Historical Studies*, xviii, no. 72, (1973), pp 524–550; Kearney, *Strafford in Ireland*, 187.

26. Knowler (ed), *Strafforde's letters*, ii, 335–337, 336; Perceval-Maxwell, 'Strafford, the Ulster Scots and the Covenanters', 542 and *passim*.

27. Knowler (ed), *Strafforde's letters*, ii, 372–373.

28. SRO Hamilton Papers, GD406/1/1025. I am indebted to John Scally for this and other references.

29. Knowler (ed), *Strafforde's letters*, ii, 391–392, 400–401. Muster roll of the Irish army 23 April 1640, endorsed by Ormond 'this was the 10,000 men raised for the expedition into Scotland,' Carte MSS, i, 181–185.

30. Carte MSS, i, ff 302–303.

31. Ibid.

32. J Rushworth, *The Tryal of Thomas Earl of Strafford* (London, 1680), 27; A Clarke, *The Old English in Ireland 1625–42*, (Ithaca and London 1966), 132.

33. Rushworth, *The Tryal of Thomas Earl of Strafford*, 27; Kearney, *Strafford in Ireland*, 188.

34. On Ormond's influence in parliamentary elections, see W Kelly, 'The early career of James Butler, twelfth Earl and first Duke of Ormond, (1610–88), 1610–43, (University of Cambridge PhD thesis, 1995), 58–60, 93–96.

35. Strafford MSS, iii, 289–90.

36. Carte MSS, i, f 106; Knowler (ed), *Strafforde's letters*, ii, 225–226.

37. Knowler (ed), *Strafforde's letters*, ii, 402–403.

38. Troops under Ormond, Lieutenant-General, HMC *Fourteenth Report*, appendix, part vii *The Manuscripts of the Marquis of Ormonde*, old series, two volumes, (London, 1885–89), 121–123; Army muster roll, written for Ormond's attention by Sir Richard Fanshawe, Secretary to the Council of War, Carte MSS, i, ff 181–185.

39. Carte MSS, i, ff 181–185, f 181.

40. Kearney, *Strafford in Ireland*, 188.

41. Carte MSS, i, ff 302–303.

42. Knowler (ed), *Strafforde's letters*, ii, 394–395; Clarke, *The Old English in Ireland*, 126.

43. *CSPD, 1639–40*, 608; Knowler (ed), *Strafforde's letters*, ii, 403–404.

44. *Journals of the House of Lords of the Kingdom of Ireland* (1634–1800), eight volumes (Dublin, 1799–1800), volume i, 101, 102. Ormond was absent on one day, 26 March, in connection with his chairmanship of the Lords' Committee of Privileges and Greivances.

45. *Journals of the House of Lords* of *the Kingdom of Ireland*, i, 112–114.

46. Ibid.

47. Ibid.

48. For a breakdown of the representation in Kilkenny see, Clarke, *The Old English in Ireland*, appendix iii, 256–261 and Kearney, *Strafford in Ireland*, appendix i, 223–259, appendix ii, 260–263; G D Burtchaell, *Members of parliament for the city and county of Kilkenny*, (Dublin 1888), 31–43.

49. Kelly, 'The Early Career of James Butler, twelfth Earl and first Duke of Ormond', 95.

50. Wharton was Lieutenant-Colonel of Ormond's regiment and later became a close confidant. He was originally from Eslington in Yorkshire. Burtchaell, *Members of parliament*, 37–38; *HMC Ormonde MSS*, os, i, 124.

51. Burtchaell, *Members of parliament*, 31–43.

52. Clarke, *The Old English in Ireland*, 128.

53. Kearney, *Strafford in Ireland*, 195–196.

54. T Carte, *The Life of James, Duke of Ormond*, (six volumes, second edition, Oxford 1851), volume i, 95.

55. Clarke, *The Old English in Ireland*, 128–129.

56. Ibid, 129.

57. Whitaker, *The life and original letters of Sir George Radcliffe*, 249–251; *Journal of the House of Commons of the Kingdom of Ireland (1613–1791)*, 28 volumes, (Dublin, 1793–91), volume i, 145–147.

58. Whitaker, *The life and original letters of Sir George Radcliffe*, 249–251; *Journals of the House of Lords of the Kingdom of Ireland*, i, 36–37; Carte MSS, i, ff 210–211.

59. Kearney, *Strafford in Ireland*, 191.

60. Whitaker, *The life and original letters of Sir George Radcliffe*, 249–251.

61. The exact date of his departure is not known but it was certainly before 10

May when Wandesford wrote to Ormond informing him of the contents of the Lord-Lieutenant's dispatches of 2 May. Ormond's out-going correspondence for this period is not extant but his concerns can be inferred from Wandesford's replies to his letters (Wandesford to Ormond, 10 May 1640, Carte MSS, i, 192).

62. Carte MSS, i, ff 212–213.

63. Sir George Radcliffe to Ormond, 22 July 1640, Carte MSS, i, ff 216–217; Wandesford to Ormond, 4 June 1640, Carte MSS, i, f 200; Wandesford to Ormond, 7 June 1640, Carte MSS, i, ff 202–203. Few of these letters survive but Wandesford's correspondence makes it clear that he forwarded letters from England to the Earl and visited him on at least one occasion. Wandesford to Ormond, 31 July 1640, Carte MSS, i, f 218.

64. T W Moody, F X Martin, and F J Bryne (eds), *New History of Ireland, III, 1534–1691* (Oxford, 1976), 277.

65. Carte MSS, i, f 194v.

66. Ibid, i, f 194v.

67. Ibid, i, ff 202–203.

68. Ibid, i, ff 208–209.

69. Ibid, i, ff 210–211.

70. St Leger for one assumed that Ormond would 'not be stayed long now that her Ladyship is brought to a fair bed' (St Leger to Ormond, 21 July 1640, Ibid, i, ff 214–215, f 214).

71. Wandesford had disappointingly informed Ormond in June that he doubted if he could find money to pay Ormond's entertainments. (Ibid, i, ff 208–209, f 208). As late as August St Leger was complaining to his commander that although the army was now ready no transports had yet arrived (Ibid, i, ff 231-2, f 231v). C.V. Wedgwood was of the opinion that Hamilton did not provide the ships out of a sense of misguided loyalty to the king knowing better than most the hatred and fear of a Catholic Irish army among the Covenanters (Wedgwood, *Wentworth*, 302, note 46).

72. The muster of the foot had originally been deferred until the beginning of June due to the delayed muster of the English army with whom it was envisaged the Irish army would coordinate operations (Carte MSS, i, f 194). The muster was again deferred for three weeks because of a lack of finance and transport for the artillery and baggage train (Carte MSS, i, ff 210–211). See also, Stevenson, *Scottish Covenanters and Irish Conferedates*, 36; Clarke, *The Old English in Ireland*, 131.

73. Carte MSS, i, f 194.

74. Military map of the coast of Scotland endorsed and annotated by Ormond, Ibid, i, f 334.

75. Ibid, i, ff 239–240.

76. Ibid, i, ff 229–230.

77. Copy of Strafford's commission as Captain-General empowering him to appoint Ormond Lieutenant-General, Ibid, i, ff 247–260. The original, (Carte MSS volume clxxvi) bears the date 3 August but Strafford had intended to return to Ireland even after this date and it is therefore unlikely he would have empowered Ormond to this degree at this time. Indeed, he was expected back as late as 22 August and his pinnace was sent to Chester to await him (Carte MSS, i, f 227, 235).

78. Ormond's queries on the Earl of Strafford's patent to be Captain-General of the army in Ireland, [undated] Ibid, i, f 198.

79. Ibid.

80. Ibid.

81. Ibid.

82. Ibid.

83. Ibid.

84. Strafford to Sir George Radcliffe, 5 November 1640, Whitaker, *The Life and original correspondence of Sir George Radcliffe*, 204.

85. Sir Charles Coote to Ormond, 16 December 1640, Carte MSS, i, f 290; Coote to Ormond, 17 December, Carte MSS, i, f 292.

86. Ulick Burke, Earl of Clanricarde, *Memoirs and Letters...*, (London, 1757), 340.

CHAPTER 4

The Making of the Radical South-West: Charles I and his Scottish Kingdom, 1625–1649

Sharon Adams

'The people throng to our sermon, as ever you saw to any Irvine communion; their number daylie increases.'[1]

With these words Robert Baillie informed his brethren in the presbytery of Irvine of the enthusiastic reception he and his fellow Scots preachers were receiving in London in 1641. By comparing the attendance at sermons in London with those in the small sea port of Irvine on the west coast of Scotland, Baillie was revealing much more than a naive parochialism. As minister of Kilwinning, and later Professor of Divinity at Glasgow University, Baillie came from an area of south-west Scotland which had, over the previous decades, developed a distinctive cast to its religious life. Robert Baillie would have been personally acquainted with the ministry of David Dickson who, as minister of Irvine, had preached at Baillie's induction into the parish of Kilwinning. Dickson gave a public sermon each Monday, the market day in Irvine. According to the contemporary commentator Robert Blair, who exercised an itinerant ministry in the south-west in the 1620s and 30s, this attracted spectators from the outlying parishes who

> went to the Monday market of Irvine with some
> little commodities as they had; but their chief
> intention was to hear the lecture that ended before
> the market began...whereby the power of religion
> was spread over that part of the country.[2]

Many of these pilgrims came from Stewarton where Blair himself had preached with similar results. During this extended period of religious revival, stretching across the 1620s and into the next decade, those affected were given spiritual counsel by a local noblewoman, Lady Robertland.[3] Similarly Anna Livingstone, the wife of Robert Baillie's patron, Alexander Montgomery, 6th Earl of Eglinton — described by yet another south-western minister, John Livingstone, as one who 'although bred at Court, yet proved a subdued and eminent

Christian'[4] — sought to persuade her husband to desist from his usual occupations of hunting and hawking in the hope that he would be influenced by the testimony of the parishioners of Stewarton.[5]

This phenomenon, which came to be known as the 'Stewarton sickness' suggests several themes pertinent to the study of south-west Scotland in the seventeenth century — the impact of the parish ministry and the role of popular preachers; the local economy, trade, and agriculture; networks and communications; the ties of family, association, and dependency and the role of the nobility in local society. A valid regional study in its own right, the political ramifications of these patterns of behaviour extend far outwith the confines of the locality into all three of Charles I's kingdoms. Stewarton introduces us to the nucleus of a cast of characters, prominent in articulating discontent with royal policies in Scotland, instrumental in organising opposition to Charles' introduction of innovations in worship, and prominent in the subscription of the National Covenant. Many would be equally diligent in pursuing this agenda throughout the 1640s. David Dickson was active in recruiting support for the Covenanting cause in the late 1630s. Robert Baillie returned to London in 1643, this time as one of the Scottish commissioners to the Westminster Assembly of Divines, where he was joined, Samuel Rutherford, formerly minister of Anwoth near Kirkcudbright. Accompanying them was George Gillespie, previously household chaplain to Viscount Kenmure at New Galloway where, in 1634, Samuel Rutherford had witnessed Kenmure's deathbed confession of his lack of resolve in the controversial Coronation Parliament of 1633. Unable to obtain a parish in Scotland due to his views on worship and church government (like John Livingstone and Robert Blair before him), Gillespie went on to minister in the household of an Ayrshire magnate, John Kennedy, 6th Earl of Cassillis. Cassillis, himself also elected as a delegate to the Westminster Assembly, would play a key role in the Covenanting administration of the 1640s, along with his fellow Ayrshire noblemen, Eglinton and John Campbell, 1st Earl of Loudoun.[6]

A cursory examination of any bibliography of seventeenth-century Scotland — and here the comparison with England during the revolutionary decades is instructive — reveals a relative lack of any detailed regional studies. Recent studies of the early modern period have recognised that Scotland can never be seen primarily as a monolithic unitary state but should be viewed instead as a composite of various regional and local identities.[7] This comment is particularly apposite in the context of the mid-seventeenth century as it has long been recognised that patterns of allegiance to 'King or Covenant' during the era of the Scottish Revolution can be defined along broadly geographical lines, with support for the Covenant being concentrated in Lowland Scotland, in Fife, the Lothians, and the south-west.[8] Contemporary observers recognised the significance and political volatility of the 'Gentlemen of the West', drawing attention to, for example, the geographical alignment of support for or against the Engagement on behalf of Charles I in 1648,[9] while Robert Baillie's promotion to Principal of Glasgow University was considered unwise in some quarters as the job

> would requyr a man of a more activ and resolut temper,
> by whose authority the ministry of the West...might
> be reduced and kept in order.[10]

This was never the complete picture of religious or political life, even in the south-west where an early adhesion to the Reformation was followed by patchy progress and in Dumfriesshire by a prolonged difficulty in attracting and financing a preaching ministry. It is perhaps not surprising, therefore, that seventeenth-century Dumfries saw public celebrations of the mass. In the 1640s the Covenanting nobles of Ayrshire were counterbalanced by a group of Royalist nobles along the western border, including the Earls of Nithsdale, Dumfries, Galloway, and Annandale. The serious and potentially factional nature of such opposing alignments is suggested by a comparison of the commanders of regiments in the Army of the First Bishops' War of 1639 and the Engager Army raised in 1648. The regiments of the first army raised in the south-west in the name of the Covenant were led by local figures prominent in the opposition to Charles I such as Cassillis, Eglinton, and Lord Kirkcudbright, all of whom retained a role in the mustering of further armies in the course of the 1640s. None of these commanders played any part in the Engagement but they were replaced by Royalists such as the Earl of Dumfries who had remained largely inactive in the conflict thus far.[11]

It is, however, the contrasting picture of religious agitation and opposition to the Crown which has received greatest attention. While all modern studies of the Covenanting decades have recognised, at least in passing, the existence of 'a radical south-west', attempts to explain this phenomenon have ranged from the inconclusive to the bizarre. This is partially a result of the deterministic nature of much of the older historiography of the period which tends either to Presbyterian hagiography or to the portrayal of committed Covenanters merely as religious fanatics.[12] Yet the events of the 1630s and 40s leave several questions unanswered. Why was the south-west so significant in organising opposition to Charles I in the 1630s? Why did so many nobles, lairds, and burgesses from the south-west, who had hitherto tended to play little part in political affairs in recent years, take so prominent a place in the Covenanting administration of the 1640s? Why, when most of the Scottish political nation was falling headlong over itself in the rush to support the monarchy in 1648, did opinion in the south-west remain ambiguous? Perhaps most intriguingly, what lay behind the insurrections of 1648 — the Mauchline Rising and the Whiggamore Raid — possibly the only time when it could be said that events in Scotland mirrored the social upheaval and unrest which was a factor in English political life in the 1640s?

It is undoubtedly true that the participants in these events represent a small section of society. One of the values, indeed one of the frustrations, of regional studies is that they often reveal local preoccupations far removed from what historians perceive to be significant events. The records of the burgh of Ayr for the key years of the 1640s reveal a community preoccupied with the effects of the plague and the administration of the town's finances. Yet, at the same time, the burgh was heavily involved in national politics, successive provosts playing a key role in Parliament and on the various Committees of Estates.[13] Given the comparative scale of activity and social diversity of those involved — members of the higher nobility; lesser nobles and lairds; office holders in burghs, as well as tenant farmers and ministers — this would seem to demand an explanation more sophisticated and more convincing than mere fanaticism.

What follows is a preliminary attempt to address the issue of why the south-west was so radical? Or, to phrase the question more accurately, why did so many of the radicals come from the south-west? In terms of methodology this initial study deliberately focuses on the revolutionaries of the 1630s and 1640s, rather than on the active supporters of the king or on that even less studied group who sought to remain neutral in the conflict. It further proceeds on the assumption that the origins of the Scottish Revolution can be found in a variety of causes and over a timespan longer than the years immediately preceding 1637. This approach seems particularly pertinent in the context of a regional study, as the argument that this was nothing more than a revolt against an unpopular monarch fails to take account of the fact that both the king and Covenant received varying levels of support from different geographical areas, implying at the very least, that Charles was more — or less — popular in different parts of his kingdom.[14]

In the context of the radical south-west, it is equally clear that religion and politics have been used in an almost interchangeable fashion. This lies at the heart of the circular debate over whether the Covenanting Movement was essentially a civil or a religious revolt. What the example of the south-west perhaps shows is that, in an attempt to clarify the issues, religious and political motivations and actions have been separated in a manner that a seventeenth-century observer would have failed to recognise and which distorts our perspective on events. Much of what follows draws upon the openly partisan writings of the participants themselves. Nevertheless, as the example of Stewarton shows, it is possible to unpack these narratives and illustrate the impact of religion in its widest sense. Could the answer lie, not in a rigid separation of religion and politics, but rather in a wider redefinition of what constitutes ecclesiastical history outside the confines of polity and discipline?

What then do we understand by the term 'radical' which as an historical label is non-specific and largely unhelpful due to indiscriminate usage? In the context of this discussion it is a term inherited rather than specifically chosen. In Scotland 'radical' has been used variously of sixteenth-century Presbyterianism, the political activities of Thomas Muir in the 1790s, and the 'Radical War' of 1820, all of which had vastly different religious, constitutional, political, or social agendas. Yet all of the above possessed one common factor: a class of activity which seemed threatening to the *status quo* of the day. Thus the conclusions reached by the editors of the *Biographical Dictionary of British Radicals in the Seventeenth Century* hold true for Scotland: radicalism must 'be judged in the context of the available spectrum of dissent at a given time...There is no radical orthodoxy as such, but a periodically shifting response to historical situation'.[15] This is particularly applicable to the south-west of Scotland where the longevity of the tradition, stretching over more than a century between the Reformation of 1560 and the arrival of William of Orange in 1689, forces a constant redefinition of what constitutes radicalism. The Gentlemen of Angus and the Mearns were just as active as the Gentlemen of the Westland during the Reformation crisis, yet seventeenth-century Angus is more commonly characterised as part of the 'conservative north' — resistant to Presbyterianism, loyal to Charles I and inimical to the Covenants — while its radical cousin went on to indulge in Covenanting, Conventicles, and the ejection of Episcopalian clergy.[16]

In the context of early modern Scotland, the label 'conservative' has been commonly applied either to Catholics, Episcopalians, or to

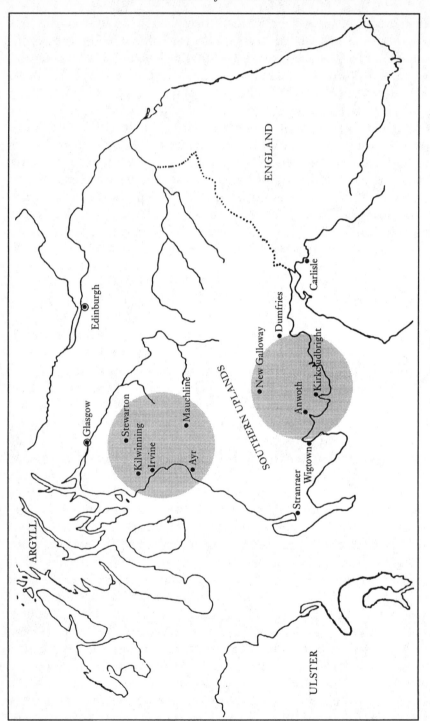

Location Map

Royalists. Consequently its antonym, 'radical', has been used in a strictly limited and specific sense to denote reformed Protestants or Presbyterians in opposition to the Crown, either because of religious principles or under the guise of religion. Thus, in 1638, subscription to the National Covenant was near normative in Lowland Scotland and non-subscription the maverick act, yet this does not make failure to subscribe radical *per se*. Radicalism does not denote any fixed political philosophy or social programme but is in essence a party or factional label. It does not, however, simply indicate fanaticism, particularly when any opposition to the Crown could be, and indeed increasingly was, construed as extreme behaviour. Arguably it was this sense of growing absolutism, evidenced in a monarch against whom no legitimate criticism or complaint could be levelled, which proved a potent factor in promoting revolution. It mattered little whether or not Charles I was a more arbitrary monarch than his predecessors: what mattered was that his subjects increasingly perceived him as such.

Yet few of the revolutionaries would have recognised themselves under the label 'radical'. The ministers saw themselves rather as the true conservatives, wishing to restore the church to her former purity, free from the corruptions in worship and polity imposed by the monarch. The nobles in the party of revolution cast their agenda in equally traditional language vowing, 'to maintaine the true worship of God, the Majesty of our King, and peace of the Kingdome'.[17] Thus the credentials for radicalism also vary according to social standing as, for example, the criteria may vary for a member of the nobility as opposed to a member of the clergy, or for those inside or outside of the circles of government and patronage. In the final analysis, 'radical' remains an inexact term, though its use as a label for a particular segment of the political spectrum is in the 1630s and 40s is broadly analogous to contemporary usage. While not recognising the term 'the radical party', contemporaries would have mentally equated it, in the context of high politics, with the faction surrounding Archibald Campbell, 8th Earl and 1st Marquis of Argyll or, in terms of social unrest and insurrection, with the fear of the 'men of the west'.[18]

The area defined loosely as 'the west' was located in the bottom left-hand corner of Scotland, behind an imaginary diagonal line stretching from the Clyde to the Solway. Today it is bounded to the north by the M8, the main route across central Scotland between Edinburgh and Glasgow, and to the west by the A74 heading northwards across the border with England from Carlisle; enclosing an area immediately to the south of Glasgow, down through Ayrshire to Galloway and east to

Dumfriesshire. Thus the south-west was at one and the same time a peripheral region (Stranraer lies as far south from Edinburgh and Glasgow as does Fort William to the north), as well as a locality immediately adjacent to the central belt. The geopolitics of the south-west were further governed by its proximity to the north of England, to Argyll, and to Ulster. A recent work on rural society defined a region which lying to the west of a natural physical boundary — the hills of the Southern Uplands — beyond which 'movement in all directions was impeded', arguing that, even until well into the nineteenth century, the hills which bordered Galloway seriously hindered contact with the central belt. Yet the same physiological features which define the region serve to divide it: such contacts as the southern parishes had with the central belt were more often based on the need to maintain administrative links with Edinburgh than links with Glasgow and the economy of the west.[19]

The relative ease of sea-borne communications with Ireland proved an attractive alternative. Many of the settlers in Ulster originated from the south-west; indeed plantation was perceived to have most chance of success where it involved men who already had links with Ireland and whose kinsmen and retainers were more likely to follow them on the short sea crossing.[20] Emigration was for a variety of reasons — during the 1626 revival at Six-Mile Water, for example, the majority of the affected were said to be Scots who had left 'for debt and want, and worse reasons'.[21] Several of their ministers were themselves Scots in voluntary exile: Josias Welsh, son of John Welsh the deposed minister of Ayr, George Dunbar, himself deposed from the ministry of Ayr, Robert Blair and John Livingstone, all ministered in Ulster in the 1620s and 30s. Several of these men retained links with the south-west, preaching frequently on the mainland and returning to the area after 1638.[22] Livingstone had been inclined to the rural parish of Straiton in Ayrshire, but was advised to go to Stranraer as it was 'so near for the advantage of our people in Ireland'.[23]

This geographical alignment has major implications for the study of the south-west. Crossing the sea, for example, was a convenient way of avoiding the levy for the Engager Army. Ulster provided a safe haven for dissidents with easy access back to Scotland. Had the 140 passengers who set sail aboard the Eagle Wing in the autumn of 1636 been successful in their attempt to emigrate to New England, this would have permanently removed not only Blair and Livingstone, but also John Stewart of Ayr, who would be active in the civil politics of the 1640s.[24] Indeed emigration was partially responsible for the eventual dissipation of the radical tradition. Although the south-west remained the stronghold of the Cameronians (later the Reformed Presbyterians) who refused to accept the Williamite settlement of 1690, links with Ulster, and through Irish Presbyterianism to the American colonies, led to increasing migration, particularly by preachers. Thus the Scottish Covenants were exported to the New World and linked with opposition to British rule overseas. William Martin, brought before Governor Cornwallis for preaching sedition during the War of Independence, claimed in his defence that he

> was raised in Scotland, educated in its literary and
> theological schools, was settled in Ireland where I
> spent the prime of my days, and emigrated to this
> country seven years ago...The Declaration of
> Independence [formulated by the Reformed Presbyterians
> in 1773 and known to Thomas Jefferson] is but a
> reiteration of what our Covenanting fathers have always
> maintained.[25]

Divorced from its radical pedigree, the south-west can be said to exist only as a geographical designation. The south-west is in no sense a coherent political unit and it would be a brave commentator who would insist on applying the same criteria to Dumfries as to Ayr and to every village in between. There is a tension inherent in any attempt to examine local politics and society for, taken to its logical extreme, any locality can be localised to the extent where it quite simply ceases to exist. Not only is the 'typical' locality nonexistent, but its bounds would be near impossible to define and its demarcation could shift with even a slight change in perspective. In north Ayrshire, the burgh of Irvine, the barony of Kilwinning, the estates of the Earls of Eglinton, the bailliary of Cunningham and the sheriffdom of Ayr, all represent valid local units, either contiguous or concurrent, each with a different constituency. Aspects of the south-west undoubtedly evidence a sense of localism or local identity but there is nothing which approximates to a sense of 'county community' as has been argued for seventeenth-century England. The point has been made that the natural bonds which shape the local community do not always coincide with administrative units[26] but are more inchoate, reflecting the ties of economy, jurisdiction, lordship, and kinship.

Territorial ambitions serve as a useful check on assumptions made about localities by historians, as family loyalties, local networks, and personal aggrandisement tend to cut across any artificial boundaries placed on the local community. The Hamiltons, the most influential family in the area immediately south of Glasgow, extended their influence into Ayrshire; while in the 1590s Hugh Campbell of Loudoun, the sheriff of Ayr, was identified as 'a highlander' and consequently identified with the policies of the Campbell Earl of Argyll, a pattern which would be repeated in the 1640s.[27] In North Ayrshire, local politics were dominated by the two magnate families, the Cunningham Earls of Glencairn and the Montgomery Earls of Eglinton, but were also heavily influenced by important lesser nobles such as Lord Boyd of Kilmarnock. Carrick was largely the province of the Kennedy family, headed by the Earl of Cassillis, whose holdings extended south into Wigtownshire. Further south and east the earldoms were all new creations of the early seventeenth century — Nithsdale in 1620, Galloway in 1623, Annandale in 1624, and Dumfries in 1633 — in an area which would otherwise exhibit an even more diverse pattern of lesser nobles and substantial lairds. The representative of a dominant family of the sixteenth century, Robert Lord Maxwell, 1st Earl of Nithsdale, had restored his fortunes at court and, while retaining an interest in his family lands (for example his erection of an elaborate Renaissance palace block at Caerlaverock Castle, one of only two strongholds in south Scotland which would be held for the king) he substantially lived the life of an absentee.[28]

These patterns of magnate power and local landlordship are as diverse across the region as they are broadly typical of Scotland as a whole, providing little clue as to the genesis of radical politics beyond suggesting the existence of a sizeable corpus of substantial and influential lesser nobles and lairds. Here the comparison can be drawn between Dumfriesshire and Fife, another Covenanting locality, which shows a similar trend towards local politics being in the hands of a number of families rather than dominated by one single line. These patterns are significant in the light of recent work on the social composition of the Covenanting Movement. Although initially dominated by the nobility — Robert Baillie describing the National Covenant as the 'nobles' Magna Charta'[29] — the enthusiasm of the higher nobility waned and the movement became increasingly dependent upon the laird and burgess classes. The Parliament of 1649, attended by few nobles but including Eglinton, Loudoun and Cassillis,[30] drew rather on the 'radical mainstream',[31] 'an oligarchic inner core able to draw on a reservoir of support among the gentry and burgesses'.[32] As the Covenanting Movement relied less on the support of the nobility, the more it drew its support from the west.[33] Further down the social scale, the Mauchline Rising of June 1648 has been seen as 'a rising of the predominantly unenfranchised but disaffected'[34] and as the flashpoint where 'radical idealism met social disconent'.[35] In the context of the south-west this would seem to argue for the combination of an alienated section of the nobility prepared to pursue its agenda throughout the 1640s with an increasingly confident gentry and a disaffected tenantry. All of these conclusions are borne out by the pattern of events, but evidence for their origins specific to the south west is harder to come by.

How significant a factor was Charles I himself? Were his policies any more obnoxious to the inhabitants of the south-west than to those of any other part of his kingdom? Certainly, if one of Charles' stated aims behind his Revocation of 1625 had been to benefit the lairds and make them dependent upon no other authority than the king, this proved a manifest failure in the south-west where the lesser nobility and the lairds were among his most vocal opponents. Several Dumfries and Galloway families held old ecclesiastical properties by virtue of the number of pre-Reformation religious houses along the Solway; similarly in Ayrshire, where Loudoun, for example, held the ecclesiastical barony of Kylesmuir, formerly belonging to Melrose Abbey. Arguably the holders of these lands could have felt alienated by the threat of losing their property under the terms of Charles's Revocation, although the holding of former-ecclesiastical lands was no more widespread in the south-west of Scotland than elsewhere. Furthermore, many of these properties had already been set aside by James VI for the support of the bishopric of Galloway, while Holywood and Dundrennan had been erected into temporal lordships for John Murray, later 1st Earl of Annandale and one of Charles' staunchest supporters.[36] Paradoxically, it was perhaps where Charles' policies were most successful that they facilitated the growth of opposition: his zeal for the temporalities of the church, the augmentation of stipends, and the increasingly successful prosecution of commission to local heritors to build and repair parish churches, created attractive charges which would draw and support well educated and ambitious ministers. It is surely no coincidence that Samuel Rutherford's parish of Anwoth had been newly created before his arrival in 1627.

Thomas Sydserff, Charles' appointment to the bishopric of Galloway in 1635, is one of the best candidates for the hypothesis that Charles sought to create a new look, active, interventionist, Arminian episcopate to be his representatives in the localities. Although Sydserff's appointment may have been in response to a pre-existing situation, he nevertheless proved diligent, banishing Samuel Rutherford to

Aberdeen in 1636. In other instances, Sydserff's jurisdiction proved more problematic. In 1635 he sought to fine and banish Alexander Gordon of Earlston for preventing the intrusion of an episcopal nominee; his sentence of banishment, however, was overturned by the Privy Council on payment of the fine. In the same year Sydserff suspended Robert Glendinning, minister of Kirkcudbright, from office and, when the burgh's magistrates protested and continued to attend Glendinning's ministry, Sydserff ordered them confined in Wigtown. Samuel Rutherford advised Marion McNaught, wife of Provost William Fullarton, to seek legal advice as to his rights in opposing an intruded minister and to encourage her husband not to co-operate with the bishop. Again it proved difficult for Sydserff to enforce his edict.[37] Here indeed the Caroline regime interfered with the mechanisms of local society, for interference in the relationship between a burgh and its parish minister and with the rights of patronage was as much a threat to personal property and jurisdiction as the Revocation had been to landholding. Where, therefore, the new deal episcopate came up against the forces of vested interest it had just as much difficulty in enforcing its remit as had the old style Presbyterian discipline.

Patterns of allegiance in the south-west appear to indicate a clear demarcation line between a provincial Covenanting nobility — Loudoun, Cassillis, Eglinton — and a Court-influenced nobility loyal to the king — Annandale, Dumfries, Galloway, Nithsdale — the primary exception being the Ayrshire based 6th Earl of Glencairn whose overall views were more pro Charles than the Covenant.[38] However, this is a crude distinction which implies that support for the National Covenant was the product of an alienated country party excluded from positions of power. Although men such as Cassillis and Eglinton had not previously played a major part in central government — partially why their behaviour in the 1640s is so significant — neither had they been deliberately excluded. The patent granted to Campbell of Lawers for his elevation to Earl of Loudoun was suspended following his opposition in the Coronation Parliament of 1633, implying a pre-existing degree of favour. The power base of all these men still lay in their localities, a power base which neither James VI nor Charles I, had been unable to erode. While there may indeed have been a distinct lack of enthusiasm for the post of Justice of the Peace, the appointments made by both James and Charles reflect the existing leadership of society rather than a desire to confound vested interests. As has been argued for the reign of James VI, new administrative bodies provided an important sphere of influence for the lairds but were largely beneath the notice of the traditional aristocracy and did not pose a threat to their influence. This may, however, reflect an increasing self-confidence among lairds and lesser nobles — Gordon of Earlston, for example, was reprimanded for overstepping the bounds of his office as Justice of Peace.[39]

At the other end of the social scale, the south-west saw a marked inflation of honours in the first half of the seventeenth century. The new peers, however, came from substantial, established families such as the Maxwells and the Crichtons of Sanquhar; only one, John Murray earl of Annandale, was elevated primarily as a result of his service to the Crown. There is no vast gulf here between either an old and new or a 'Court and Country' nobility, although proximity to the king certainly helped to condition allegiances. Cassillis and Eglinton would have spent much of their life under an absentee monarchy and came to their political maturity in the years when the problems of the dual monarchy were becoming apparent. As Keith Brown has pointed out, they, like other provincial noblemen, had little personal reason to fight for a king they barely knew.[40] Conversely Charles's political failure to create a strong Royalist party in the localities had serious consequences. While Annandale *et al* never became wholly divorced from the localities, their customary influence was qualitatively less than that of their more traditional Ayrshire counterparts. As Earl of Nithsdale, Robert Maxwell (his impressive taste in architecture aside) was unable to command the same local prestige his predecessors had enjoyed as Lords Maxwell.[41] This may have encouraged a greater independence of activity and choice of allegiance among the lesser nobility of Dumfries and Galloway. They chose, however, to use their freedom in different ways. On the occasion of his Scottish Coronation Charles honoured both Lord Kirkcudbright and Lord Johnstone of Lochwood. Kirkcudbright's nephews, the 2nd and 3rd lords Kirkcudbright, adhered to the National Covenant, raising successive armies in the course of the 1640s to the ruin of their estates. Lord Johnstone initially subscribed the National Covenant, ensuring his tenants did likewise, and raised a regiment in the First Bishops' War, but he went on to sign the Royalist Cumbernauld Band. Johnstone repudiated the Cumbernauld Bond but was associated with Montrose's campaigns, arrested, imprisoned, fined and made to find caution. Whether Johnstone was more swayed by the £29,000 owed to him for his regiment or by Charles's offer of the title of Earl of Hartfell in 1643 is anyone's guess.[42] What is clear, however, is that lesser nobles and lairds loyal to the Covenant can be found in all sectors of the south-west, regardless of the politics of the higher nobility. In the context of the 1640s, the key issue is not aristocratic dominance, but the need to explain why a small number of committed Covenanting nobles behaved in a seemingly uncharacteristic fashion.

Both Cassillis and Eglinton have been used as examples of the changing requirements and expectations of the Scottish nobility in the seventeenth century:[43] it has been argued that noblemen raised 'regiments not retinues' and that Eglinton raised his supporters as the colonel of the shire rather than as a feudal landlord.[44] The pace of change was slow before 1637 and it could be argued that many nobles would have seen themselves simply as reverting to their traditional role as the military leaders of local society. One of the historiographical problems posed by the events of the 1640s and 50s is that the immense changes wrought by the events of the Revolution and the Interregnum cannot be read back into the decades prior to 1637. One major factor was, however, of increasing importance to nobiliar prestige in the late sixteenth and early seventeenth centuries — financial liquidity. Economic insecurity was a key issue for contemporary complainants and has become one of the most commonly quoted causes of the Covenanting revolt.

The prerequisite for income and status was land. The agrarian map of the south-west was diverse, ranging from high quality farmland to the north and in Ayrshire, to barely cultivatable upland areas. The burghs of south-west Scotland — Ayr, Irvine, Dumfries, Kirkcudbright etc — were predominantly coastal. The sixteenth and seventeenth centuries, however, saw a number of new foundations of urban centres and rural markets, some inland, most, like Stranraer and New Galloway, remained small and struggling throughout the seventeenth century.[45] As a broad generalisation, although crops were certainly grown, particularly in the north of Ayrshire, the agricultural economy of the south-west was primarily pastoral in nature — a conclusion borne out by the findings of an English military report of the 1560s which declared Carrick to be a 'barrant cuntreee but for bestiall'.[46] This pattern is by no means specific to the south-west and is, for example, repeated in the east Borders. Nor is it possible to detect any trace of a distinctive pastoral-based rural community.[47] It has, however, been argued that rents in the south-west tended to be paid as a composite of cash and kind, leading Walter Makey to suggest that landlords were forced to insulate themselves from some of the effects of inflation by augmenting the money rent from their unfeued lands. Thus one tenant could still be paying at the levels of the 1540s while his neighbour was paying an augmentation three, five, or ten times that amount, a potentially socially explosive situation.[48]

If, however, substantial rent increases proved possible, this would cushion noble incomes against inflation, partially cancelling the effects of the increasing incidence of noble indebtedness. Nobles from the south-west undoubtedly experienced some degree of financial retrenchment in the first half of the seventeenth century. The fifth Earl of Cassillis, for example, contracted an increasing number of mortgages on his estates. Although many of these were later redeemed, given the range of his wadsetters and the sums of money involved, it seems likely that this represented more than local patronage in land.[49] Western nobles, however, experienced no greater financial difficulties than those elsewhere and the severest fiscal penalties were exacted by the stresses of the 1640s and 1650s upon those who adhered to either side. In the long term this makes the behaviour of figures such as Cassillis seem less explicable. The 7th Earl of Cassillis, 'following the laudable custom of his forefathers,'[50] experienced persistent difficulties in his reluctance to suppress conventicles on his estates in the 1670s and 80s. As a result of financial penalties incurred in this respect and difficulty in recovering the sums of money advanced by his Covenanting father during the Revolution (which were not declared a public debt until 1681), the 7th Earl was forced to sell the southern part of his estates — a rare example of a noble putting principle above his bank balance![51]

Makey's conclusions have been critically examined by Alan Macinnes with reference to the five presbyteries around Glasgow. Macinnes reached a substantially different conclusion, suggesting that a balance between crops and livestock ensured that victual rents kept pace with inflation which was countered by increased entry-fines rather than rack renting and where tenants acquiesced in a 'commercial re-orientation of estates'.[52] Both studies centred on the Hamilton estates and there are insufficient consecutive rentals pertaining to estates further south to make definitive conclusions possible. What is clear, however, is that the perception of rent rises was a contemporary issue for debate. In 1639 Charles I discharged the tenants of rebels from paying rents, further promising a long lease to any who left their masters to become tenants of the king, together with a rent reduction of at least a third.[53] Whether or not higher rents encouraged tenants to fight is less clear-cut. One English correspondent felt augmented rents made tenants less likely to follow nobles into battle as they were 'repining to pay dear rents and buy armour,'[54] while a colleague reported the Marquis of Hamilton as suggesting that

the common sort have so exhausted themselves with
making provision for war, that they want money to buy
read, insomuch that, though the heads of the army would
be content to be quiet, yet the body will not suffer
them, out of hope to repair their necessity in a more
abundent country.[55]

It was the common sort who mustered at Mauchline Moor in June
1648, but a common sort of some substance. More than half came on
horseback and many appear to have been fairly prosperous tenant
farmers such as William Hendry of Stewarton who appealed to the
English Parliament for the redress of the loss of his two good horses,
sword, pistols, and purse taken from him on the battlefield.[56] Whether
or not such men were protesting at their lack of political power or were
alienated by rent rises, they represented those who, unlike their
superiors, wereunable to protect themselves from the unwelcome
levying for the Army of the Engagement. The stresses of nearly a
decade of war must have had a potent effect in encouraging disaffection
amongst those who had to do the actual fighting. Robert Baillie
attributed the Mauchline Rising to a combination of 'the extreme great
oppression' of the military and the impact of 'our preaching and
discours'.[57] Baillie introduces a largely overlooked aspect of the south-
west, but one which has a direct bearing on motivations and actions —
the effect of outside ideological stimuli. Most commentators have, at
the very least, agreed that the Covenanters used religious issues as a
pretext or vehicle for insurrection. As participants from the south-west
tended to be more committed to the revolt, might it not be possible that
they were more committed to these religious principles?

The radical south-west in the reign of Charles I was, in essence,
composed of two local networks, each of about twenty miles radius,
one centred round Irvine and the other centred round Kirkcudbright.
These represent both the main population densities and an important
network of local religious contacts. It is in this sphere that we find
connections between the nobility and radical ministers, whether as
patrons or as household chaplains — David Dickson dedicated a
volume of his commentary on the psalms to the Earl of Eglinton to pay
'the old debt I owe to your lordship...for countenancing and
encouraging me openly in my ministry, all the while I was in Irvine'.[58]
Such support could also take the form of material aid. When John
Livingstone was temporarily deposed from his Irish ministry he
received financial support from a number of noblewomen including
Lady Boyd of Kilmarnock and the Countess of Eglinton.[59] The breadth

of such contacts is illustrated by the diversity of Samuel Rutherford's correspondents, themselves a 'who's who' of the radical party'.

Religious networks are also the sphere that we find contact between the south-west and other Covenanting localities — Lady Melville of Culross in Fife lamented that she went to 'preachings and communions here and there, neglecting the care of my family'.[60] When Robert Baillie compared his London audiences with an 'Irvine communion' he was making a serious point; private religious meetings and sizeable gathered communions were increasingly frequent in the south-west from the last years of the reign of James VI, possibly as a reaction to the process of liturgical innovation. Unlike the Conventicles of the Restoration era, these meetings tended to occur in easily accessible sites, often in or near the major population centres. It was in this context that the middling sort of the Covenanting Movement became acquainted with one another in the years before the Revolution, providing much of the organisational impetus for the swift response to Charles's innovations in 1637. Leigh Eric Schmidt, documenting the impact of Scottish-style communion seasons in eighteenth-century America, commented on how sacramental seasons provided a sense of community in the scattered rural communities of the frontier counties of Virginia and the south-eastern states.[61] This argument can be read back into forerunners of these seasons in south-west Scotland, in particular the concept of creating a community within a community, a gathering of the godly within society and, more importantly, within the church. In 1626 John Livingstone preached extensively in Galloway: at a communion in Borgue — 'where was many good people that come out of Kirkcudbright' — and at several private meetings.[62] Livingstone was in effect commenting on gatherings of the future supporters of the National Covenant, for whom these meetings were possibly an embryonic vehicle of insurrection and certainly a protest against the prevailing trend of ecclesiastical reform. Perhaps this is the truly radical aspect of south-west Scotland in the reign of Charles I — whether it is unique to the south-west, however, must await the findings of further regional studies.

NOTES

1. R Baillie, *Letters and Journals*, 1637–62, D Laing (ed), three volumes, (Bannatyne Club, Edinburgh, 1841–42), I, 295.

2. *Autobiography and Life of Mr Robert Blair*, T McRie (ed), (Wodrow Society, Edinburgh, 1848), 19.

3. Ibid, 19; M Lynch, 'Preaching to the Converted?', in A MacDonald, M Lynch, & I Cowan (eds), *The Renaissance in Scotland* (Leiden, 1994), 337–338.

4. *Livingstone's Characteristics*, in *Select Biographies*, W Tweedie (ed), two volumes, (Wodrow Society, Edinburgh, 1845–47), i, 347.

5. *Life of Blair*, 19.

6. *The Last and Heavenly Speeches of Viscount Kenmure*, in *Select Biographies*, ii, 374–375. For the role of Dickson and the general contribution of the west to the petitioning against the new Service Book, see the relevant chapters in A I Macinnes, *Charles I and the Making of the Covenanting Movement, 1625–1641* (Edinburgh, 1991) and D. Stevenson, *The Scottish Revolution 1637–1644. The Triumph of the Covenanters* (Newton Abbot, 1973). The involvement of the south-west in the Covenanting administration is documented in J R Young, 'The Scottish Parliament 1639–1661: A Political and Constitutional Analysis' (University of Glasgow, PhD thesis, three volumes, 1993) and D Stevenson (ed), *The Government of Scotland Under the Covenanters, 1637–51* (SHS, Edinburgh, 1982). See also F McCoy, *Robert Baillie and the Second Scots Reformation* (Berkeley, 1974). For Blair, Dickson, Gillespie, Livingstone, and Rutherford, see the *Dictionary of Scottish Church History and Theology*, N Cameron *et al* (Edinburgh, 1993), 81–82, 243, 359–360, 392–393, 735–736. For Eglinton, see *The Scots Peerage*, Sir J Balfour Paul (ed), nine volumes (Edinburgh, 1904–1914), iii, 445–446. For Cassillis, see *Scots Peerage*, ii, 477–481. For Loudoun, see *Scots Peerage*, v, 506–507.

7. This approach has been taken in recent general histories such as J Wormald, *Court, Kirk, and Community. Scotland 1470–1625* (London, 1981) and M Lynch, *Scotland: A New History* (London, 1991). Also see David Stevenson's often quoted comment that Scotland was 'virtually all country and no court' (*Scottish Revolution*, 324).

8. Regional studies specific to the Covenanting decades have included R Bensen, 'South-west Fife and the Scottish Revolution: the Presbytery of Dunfermline 1633–52' (University of Edinburgh, M Litt thesis, 1978). The most suggestive analysis so far in relation to the west is AI Macinnes, 'The Origin and Organisation of the Covenanting Movement during the reign of Charles I; with a particular reference to the west of Scotland', (University of Glasgow, PhD thesis, two volumes, 1987). The last chapter of this thesis forms a case study of the area around Glasgow and critically assesses many of the issues raised in pioneering discussions of the origins of the radical

south-west by W Makey in both *The Church of the Covenant 1637–1651* (Edinburgh, 1979) and 'Presbyterian and Canterburian in the Scottish Revolution', in N MacDougall (ed), *Church, Politics and Society: Scotland, 1408–1929* (Edinburgh, 1983). See also D Stevenson, 'The Battle of Mauchline Moor 1648', *Ayrshire Collections*, XI (1973) and 'The Western Association 1648–50', *Ayrshire Collections*, XII (1983).

9. See, for example, *Life of Blair*, 204.

10. Baillie, *Letters and Journals*, I, lxxv.

11. E Furgol, *A Regimental History of the Covenanting Armies 1639–1651* (Edinburgh,1990), 19–20, 23, 27, 274. For a reminder that regional trends do not form hard and fast rules see Furgol, 'The Northern Highland Covenanter Clans 1639–51', *Northern Scotland*, vii (1987).

12. An example of this is the early-twentieth century biographer of John, Duke of Lauderdale, who blamed the troubles on 'the temper of the peasantry of the south west of Scotland' and the 'well grounded differentiation' that 'in the domain of religion Celtic fervour is peculiarly assertive and uncompromisisng; W C Mackenzie, *The Life and Times of John Maitland Duke of Lauderdale (1616–1682)* (London, 1923), 131–132.

13. Ayr Carnegie Library, B6/18/2, Ayr Council Minutes 29/09/1647–24/08/1669; *The Parliaments of Scotland. Burgh and Shire Commissioners*, M Young (ed), two volumes, (Edinburgh, 1992–93), volume one, 388–389.

14. Recent works by Keith Brown, Allan Macinnes and Walter Makey have suggested new ways of assessing the social and economic contexts of the Covenanting Revolution. An analysis of potential avenues of exploration can also be found in K Brown, 'Aristocratic finances and the origins of the Scottish revolution', *EHR*, 54, (1989), 46–87. See also E J Cowan, 'The Making of the National Covenant', in J Morrill (ed), *The Scottish National Covenant in its British Context* (Edinburgh, 1990), 68–890. For an alternative viewpoint, see M Lee, jr, *The Road to Revolution: Scotland under Charles I, 1625–37* (Urbana & Chicago, 1985).

15. R Greaves & R Zaller (eds), *Biographical Dictionary of British Radicals in the Seventeenth Century*, three volumes, (Brighton, 1982), I, ix–x.

16. See G Donaldson, 'Scotland's Conservative North in the Sixteenth and Seventeenth Centuries', in *TRHS*, 5th series, xvi, 65–79.

17. This fits to some extent with Greaves and Zaller's definition of radicals as 'those who sought fundamental change by striking at the very root at contemporary assumptions and institutions, often in order to revert to what they judged to be the proper historic roots,' (*Bibliographical Dictionary of British Radicals*, I, viii), The quotation comes from the National Covenant, see G Donaldson, *Scottish Historical Documents* (Edinburgh, 1974), 199.

18. For the use of 'radical' as a party label, see Young, 'The Scottish Parliament', volume one, 1.

19. R Campbell, *Owners and Occupiers. Changes in Rural Society in South West Scotland Before 1914* (Aberdeen, 1992), 3–5.

20. M Perceval-Maxwell, *The Scottish Migration to Ulster in the Reign of James I* (London, 1990), 105, 286–289.

21. *The Life of Mr John Livingstone*, in Select *Bibliographies*, i, 141–144.

22. D Stevenson, *Scottish Covenanters and Irish Confederates* (Belfast, 1981), 12–13.

23. *Life of Livingstone*, 161.

24. D Stevenson, *Revolution and Counter-Revolution in Scotland, 1644–51* (London, 1977), 108; *Life of Livingstone*, 153.

25. A Loughridge, *The Covenanters in Ireland, A History of the Reformed Presbyterian Church of Ireland* (Belfast, 1984), 39. The 'Declaration of Independence' referred to was known to Thomas Jefferson and formulated by the Reformed Presbyterians a year before the Declaration of Independence of 4 July 1776.

26. Lynch, *New History*, 180–181.

27. *Calendar of State Papers Relating to Scotland, 1547–1603*, J Bain *et al* (eds), thirteen volumes, (Edinburgh, 1898–1969), xi, 338, 527.

28. A study of the complex nature of family networks in North Ayrshire in the context of the Cunningham/Montgomery feud can be found in K M Brown, *Bloodfeud in Scotland 1573–1625: Violence, Justice and Politics in Early Modern Scotland* (Edinburgh, 1986), 85–102; *Calendar of State Papers Relating to Scotland, 1547–1603*, ed. J. Bain *et al*, 13 volumes (1898–1969), xi, 338, 527; K M Brown, 'Courtiers and Cavaliers: Service, Anglicization and Loyalty among the Royalist Nobility', in Morrill (ed), *The Scottish National Covenant in its British Context*, 175.

29. Baillie, *Letters and Journals*, I, 38.

30. *APS*, vi, ii, 124.

31. A I Macinnes, 'The Scottish Constitution, 1638–1651: The Rise and Fall of Oligarchic Centralism', in Morrill (ed), *The Scottish National Covenant*, 107.

32. Ibid, 124.

33. Young, 'The Scottish Parliament' (PhD thesis), volume one, chapters nine and ten.

34. Macinnes, 'The Scottish Constitution, 1638–1651', 126.

35. Makey, *The Church of the Covenant*, 178.

36. Macinnes, *Charles I and the Making of the Covenanting Movement*, 53; I Cowan & D Easson, *Medieval Religious Houses in Scotland* (London, 1976), 74–75, 102–103. The one potentially threatening exception was Charles' allocation of the revenues of the New Abbey in Galloway to support his new

bishopric of Edinburgh in 1633 (Makey, 'Presbyterian and Canterburian', 161–162).

37. *RPCS*, second series, eight volumes (Edinburgh, 1899–1908), vi, 507; *The Letters of Samuel Rutherford*, A Bonar (ed), (Edinburgh, 1891), 125; Baillie, *Letters and Journals*, I, 16.

38. For a breakdown of nobles associated with the court in 1638, see K M Brown, 'Courtiers and Cavaliers', 157.

39. Macinnes, *Charles I and the Making of the Covenanting Movement*, 94–96; *RPCS*, second series, v, 378–383, vi, 390; *RPCS*, ix (?), 77; M Meikle, 'The Invisible Divide: The Greater Lairds and the Nobility of Jacobean Scotland', *SHR*, LXXI, (1992), 71, 79–80.

40. Brown, 'Courtiers and Cavaliers', 179.

41. For the Eighth Lord Maxwell, see K Brown, 'The Making of a *Politique*: The Counter Reformation and the Regional Politics of John, Eighth Lord Maxwell', *SHR*, LXVI, (1987), 152–175.

42. *The Scots Peerage*, i, 254–259, 267–268; W Fraser, *The Annandale Family Book of the Johnstones*, two volumes, (Edinburgh, 1894), volume i, clxxx–cxcix.

43. J Goodare, 'The Nobility and the Absolutist State in Scotland, 1584–1638', *History*, 78, (1993), 175; K Brown, 'From Scottish Lords to British Officers: State Building, Elite Integration and the Army in the Seventeenth Century', in N MacDougall (ed), *Scotland and War* (Edinburgh, 1991), 140.

44. Brown, 'From Scottish Lords to British Officers', 140.

45. *Historic Stranraer: the archaeological implications of development*, E P Dennison Torrie & R Coleman (Scottish Burgh Survey, Aberdeen, 1995), 19.

46. 'Military Report on the districts of Carrick, Kyle and Cunningham', *Archaeological and Historical Collections Relating to Ayr and Wigtown*, volume iv, (Edinburgh, 1884), 18.

47. cf D Underdown, *Revel, Riot and Rebellion. Popular Politics and Culture in England 1603–1660* (Oxford, 1985). See also J Morrill, 'The Ecology of Allegiance in the English Civil War', in the *Journal of British Studies*, 26, (1987); this is reprinted in J Morrill, *The Nature of the English Revolution* (London, 1993), 224–241.

48. Makey, *The Church of the Covenant*, 169–173.

49. See for example, SRO Ailsa Muniments, GD 25/3/14.

50. *The Lauderdale Papers*, O Airy (ed), three volumes, (Camden Society, London, 1884–85), ii, 200n.

51. *The Scots Peerage*, ii, 483.

52. Macinnes, *Charles I and the Making of the Covenanting Movement*, 6.

53. *CSPD 1639*, 79.

54. *CSPD 1638–1639*, 152, 303.

55. Ibid, 152.

56. Stevenson, 'The Battle of Mauchline Moor', 7; PRO SP 18/2, 7 August 1649.

57. Baillie, *Letters and Journals*, III, 49.

58. D Dickson, *Psalms* (reprint, one volume, Edinburgh, 1985), vii. The other two volumes were dedicated to the Marchioness of Argyll and to the 6th Earl of Cassillis.

59. *Life of Livingstone*, 148.

60. *Livingstone's Characteristics*, 339.

61. Leigh Eric Schmidt, *Holy Fairs: Scottish Communions and American Revivals in the Early Modern Period* (Princeton, 1989), 73–74, 94–100.

62. D Stevenson, 'Conventicles in the Kirk 1619–37: The Emergence of a Radical Party', *RSCHS*, XVII, (1973), 99–114; *Life of Livingstone*, 135–136. A number of private meetings also took place in Edinburgh.

CHAPTER 5

Samuel Rutherford and the Political Thought of the Scottish Covenanters

John Coffey

Samuel Rutherford is generally acknowledged to have been one of the most important intellectual figures in seventeenth-century Scotland. Michael Lynch sees him as 'the leading theoretician of the Covenanting kirk',[1] and Arthur Williamson has described him as 'the Scottish Revolution's most distinguished theorist'.[2] Rutherford's major treatise, *Lex, Rex, or The Law and The Prince*, published in 1644 to justify the rebellion against Charles I is often seen as the classic statement of Covenanting political thought. David Stevenson, for example, calls it 'the most influential Scottish work on political theory' in the mid-seventeenth century.[3] Moreover, according to W H Makey, Rutherford understood better than any of his contemporaries the nature of the revolutionary process; he knew where he was going and why he failed.[4]

However, despite this widespread acknowledgement of his importance, there has been little work on Rutherford's political thought. The last major study of his ideas was a PhD thesis written at Edinburgh University in the 1930s.[5] Fortunately, the recent revival of interest in the history of Scottish ideas has brought with it a reassessment of *Lex, Rex* by John Ford, in an essay published in Roger Mason's *Scots and Britons*.[6] I am indebted to Ford's meticulous work, but since it deals specifically with Rutherford's views on the origins of government, much remains to be said about his political thought more generally.

Consequently, after providing a brief sketch of Rutherford's life, the rest of this paper will discuss his political ideas. I will begin by outlining the natural law arguments for resistance which Rutherford presents in *Lex, Rex*. But I will then go on to argue that although *Lex, Rex* is predominantly an exercise in natural law theorising, it contains a powerful undercurrent which stresses the paramount importance of the nation's covenant with God. Rutherford's deepest reason for believing that the king must be resisted is that he has violated this covenant by fostering idolatry. In order to explain this I will reconstruct Rutherford's understanding of national covenants, something that throws considerable light on how the clergy at least saw the Covenant of 1638. I will then conclude that after the Engagement in 1648, Rutherford's commitment to a purist vision of the national religious covenant undermined his natural law theory and alienated him from his more moderate colleagues within the Covenanting Movement.

I

Rutherford was born in the south-east of Scotland around the year 1600.[7] He grew up under the ministry of David Calderwood, the prolific Presbyterian controversialist, and received a scholastic education at Edinburgh University from 1617 to 1621. After his graduation he became a regent at the university, and he also seems to have been involved with the illegal conventicles which flourished in the city in the early 1620s. By consolidating Calderwood's influence, these conventicles ensured that Rutherford became a fierce opponent of the liturgical innovations — such as kneeling to receive communion — which were introduced into the kirk by James VI and his son Charles. In 1627, Rutherford became minister of Anwoth, just several miles from Kirkcudbright. Over the next eight years he worked closely with a network of fellow nonconformists, led conventicles, co-ordinated protests against 'popish ceremonies', wrote a Latin treatise against Arminian theology, and organised seasons of fasting and humiliation over the corruption of the church. His subversive activities soon came to the attention of the bishops and in 1636, Thomas Sydserff, the new Bishop of Galloway, had him summoned before the Court of High Commission in Edinburgh, where he was deprived of his charge and sentenced to be confined to Aberdeen, where it was hoped that he would come under the moderating influence of a group of theologians known as the Aberdeen Doctors. The hope was a vain one, because Rutherford simply engaged in vociferous debate with the Doctors and released a torrent of letters to those who sympathised with his cause around Scotland. In these letters he lamented Scotland's apostasy, warned of impending judgement on the land, and even contemplated emigration to the New World.

However, the success of the riot against the new Scottish Prayer Book and the establishment of an alternative government by those disaffected with Charles's rule, transformed the political situation. Shortly after the signing of the National Covenant in February 1638, Rutherford left Aberdeen and returned to Anwoth. At the Glasgow General Assembly of November 1638, he was exonerated from all church censures and took his place as one of the clerical leaders of the Covenanting Movement, rejoicing in the abolition of Episcopacy. In

1640 he moved to St Andrews University where he took up the Professorship of Divinity at New College, and over the next four years he was immersed in church and university business. His decisive break came in 1643, when he was chosen as one of the Scottish commissioners to the Westminster Assembly, which was established to decide on a new form of church government, liturgy, and confession of faith for England. Rutherford stayed in England from 1643 to 1647, and in these four years he was immensely productive, participating in the debates and committees of the assembly and publishing treatises in defence of Reformed orthodoxy and Presbyterian ecclesiology.

It was also while in London that Rutherford published *Lex, Rex*, his famous defence of the Covenanting Revolution. Although there is evidence that he had been working on a similar theoretical project whilst still in Scotland, *Lex, Rex* was written to refute a Royalist treatise which appeared in January 1644: *Sacro-Sancta Regum Majestas; or the Sacred and Royal Prerogative of Christian Kings*. Its author, John Maxwell, had been Bishop of Ross and one of the major architects of the Scottish Prayer Book, and one suspects that this is one of the reasons for Rutherford's eagerness to respond to him — throughout the work he refers to his opponent as the 'popish prelate'.

Maxwell had defended the divine right theory of kingship. This asserted that though the people may have originally designated individuals to the kingship, the sovereign authority of the king was given by God alone. Maxwell concluded from this that divine prerogatives were inherent in the king and untransferable to the people, and that resistance by force of arms was always unlawful. In response, Rutherford reasserted the radical scholastic theory that God gives political power to the community, which subsequently delegates it under certain conditions to the magistrate, retaining the right to resist him if he becomes tyrannical. This natural law contractualism originated with the medieval conciliarists, and had been revived in the late sixteenth century by Jesuit theorists like Suarez and Calvinists like the French Huguenots, George Buchanan, and Johannes Althusius.[8] By the seventeenth century it had become 'the leading mode of anti-absolutist argument' in Europe.[9] When the Scottish Covenanters (and subsequently the English Parliamentarians) came to justify their resistance against Charles I, it was to this tradition and to its sixteenth century proponents that they turned. Consequently, little of *Lex, Rex* is particularly novel; its author was drawing on a long tradition and summing up the case for resistance made by both Scottish and English theorists since 1638.[10]

It is striking that *Lex, Rex* leans at least as heavily on Catholic natural law theorists as on Calvinist writers. This becomes apparent in the first two chapters of the book, where of the ten authors whom Rutherford quotes, one is Aristotle and the rest are Catholics, six of them being sixteenth century Spanish neo-Thomists (Vitoria, de Soto, Suarez, Molina, Covarruvias, and Vasquez). Rutherford praises Aristotle as 'the flowre of nature's wit'[11] and he quotes with approval Aquinas' maxim 'grace does not abolish nature but perfects it'[12]. Like Aquinas, Rutherford believes that the deductions of natural reason and the deliverances of divine revelation can be harmonised, since Scripture is in large measure a republication of natural law. Consequently, he continually corroborates his natural law arguments with copious biblical references.

As one would expect in a natural law theory, the argument takes off from certain assumptions about human nature. In particular, Rutherford agrees with Aristotle that man is 'a social creature, and one who inclineth to be governed by man'[13]. Man's natural state, as he sees it, is one of community life under heads of families. Yet he does not accept the patriarchalist claim that the power of magistrates and kings grows naturally from paternal authority (Question XV). Government by magistrates, he argues, is of an entirely different order. Man's natural sociability might incline him to political life, but we must also remember that

> Every man by nature is a freeman born, that is by nature
> no man cometh out of the womb under any civil subjection
> to king, prince, or judge.[14]

Because 'King and beggar spring of one clay'[15], political authority and subjection is not completely natural. Man's natural freedom and his instinct for self-preservation cause him to shy away from establishing magistrates with the authority to inflict the ultimate punishment on lawbreakers.

How then is government among men established? Rutherford gives his answer by way of analogy. Whilst our natural instinct might lead us to resist the amputation of a limb, 'reason in cold blood' tells us that it is absolutely necessary if our lives are to be saved.[16] So too with magistrates; whilst instinct rebels against such political authority, rational reflection leads us towards it, particularly since in our fallen condition government by magistrates is essential 'as a remedy of violence and injustice'.[17] Consequently, 'Men being reasonable creatures, united in society' under heads of families, put their 'power of warding off violence in the hands of one or more rulers, to defend themselves by magistrates'.[18]

The mechanism by which government is set up, Rutherford claims, is that of a covenant between king and people. However, in contrast to Locke he does not believe that this covenant works by means of a transfer to the state of the natural rights of individuals. He agrees with Maxwell that individuals do not 'have in them formally any ray of royalty or magistratical authority'. Instead, he maintains that only the community as a 'joint political body' possesses a God-given power of government which it can use to establish magistrates.[19] In the original community, this power is latent, but it is activated when it is placed in the hands of a magistrate. By arguing in this way Rutherford avoids Maxwell's jibe that Puritans make kings to be the derivatives of the irrational commonality. 'We make not the multitude, but the three estates, including the nobles and gentry to be as rational creatures', he writes.[20] Thus *Lex, Rex* reinforces the position of the traditional ruling elite of Scotland.

It is this account of the origins of government which provides Rutherford with the basis of his theory of limited government and the right to resist. He argues that because communities establish government by covenant — that is, by a calculated, rational act — they take care to impose stringent restrictions on their magistrates. When the community tells the king, 'Reign thou over us', it can hardly mean, 'Come thou and play the tyrant over us, and let thy lust and will be a law to us'.[21] Instead when the people appoint a ruler over them,

they measure out, by ounce weights, so much royal power,
and no more and no less. So as they may limit, moderate
and set banks and marches to the exercise.[22]

One such limitation on royal power is the stipulation that the king must rule with the representatives of the original community, the Estates of Parliament. It is true, Rutherford admits, that 'the king is the head of the kingdom; but the states of the kingdom are as temples of the head'. The Parliament is 'co-ordinate' with the king in making laws, but it is also superior to the king because it is the fountain of his own power.[23] Together King and Parliament must enact legislation which derives from either the divine law of Scripture or natural law[24], and everything must be done with reference to the Ciceronian principle that the welfare of the people is the supreme rule of government.[25] Moreover, the judiciary must be fully independent, even if they are appointed by the king; they judge not for him but for God, and according to their consciences (Question XX).

Rutherford has given the supreme magistrate little room for manoeuvre. He denies that he has turned the king into a mere delegate, and says that in the executive power of the law, the king 'is really sovereign above the people'. However, this clearly implies that in legislative and judicial functions the king is not sovereign over the estates and the judges. One suspects that Rutherford has not really answered Maxwell's jibe that under the Covenanters 'the king is in a poor case'.[26] This suspicion is confirmed by his statement that

> the duke of Venice, to me, cometh nearest to the king
> moulded by God in respect of power, *de jure*, of any king
> I know in Europe.[27]

Moreover, as well as being strictly limited in his official powers, Rutherford's king also forfeits his authority whenever he transgresses the boundaries the people have set for him. This is because they only give him the power of government

> upon this and that condition, that they may take again to
> themselves what they gave out upon this condition, if the
> condition is violated.[28]

As a good Reformed theologian, Rutherford declares that 'The goodness of the king, a sinful man, inclined from the womb to all sin, and so to tyranny, is no restraint'.[29] Political power is 'a birthright of the people borrowed from them; they may let it out for their own good, and resume it when a man is drunk with it'.[30]

'The people', however, as we noted earlier, are not the multitude but their representatives — institutions like the Scottish Estates (Parliament). Rutherford is at one with the Huguenot resistance theorists and the German Calvinist Althusius in arguing that rebellion against a tyrant cannot be instigated by private individuals. If the king becomes a tyrant, it is the estates who are 'to use their fountain-power' against him. In particular, when the king attacks his people, defensive wars led by properly constituted inferior magistrates are entirely legitimate.[31]

In the penultimate chapter of *Lex, Rex* Rutherford tries to demonstrate that Scottish historical practice is in accord with the natural law principles he has uncovered (Question XLIII). Drawing heavily on George Buchanan's *History*, he argues that the Scottish tradition is that 'a parliament must be before the king'.[32] Fergus — the first of Scotland's one hundred and seven kings — had been 'freely elected' to his throne by the Estates of the kingdom, and had not attained it by conquest and all subsequent Scottish monarchs had been bound by their coronation-oaths 'to govern by law', and could have 'no prerogative above the law'. Whenever they had violated their oaths, they had been censured by the nobility and Parliament.[33]

Together with the natural law argument, this Scottish ancient constitutionalism was used by Rutherford to justify the actions of the Covenanters since 1637. When the aristocracy had set up their own government, the Tables, they were in Rutherford's terms simply using their 'fountain power' as 'inferior magistrates' to restore constitutional balance. The popular support they received was fully justified, because whenever a king violated his solemn 'coronation-covenant' to be 'the keeper and preserver of all good laws', the people immediately became obliged to follow the lead of inferior magistrates.

II

It would be easy to finish our analysis of *Lex, Rex* at this point, for the bulk of the book is simply advancing this natural law argument, one which is largely secular in tone. Yet this would be to make a great mistake. Rutherford's case against Charles I is, I think, not primarily a secular constitutionalist one; it is religious. It is based on the assumption that resistance to a king is legitimate if he has violated a nation's covenant with God. In order to understand this we need to undertake a detailed reconstruction of Rutherford's concept of national covenanting.

The origins of the national covenant concept in Scotland have been much discussed. Historians have pointed to several possible sources: the Scottish custom of 'banding' for political, economic, or religious purposes; the medieval notion of a contract of government, such as the one Rutherford himself described; and the covenant theology which became popular in Scotland from the late sixteenth century.[34] However, there is a major problem with looking to covenant theology to explain the emergence of the national covenant idea. The widespread popularity of covenant theology clearly made it natural to think in terms of covenant relationships with God, but how did theologians move from the *covenant of grace*, made between God and the elect, to the *national Covenant*, made with an entire nation? After all, the whole idea of a national covenant with God was wide open to attack on Calvinist grounds: since every nation contained large numbers of reprobates along with the elect, how could God enter into a covenant with such a mixed body?

The Covenanting leadership clearly recognised this problem. As John Ford has pointed out in a recent article, they did all they could to ensure that national covenanters became what Rutherford called 'heart covenanters'.[35] The National Covenant itself urged subscribers to renew their personal covenants with God. Ford concludes from this that

what mattered [to the Covenanter clergy] was not so much
that subscribers belonged to a godly nation as that the
nation could be godly because elect and covenanted people
belonged to it.[36]

Ford also claims that because the Covenanters were concerned to re-
establish God-given laws which had been undermined by the
ceremonial innovations of Charles I, the Covenant had 'less to do with
asserting the particular heritage and destiny of the Scottish church and
nation than with retying the bonds of the universal law of God'.[37]

The difficulty with both these claims is that they make it hard to see
why the 1638 covenant was called a *National* Covenant. The godly
Covenanting leaders were undoubtedly convinced of the *particular*
importance of the elect, and of the centrality of the *universal* law of
God. However, they also had a clearly worked out concept of a *national*
covenant, which historians have so far overlooked.[38] In three different
books, Rutherford explicitly stated that the Scottish belief in national
covenants rested on the traditional Reformed distinction between the
internal and the external covenant of grace.[39] The 'internal' covenant
of grace, he explained, was a 'personal' covenant. Those who were
party to it were the elect, the members of the invisible church. By
contrast, national covenants were 'federal' or 'external', and included
every baptised member of the visible national church. Although many
of these people had no 'personal' holiness, they were all partakers of a
'federal' holiness derived from their godly forefathers.

Rutherford's basis for believing that such a 'federal' national
covenant was possible was biblical. Biblical revelation not only
substantiated natural knowledge, it also perfected nature, by adding
something to what one could know by means of reason. In particular,
it revealed the truth about God, and in Old Testament Israel, it provided
a model which all nations were called to follow. Rutherford did not, of
course, believe that every aspect of the polity of the Hebrews had to
be slavishly imitated by Christian nations. He agreed with Calvin that
the judicial law of Moses was no longer binding, and that magistrates
were free to punish crime in the way they thought most appropriate.
Rutherford had no wish to overturn centuries of Scottish constitutional
tradition. But he was convinced that certain aspects of Israel's polity
were part of the perpetual moral law (rather than the ceremonial or
judicial law which was only typical) and hence were binding on all
nations. In particular, he followed Aquinas and Calvin in assuming that
the zeal for true religion demonstrated by Israel's rulers, set a pattern
to be followed by modern Christian magistrates. When in 1649 he

published *A Free Disputation against Pretended Liberty of Conscience* —
a tract which Owen Chadwick has described as 'the ablest defence of
persecution in the seventeenth century'[40] — his central arguments
depended on the assumption that the Christian magistrate was to
imitate Moses in the remorselessness with which he prosecuted
heretics and idolaters. In addition, Rutherford believed that the Jewish
practice of national covenanting was also part of the moral law. The
Old Testament itself, he maintained, had prophesied the existence of
covenanted nations in the Church Age. In Psalm 2, for example, God
had promised to give Christ the ends of the earth and the isles of the
sea. This was 'Christs charter', and it included every nation. So the
belief that modern nations could be in a covenant with God analogous
to that of ancient Israel, was supported by Old Testament prophecy.

Several major implications flow from Rutherford's exposition of the
theological concept of national covenanting. The first is that Scotland's
National Covenant was not regarded as unique and unprecedented.
Much has been made of Rutherford's exclamation in a sermon
preached in 1634, 'Now, O Scotland, God be thanked, they name is in
the Bible'.[41] S A Burrell, for one, believed that this illustrated the
Covenanters belief that the Scots 'were the Christian successors of the
Israelites specially chosen for the fulfillment of prophecy'.[42] Yet this
is simply untrue. The text on which Rutherford was preaching was
Psalm 2, which he took to be a reference to the fact that all nations
were in Christ's charter. This excited Rutherford in 1634 not because
it confirmed his confidence in his nation, but because it provided an
assurance that despite Scotland's dreadful apostasy, the nation would
still become a part of Christ's inheritance one day. As he preached in a
later sermon, 'Christ's geographie is through all the parts of the world
he maketh all the world the holy land'. Scotland was simply 'a part of
the aikers of Immanuels land'.[43] Other nations may not have covenanted
with God as explicitly as the Scots did in 1638, but this did not affect
their covenanted status.

Secondly, Rutherford's exposition of the idea of a covenanted nation
should remind us that the 1638 Covenant was not meant to establish
something radically new. It was rather the renewal of the 'external'
covenant with God which had first been established at the time of
Scotland's conversion to Christianity, but had been repeatedly broken
since through national apostasy. Rutherford had an historical narrative
about the Church of Scotland to illustrate this, one which he derived
in large measure from Calderwood and which he used to complement
Buchanan's story of Scotland's ancient constitution. This told how the

king and nobility of Scotland had received the Christian gospel around 205 AD and how 'in a short time the whole nation became Christians' (clearly in the external, federal sense, we have already noted). At this time, we may assume, a religious covenant was welded onto the secular covenant established at Fergus's coronation in 330 BC. For many generations after this the Scottish people were godly and pious, but then they fell into bondage to popish superstitions and idolatry. Only at the Reformation of 1560 had the broken national covenant with God been repaired. This covenant was renewed by the Negative Confession of 1581, when king and people pledged to defend pure Protestant religion. But tragically, it was soon undermined once more, by the assaults of James VI on Presbyterianism and by the liturgical innovations which he and his son introduced.[44] As Rutherford put it in his inimitable prose, 'Wearied Jesus, after he had travelled from Geneva, by the ministry of worthy Mr Knox', had just gotten to sleep in Scotland, when he was disturbed by 'irreverent bishops' and greedy nobles, who forced Him, like 'an ill-handled stranger', to put on His clothes and 'go to other lands'.[45] The National Covenant of 1638, therefore, was intended — in the eyes of radical clergy like Rutherford at least — to undo the apostasy and spiritual adultery of the past half-century, and restore the relationship with God which the nation had enjoyed in 1581, 1560, and 205 AD.

The third great implication of Rutherford's understanding of national covenanting concerns Charles I. The king is condemned in Rutherford's eyes, primarily because he has violated Scotland's covenant with God by endeavouring to promote popish idolatry. This is the emotional heart of *Lex, Rex*. What really motivates Rutherford is not a scholastic belief in the popular origins of royal authority, but a passionate conviction that Charles is destroying Scotland's covenant with God. The following passage reveals the fury which hot Protestants like Rutherford felt towards the king's religious policies:

> a king may command an idolatrous and superstitious
> worship — send an army of cut-throats against [his
> people], because they refuse that worship, and may
> reward papists, prelates, and other corrupt men, and may
> advance them to places of state and honour because they
> kneel to a tree altar — pray to the east — adore the
> letters and sound of the word Jesus — teach and write
> Arminianism, and may imprison, deprive, confine, cut the
> ears, slit the noses and burn the faces of those who
> speak and preach and write the truth of God; and may send

armies of cut-throats, Irish rebels, and other papists
and malignant atheists, to destroy and murder the judges
of the land, and innocent defenders of the reformed
religion.[46]

These bitter references to the Laudian policies of the 1630s, to the punishment of English Puritans, to Rutherford's own confinement in Aberdeen, and to the king's wars against the Covenanters occur throughout *Lex, Rex*. The prelates, Rutherford fulminated, had taught Charles that he had a greater power than 'the great Turk' who commanded his subjects to cast themselves into the fire for his entertainment; Charles had in effect ordered his subjects 'to cast themselves into hell-fire' by following a Service Book 'as abominable as the worshipping of Dagon or the Sidonian gods'.[47] When they had refused he had invited

a bloody conqueror [the confederate Irish] to come in
with an army of men to destroy his people, and impose
upon their conscience an idolatrous religion.[48]

Moreover, this had not been done in a fit of madness, but after he had 'slept upon this prelatical resolution many months'.[49] Not without reason, therefore, could Rutherford appeal to the example of Nero, 'wasting Rome, burning, crucifying Paul, and torturing Christians'.[50]

Rutherford's direct attacks upon the king would have probably been fairly shocking in 1644, when many still followed the convention of blaming royal counsellors for the monarch's errors. One of Rutherford's colleagues at St Andrews, Andrew Honyman, later wrote that he was appalled by Rutherford's 'infinite inhumane bitterness against the late king'. *Lex Rex* had portrayed Charles I as

a great persecutor of Religion, intending the total ruine
and destruction of the Protestant profession, and the
total ruine and destruction of the whole people of the
land,

when the reality was that 'the king lived and died a Protestant being exemplary devote'. Moreover, by suggesting that the people, and not just the king, had a duty to ensure that the religious covenant was publicly maintained, Rutherford seemed to leave the commonwealth forever exposed to the danger of religious wars.[51]

This final argument was scorned by Rutherford. In response to Maxwell's claim that 'the kingdom had peace and plenty in the prelates' time', Rutherford retorted: 'A belly argument. We had plenty when we sacrificed to the queen of heaven'.[52] When the survival of the nation's covenant with God was at stake, everything else faded into insignificance. At one point in *Lex, Rex*, Rutherford appealed to Psalm

2, which had so entranced him in that 1634 sermon. He argued that once a nation passed into Christ's hands, in fulfillment of this prophecy, it must never again be abandoned to Antichrist.[53] And Rutherford saw Charles I as an agent of Antichrist. Looking back on 1638 later in his life, he maintained that the National Covenant was essential because the Scots were being 'compelled to quit Christian Religion', and 'thralled to embrace popery by the domineering power of the Prelates'.[54]

The willingness of Rutherford and other radical Presbyterians to leap to such drastic conclusions stemmed in large measure from their paranoia about popery, a paranoia intensified by their apocalyptic beliefs. As Arthur Williamson has demonstrated, godly Presbyterians like Rutherford — in common with many other European Protestants — believed in the imminency of three great apocalyptic events: the downfall of the Popish Antichrist, the conversion of the Jews, and the establishment of Christ's rule among all the Gentile nations.[55] During the Thirty Years' War, in particular, apocalyptic speculation was rife. To many Protestants it seemed as if the fate of their religion hung in the balance. After the defeat of the Protestant champion Gustavus Adolphus, Rutherford thought it possible that God was allowing 'the whore of Rome' to 'smite Scotland, and make it a den of dragons'.[56] In such a climate of apocalyptic apprehension, the fact that ceremonies such as kneeling at communion looked Catholic was enough to have them condemned as Antichristian.

The renewal of Scotland's national covenant in 1638, of course, put things into a rather different perspective. It was now evident to Rutherford that Christ was not going to abandon Scotland to the Antichrist. Indeed, the Saviour was once again on horseback, 'hunting and pursuing the Beast'.[57] By August 1640, when the Scottish army was preparing to enter England in the Second Bishops' War, Rutherford began to suspect that the climax of history was nigh:

> who knows but this great work which is begun in Scotland
> now when it is going into England, and it has tane some
> footing there, but the Lord he will make it go over the
> sea? Who knows but the Lord will make Scotland, who is
> a worm indeed in comparison of other nations, to be a
> sharp threshing instrument, to thresh the mountains and
> to beat the hills to pieces?[58]

This was an awesome thought: the Scottish National Covenant might just be the trigger to set off a series of events culminating in the fall of the Antichrist and the establishment of Christ's rule over all the nations. And how beautifully appropriate this would be, for God —

who refused to share His glory with another and chose the weak and despised things of this world to shame the powerful — would have allowed the great Gustavus to fall but then taken up Scotland, a 'worm' of a nation at the ends of the earth, to accomplish His purpose!

As the alliance with the English Parliament grew stronger, such an expectation seemed to be confirmed. In the preface to the first book he had published in London in 1642, Rutherford described his dream of the two sisters, 'Britaines Israel and Judah, England and Scotland comming together, weeping and asking the way to Sion'.[59] Appointed as a commissioner to the Westminster Assembly, he was overwhelmed by 'the honour of being a mason to lay the foundation for many generations, and to build the waste places of Zion in another kingdom'.[60] In a sermon preached to the English House of Commons in March 1644, Rutherford's colleague, George Gillespie went so far as to date the 1260 years of the reign of the Beast from the Pope's ascendancy in AD 383 to the year 1643, in which the Westminster Assembly had begun to meet![61] When Rutherford preached to the Commons in January 1644, he revealed the same heightened sense of the fulfillment of prophecy opening up extraordinary possibilities. 'The rise of the Gospel-sun' was like a comet warning of 'woe to the Pope, king of the bottomlesse Pit, and his bloody lady Babel'. He reminded Parliament that they had 'the power and opportunitie to send the Glory of Christ over sea, to all Europe'.[62]

It is important to remember that Rutherford preached like this in 1644, the very year in which he wrote that solidly scholastic treatise, *Lex, Rex*. It is strange to think that at one moment he was exulting in the imminent destruction of the Pope, and at the next he was drawing appreciatively on the natural law theory of papists like Aquinas and Suarez. Yet it was commonplace in the early modern period for one theorist to employ a variety of modes of political discourse. We have identified four in Rutherford's works. The two most important lie side by side in *Lex, Rex* — they are the language of *natural law* and the language of *covenant*. However, also significant are the *ancient constitutionalism* and the *apocalypticism* which Williamson has seen as merging to produce 'Scotland's heroic moment' in 1638.[63] In fact we can argue that from 1638 all four modes of discourse were fused to create a multi-faceted case for the Covenanting revolution. However different, each of them could be used to assert the legitimacy of active resistance to Charles I. Two of these languages (natural law and ancient constitutionalism) were basically secular and stressed the role of the nobility, whilst two (covenantalism and apocalypticism) were intensely religious and emphasised the importance of the godly. For this reason they were together capable of doing justice to both the aristocratic and the clerical components of the Covenanting alliance. They also gave the Covenanters a strong sense of their place in history. As Michael Lynch has pointed out, Buchanan's history of Scotland's constitution and Calderwood's 'one-eyed reading of the history of the kirk' were the 'two historical myths' underpinning the 1638 revolution.[64] The apocalyptic story, we might add, was the grand meta-narrative into which radical Covenanters fitted these sub-narratives concerning Scotland's church and state.

III

However, the snugness of the fit between these very different ways of thinking about politics was illusory. The unity of 1638 and the ease with which Rutherford could combine contrasting languages in 1644, masked fundamental tensions. At first it seemed as if godly reformation could be advanced through traditional constitutional mechanisms. But eventually the interests of the nobility and the godly were to collide, and the languages of grace were to point in a very different direction than the languages of nature.

This only really became apparent in the late 1640s.[65] Throughout that decade Rutherford had watched his dreams of a great European apocalypse come to nothing. Not only was the reformation not transported to the continent, it was also in jeopardy in England, due to the influence of the powerful Independent party led by Cromwell. When Rutherford returned to Scotland at the close of 1647, the tide of apocalyptic internationalism was fast receding and the retreat to 'presbyterianism in one country' had already begun. Yet even this was to be threatened by the Engagement (1647–48) agreed between the king and the majority of the Scottish nobility. This marked the breakdown of the alliance between nobility and clergy which had made the Covenanting Revolution possible, for the kirk rejected the Engagement — though only by a small majority. As far as Rutherford and the radical clergy were concerned, the nobility were acting according to the logic of natural reason alone, and failing to take into account the preeminent importance of the nation's covenant with God. In their desire for peace, and the re-establishment of a constitutional monarchy, the aristocracy were — despite their protests to the contrary — selling out the Covenants, which could never be secure in the hands of Charles I.

The radical ministers warned that this betrayal of the religious covenant by the majority of the political nation would inevitably result in the wrath of God being poured upon the land. The only way in which this could be averted was through the purging from all public of the 'malignants' who were responsible. When the Engagers were defeated by Cromwell at the Battle of Preston in August 1648, such a programme of purging suddenly became possible. Under the 'kirk party' regime which came to power after Preston, there took place one of the most intense campaigns against witchcraft in the history of early modern Scotland, and in January 1649 Parliament passed the Act of Classes, which excluded Engagers and all other 'malignants' from civil office. In the same month, Charles I was executed in England, by men who were following a similar ideology of purging — the king was regarded as a man of blood who had to be destroyed if God's wrath was to be averted.[66] Yet despite their affinity with English Puritans such as Cromwell and their antipathy towards the late king, the godly party in Scotland were still monarchists, and they duly proclaimed Charles's son King of Britain and Ireland. This was seen by the English Republicans as a direct challenge to their government, and Cromwell prepared to invade Scotland after he had pacified Ireland. Knowing that they would be facing another 'godly' army on the battlefield, the Covenanters continued their policy of purging, inspired by the biblical example of Gideon, who after ruthlessly reducing his forces to a group of just three hundred men, had defeated a vast army of Midianites. In August 1650, Rutherford wrote to a colonel in the Scottish army, that all the swords in Britain were but 'cyphers making no number' to God, who had put all his influence in 'Gideon's sword'. In the same month, several thousand officers and men were expelled from the army because they fell short of the standard of godliness required. Rutherford was convinced that God would honour such wholehearted purging, and he revelled once more in dreams of Christ's rule: 'a throne shall be set up for Christ in this island of Britain', he declared.[67]

Yet such hopes were to be cruelly dashed. On 3 September 1650, Cromwell's army inflicted a devastating defeat on the Scots at Dunbar, killing three thousand men and imprisoning ten thousand. Rutherford was devastated: 'I have suffered much', he declared, 'but this is the thickest darkness and the straitest step of the way I have yet trodden'.[68] Yet he was convinced that Dunbar did not signal God's favour towards Cromwell, but his anger towards an unfaithful Scotland. If only the army was purged further, he argued, God would show mercy to Scotland. Faith in numbers, he wrote, was but 'carnal confidence' for 'the most wonderful works of God have been done with the fewest men'. 'O what strength is there in Christ's little finger'.[69]

The majority of Rutherford's ministerial colleaques came to a quite different conclusion. Dunbar had happened because the army had been purged too drastically. Appeals to divine sovereignty could not be used to justify neglect of human means; in the face of English invasion, the Engagers had to be readmitted to the army and to civil office. This was after all, as Rutherford's opponents pointed out, entirely consistent with the natural law theory of *Lex, Rex*. According to the law of nature and nations, on which Rutherford had written at such length, the people had a natural obligation to defend their lives, liberties, and estates against invasion, and governments had the right to call all those under its protection to its defence.[70]

Rutherford, however, would hear none of this. The crisis had to be interpreted in terms of covenant, not of natural law. Where there was a conflict between natural law principles and true religion, religion took precedence. When asked how it could be legitimate to prevent men defending their liberties, lives and estates against an invader, Rutherford was emphatic:

> Light of nature is no rule for a christian man; he has
> something dearer to him than these. When religion and the
> people of God [cannot] be preserved but with the loss of
> men's natural interests, the one must give place to the
> other; otherwise excommunicate men, and papists and
> idolaters could not be debarred.[71]

In short, grace could not only perfect nature, but also destroy it. But by admitting this, Rutherford was abandoning the careful synthesis of natural law theory and religious covenantalism which he had elaborated in *Lex, Rex*. He now seemed to be advocating something very similar to the rule of the saints, a policy which he had rejected in the 1640s.

The more moderate Presbyterians — who included some of Rutherford's closest friends — were unwilling to take this line, but their policy of readmitting the Engagers did not prevent the Cromwellian conquest of Scotland. Rutherford felt justified in his analysis. Scotland had been defeated at Dunbar and then at Worcester (3 September 1651) because of her unfaithfulness to the Covenants, and her easy acceptance of malignants (including Charles II). Cromwellian rule was God's punishment on their disobedience. It was wrong to foment rebellion against the English usurper, Rutherford argued in an unpublished manuscript, for the Scots were meant 'to stande under him as the first punishment of our inquitie'. He recommended two biblical texts for the Scottish people: 'I will bear the Indignation of the Lord becaus I have sinned' and 'I was dumb and opened not my mouth because [God] did it'.[72]

Throughout the 1650s, Rutherford remained estranged from the majority of the kirk, whom he never forgave for their laxity towards 'malignants'. He and the minority party — the Protesters — continued to produce periodic condemnations of Scotland's apostasy, the most famous of which was James Guthrie's *Causes of the Lord's Wrath against Scotland*, published in 1653. As a party the Protesters were increasingly marginalised, despite attracting a large popular following among the godly. Rutherford was forced to return to the role he had occupied in the 1630s, that of a Jeremiah lamenting the nation's sins.

Thus the Scottish Revolution's most distinguished theorist was by no means its most representative. His zealous vision of a godly commonwealth was one which had never really been embraced by the mainstream of the political nation. The nobility may have been attracted to ancient constitutionalism and natural law contractualism, since these assigned to them a pivotal political role, but by taking the Engagement in 1648 they indicated their lack of enthusiasm for rigorous and anti-monarchical versions of godly rule. Even in the kirk, the radical party who controlled the General Assemblies were — as David Stevenson has shown — out of step with the more moderate and less organised majority. And Rutherford himself belonged to the extreme wing of this radical party; several of its members, despite being his close allies since the 1620s, followed the moderate line after Dunbar.[73]

Consequently, Rutherford felt isolated, and he began to question his own extremism. The destruction of his dreams between 1643 and 1651 bewildered and perplexed him. He was now no longer so sure that he could read 'the book of providence'. 'Oh, how little of God do we see, and how mysterious is He', he confessed.[74] On his deathbed, as the Covenanting legislation was being swept away by the Restoration Parliament, Rutherford did not abandon his belief that Christ would 'reign a victorious conquering king, to the ends of the earth'. However, he regretted the attempt of his party to set up 'a state opposite a state', and he wished that they had endeavoured to promote a kinder, gentler Presbyterianism:

> We might have driven gently, as our Master Christ, who
> loves not to overdrive; but carries the Lambs in his
> Bosom.[75]

NOTES

1. M Lynch, *Scotland. A New History* (Edinburgh, 1991), 251.

2. A Williamson, 'The Jewish Dimension of the Scottish Apocalypse: Climate, Covenant and World Renewal', in Y Kaplan, H Mechoulan, and R H Popkin (eds), *Menasseh ben Israel and His World* (Leiden, 1989), 25.

3. D Stevenson, *Revolution and Counter-Revolution in Scotland, 1644–51* (London, 1977), 235.

4. W H Makey, *The Church of the Covenant 1637–1651* (Edinburgh, 1979), 91.

5. W Campbell, 'Samuel Rutherford: Propagandist and Exponent of Scottish Presbyterianism', (University of Edinburgh, PhD thesis, 1938). See also his 'Lex, Rex and its Author', *RSCHS*, 7, (1939), 204–228.

6. J D Ford, '*Lex, rex iusto posita*: Samuel Rutherford on the origins of government', in R A Mason (ed), *Scots and Britons. Scottish Political Thought and the Union of 1603* (Cambridge, 1994), 262–290.

7. For Rutherford's life, see Campbell, 'Samuel Rutherford', and T Murray, *Life of Rutherfurd* (Edinburgh, 1828). See also J Coffey, 'Samuel Rutherford (c. 1600–61) and the British Revolutions', (University of Cambridge, PhD thesis, 1994).

8. The evolution of the theory is described in Q Skinner, *The Foundations of Modern Political Thought, II: The Age of Reformation* (Cambridge, 1978).

9. J Sommerville, *Politics and Ideology in England, 1603–40* (Harlow, 1986), 59.

10. On the earlier resistance treatises of the British Civil Wars, see J Sanderson, '*But the People's Creatures*': *The Philosophical Basis of the English Civil War* (Manchester, 1989), chapter one; I M Smart, 'The Political Ideas of the Scottish Covenanters', *History of Political Thought*, 1, (1980), 167–175. On the influence of the Huguenots and Althusius on the Covenanters, see E J Cowan, 'The Making of the National Covenant', in J Morrill (ed), *The Scottish National Covenant in its British Context 1638–51* (Edinburgh, 1990), 68–82.

11. Samuel Rutherford, *Lex, Rex* (1644), 79.

12. Ibid, 122, 324, 327.

13. Ibid, 2.

14. Ibid, 91.

15. Ibid, 3.

16. Ibid, 4.

17. Ibid, 213.

18. Ibid, 2, 10.

19. Ibid, 44.

20. Ibid, 38.

21. Ibid, 59.

22. Ibid, 10.

23. Ibid, 210.

24. Ibid, 207–208.

25. Ibid, 218.

26. Ibid, 417.

27. Ibid, 259.

28. Ibid, 10.

29. Ibid, 215.

30. Ibid, 226.

31. Ibid, 210.

32. Ibid, 449.

33. Ibid, 448–454.

34. A useful summary is to be found in D Stevenson, *The Covenanters* (1988), 28–34. On the importance of covenant theology, see J B Torrance, 'The Covenant Concept in Scottish Theology and Politics and its Legacy', *Scottish Journal of Theology*, 34, (1981), 232–238; M Steele, 'The Politick Christian: The Theological Background to the National Covenant', in Morrill (ed), *The Scottish National Covenant in its British Context*, 31–67.

35. S Rutherford, *Quaint Sermons*, A Bonar (ed), (1885), 61, 92–93.

36. J Ford, 'The Lawful Bonds of Scottish Society: The Five Articles of Perth, the Negative Confession and the National Covenant', *HJ*, 37, (1994), 63–64.

37. Ibid.

38. The one partial exception is J B Torrance, 'Covenant or Contract? A Study of the Theological Background of Worship in Seventeenth Century Scotland', *Scottish Journal of Theology*, 23, (1970), 70, which mentions in passing the crucial distinction between the internal and the external covenant of grace.

39. For what follows see *A Peaceable Plea for Pauls Presbyterie* (London, 1644), 164–183; *The Covenant of Life Opened* (Edinburgh, 1655), 72–117; and *A Survey of...Thomas Hooker* (London, 1658), 474–483.

40. O Chadwick, *The Reformation* (Harmondsworth, 1964), 403.

41 S Rutherford, *Fourteen Communion Sermons*, A Bonar (ed), (Edinburgh, 1877), 115–116.

42. S A Burrell, 'The Apocalyptic Vision of the Early Covenanters', *SHR*, 43, (1964), 2, 16.

43. Unpublished manuscript sermon on Genesis 28 in EUL, Dc 5 30 np.

44. *A Testimony to the Truth of Jesus Christ...by the ministers of Perth and Fife* (Kilmarnock, 1783; original edition, Edinburgh, 1660), 93–95. As Rutherford

was the first signatory to this declaration it is reasonable to assume that he was its author; he certainly subscribed to its content.

45. *Letters of Samuel Rutherford*, A Bonar (ed), (Edinburgh, 1891), 167.

46. Rutherford, *Lex, Rex*, 267–268.

47. Ibid, 180, 369.

48. Ibid, 373.

49. Ibid, 64.

50. Ibid, 274.

51. See [Andrew Honyman], *A Survey of Naphtali* (1668), 72, 20, 84–85.

52. Rutherford, *Lex, Rex*, 432.

53. Ibid, 328.

54. *Survey of Hooker*, 480.

55. Williamson, 'The Jewish Dimension of the Scottish Apocalypse', 7–30; A H Williamson, *Scottish National Consciousness in the Age of James VI* (Edinburgh, 1979); A H Williamson, 'Latter Day Judah, Latter Day Israel: The Millenium, the Jews and the British Future', *Pietismus und Neuzeit*, 14, (1988), 149–165.

56. Rutherford, *Fourteen Communion Sermons*, 32.

57. *Letters of Samuel Rutherford*, 577.

58. Rutherford, *Quaint Sermons*, 36.

59. *Peaceable Plea*, preface.

60. *Letters of Samuel Rutherford*, 615.

61. George Gillespie, *Sermon to the Commons*, in *The Works of George Gillespe*, two volumes, (Edinburgh, 1846), I, 7–9.

62. Samuel Rutherford, *A Sermon preached before the Honourable House of Commons* (London, 1644), preface, 7.

63. A Williamson, 'A Patriot Nobility? Calvinism, Kin-ties and Civic Humanism', *SHR*, 72, (1993), 1–21.

64. Lynch, *Scotland. A New History*, 264.

65. For what follows, see Stevenson, *Revolution and Counter-Revolution in Scotland*, chapters 3–5.

66. See C Hill, *The English Bible and the Seventeenth-Century Revolution* (Harmondsworth, 1993), chapter 15.

67. *Letters of Samuel Rutherford*, 650.

68. Ibid, 653.

69. Unpublished manuscript sermon on Genesis 28, EUL, Dc 5 30 np.

70. See W Stephen (ed), *Register of the Consultations of the Ministers of Edinburgh*, two volumes, (Edinburgh, 1921), I, 307.

71. See *The Diary of Alexander Brodie, 1652–80, and of his son, James Brodie of Brodie, 1680–85*, D Laing (ed) (Aberdeen, 1863), 48.

72. 'The Power of the Civil Magistrate in Matters of Religion', EUL Laing Manuscript III, 69 number 5, folio 9.

73. See D Stevenson, 'The Radical Party in the Kirk, 1637–45', *Journal of Ecclesiastical History*, 25, (1974), 135–165; D Stevenson, 'The General Assembly and the Commission of the Kirk, 1638–51' *RSCHS*, 19, (1975) 59–79.

74. *Letters of Samuel Rutherford*, 655.

75. Samuel Rutherford, *A Testimony to the Work of Reformatione in Britaine and Ireland* (Glasgow, 1719), 6–7.

CHAPTER 6

Rebels and Confederates: The Stance of the Irish Clergy in the 1640s

Tadhg ó hAnnracháin

The position of the clergy among the Confederate Catholics of Ireland during the 1640s has attracted little attention in the past. This is particularly surprising because the clergy clearly played a vital role in Confederate affairs: the formation of the Confederate Association itself was crucially influenced by the National Synod of the Irish church in Kilkenny in May 1642[1] and, thereafter, the clergy played an important role in legitimizing the authority of Confederate government. It was the difficulty of satisfying the demands of the clergy which chiefly obstructed the conclusion of peace between the Confederates and Charles I between 1645 and 1649.[2] In 1646, when the First Ormond Peace was concluded, it was rapidly overturned by a convocation of the clergy in a national synod.[3] Two years later, the resolution of the great crisis of the Inchiquin truce revolved to a considerable degree around the disunity of the clergy, while the conclusion of the Second Ormond Peace of 1649 and the dissolution of the Confederate Association owed a great deal to the initiative of members of the Irish hierarchy, in particular Nicholas French, the Bishop of Ferns.[4]

One of the reasons why the Irish clergy have attracted relatively little attention is undoubtedly the commanding figure of GianBattista Rinuccini, who was appointed as Nuncio to the Confederate Catholics of Ireland by Pope Innocent X in 1645.[5] Rinuccini's arrival in Ireland in October of that year was certainly one of the pivotal events of this entire period. Yet many of the positions which Rinuccini was to espouse had been maintained by members of the Irish clergy prior to his arrival. Moreover, it is clear that much of the strength of the Nuncio's position derived from the fact that during the first three years of his *nunziatura* he enjoyed the consistent and loyal support of the Irish clergy. The importance of this was demonstrated in the great excommunication crises of 1646 and 1648. At the apex of his success in 1646, Rinuccini received unanimous endorsement for his position from a National Synod of the entire Irish church. In 1648, Rinuccini was prevented from holding a similar synod and the outright opposition

96

of a considerable proportion of the Irish clergy significantly undermined his influence.[6]

Too great a concentration on Rinuccini thus runs the risk of obscuring the vital role of the native Irish clergy. Indeed, for the understanding of Rinuccini's own mission, it is necessary to clarify the precise role played by the clergy in the years which followed the rebellion of 1641. I propose to trace the church's involvement in the Confederate Association and the evolution in the stance of the clergy between 1641 and 1645. What I hope to demonstrate is that the support of the church was vital to the Confederate Catholics from the outset but that the influence of the clergy within Confederate government did not reflect their overall contribution to the stability of the association. I wish to suggest further that, having initially acquiesced in their own marginalisation, the clergy were gradually becoming more assertive in the period immediately prior to Rinuccini's arrival, spurred on by discontent with the manner of Confederate government and negotiation. Rinuccini's contribution, therefore, was not so much to introduce new clerical demands but to provide the clergy with more efficient leadership in pursuit of what they had already been seeking prior to his arrival.

In investigating this topic, I intend to concentrate in particular on the Irish hierarchy. The chief reason for this is that by the 1640s the Catholic church in Ireland was dominated by its episcopacy. Between 1618 and 1630, the Vatican had revived a functioning pastoral hierarchy of bishops in Ireland. All four archbishoprics had been filled with resident prelates by this date, while almost half of the remaining dioceses were also the seat of a resident bishop. In several other sees, vicars apostolic, effectively surrogate bishops, continued to act as the dominant ecclesiastical authority. As a result, when the 1641 rebellion engulfed Ireland, an extremely experienced Catholic hierarchy was already in existence in the island.[7]

This hierarchy had little or no involvement in the planning of the actual rebellion. Emer MacMahon, then Vicar Apostolic of Clogher, seems to have been Owen Roe O'Neill's envoy and was thus probably aware of some of the background but his role was not evidently of great importance.[8] The first organised declaration by the higher clergy with regard to the rebellion was not until the provincial Synod of Armagh in March 1642.[9] Prior to this, individual clerics had been involved in a personal capacity in the events associated with the rebellion. The guardian of the Franciscan convent in Dundalk, Thomas MacKiernan, played a prominent part in capturing the town in conjunction with Sir Phelim O'Neill.[10] In Kilkenny, Viscount Mountgarrett was evidently put under some pressure by his clerical advisors to join the rebellion, while the Archbishop of Dublin, Thomas Fleming, seems to have influenced Lord Clanmorish's participation.[11] Local priests seem, in some cases, to have attempted to control and channel the violence which occurred, by insisting that settlers be given the opportunity to convert to Catholicism in order to save themselves from expulsion.[12] In Kerry, Richard O'Connell, the Bishop of Ardfert, offered terms of this nature to Sir Edward Denny and the other Protestants in Tralee, pledging himself to protect their lives and property if they changed religion and joined the rebellion.[13] The forceful Archbishop of Tuam, Malachy O'Queely, was so appalled at the looting and violence which accompanied the rebellion in his diocese that he appears to have raised something of a private army to help control it.[14] A shared concern with 'repressing the destructive rapine of the multitude'[15] also seems to have been responsible for some initial tacit cooperation between Clanrickard (who opposed the rebellion) and the clergy of Clonfert and Tuam (who accepted the legitimacy of what they saw as a war but not of much which accompanied it).

Such a stance on the part of the clergy was clearly welcomed by the prosperous Catholic gentry of Ireland who were deeply worried at the social unrest which the rebellion had unleashed. Fear that they themselves would become targets of attacks, similar to those already being launched against Protestants throughout the country, was evidently a factor in encouraging many gentry to join the rebellion. Richard Bellings, the Confederate Secretary, later explained the decision of his father-in-law, Viscount Mountgarrett, to throw in his lot with the insurgents as influenced by:

> the apprehensions he had of the height to which the
> meaner sort of people might grow up against the nobility
> and gentry.[16]

For Catholics of this stamp, who believed that they had more to lose than gain in the tumult of the rebellion, the synods of the clergy of Armagh in March 1642 and of the entire Irish church in May of the same year,[17] offered a considerable measure of reassurance. In the first place, the clergy explicitly legitimised participation in the rebellion on the grounds of protection of the Catholic religion. Second, the synods offered protection for Catholic property. They denounced crimes such as unauthorised occupation of lands and the extortion of money in the most uncompromising terms and declared the guilty parties excommunicated. Third, the clergy used these gatherings to advance the development of a political structure to replace that shattered by the rebellion. In March, the Synod of Armagh expressed the desire for a union of ecclesiastical and secular authority to control the rebellion.[18] The General Synod of the Irish church, held in May of the same year, advanced more detailed plans for a unified authority which were eventually to be fulfilled in the Confederate Association.[19]

The vast majority of the Irish clergy followed the leadership of the hierarchy in 1642 in its endorsement of a war for Catholic liberties and this crucially strengthened the movement towards greater organisation. The most important exception to this rule of clerical unanimity was Thomas Dease, Bishop of Meath, who denied the legitimacy of the rebellion. Yet even Dease had been forced to toe the majority line of the hierarchy by 1643.[20] Thereafter, dissenting voices from the official church position were largely confined to a small group of priests centred around the household of the Royalist Marquis of Clanricard, several of whom were actually English and who appear to have accompanied Clanricard's wife to Ireland in the 1640s.[21]

The unity of the church and the leadership it was able to provide was thus an important factor in the movement which ultimately culminated in the first assembly of the Confederate Catholics in October 1642. The clergy also played a vital role in conferring legitimacy on the authority of the new organisation. Partly inspired by the Scottish National Covenant, the Confederates tackled the awkward problem of legitimising the structure which they had created through an Oath of Association.[22]

This oath obliged the taker to defend the lives, just freedoms, possessions, patrimonies, and rights of every person who had sworn or who would swear the oath in future. It forbade any attempt by any Confederate to seek a separate peace or pardon without permission from the Supreme Council and it enjoined obedience to the Confederate executive (the Supreme Council) in every matter concerning the common cause.[23] It was thus both an oath of obedience and association which established a brotherhood or society of 'Confederate Catholics' committed to the achievement of certain goals. The oath's force was greatly enhanced by the manner in which it was administered by the clergy. It was sworn in the parish church of the taker after he had confessed his sins and received communion and it was witnessed by the local priest. The taker's name was then enrolled in a parish list of Confederates, a copy of which was sent to the local ordinary, from there to the metropolitan, and finally to the Supreme Council.[24] The authority of the church and its sacraments was thus thrown behind the oath, which emphasised the enormity of the sin which perjury would entail.

It is likely that this idealised system did not work quite so perfectly in practice. Nevertheless, the development of a relatively efficient parochial organisation in the previous thirty years meant that the clergy were in a position to administer the oath to much of the population and also in a sense to police it. Any perjurer was likely to be known to his local priest and the reform movement of the previous decades had done much to ensure that the parish clergy were both respected and trustworthy enough to invigilate the oath among the general population. Perhaps most importantly in terms of Rinuccini's later career, the manner in which the oath was taken clearly strengthened the clergy's claim to be the legitimate interpreters of what constituted a breach of the oath. In 1646, when the National Synod of the church claimed that the those who accepted the Ormond Peace were in violation of their oath, significant elements of the general population were prepared to accept them at their word.[25]

In 1642, however, such breaches lay in the future and the new and secular dominated Supreme Council was well aware of the vital role which the clergy played in legitimising their authority. As the Secretary of the Council later admitted:

> the reverence borne to the Catholicke cause, which had
> soe powerfull and universall an influence upon those of
> that nation, did secure the Councell from anie feare they
> might entertaine of the people's aversion to the new
> Government.[26]

The arrival of PierFrancesco Scarampi, a papal agent accredited to the Supreme Council, further consolidated the Council's authority. Richard Bellings noted that Scarampi was extremely useful to the Council by

> drawing the laity to pay a perfect obedience to their
> commands, who were thought worthy of being seconded by so
> awful and much reverenced an authority.[27]

It was largely because of this that the Council unsuccessfully requested Rome to dignify Scarampi with the official title of Nuncio,[28] a request which in some ways was to return to haunt them in the person of Rinuccini.

Not only did the church's support underpin the authority of the new oathbound organisation but its excommunications were also directed against any Catholic who remained outside the Association.[29] This failed to convince Ulick Burke, fifth Earl and later first Marquis of Clanricard, the greatest Catholic nobleman in the country, to join the Confederates Catholics. Nevertheless, few other Irish Catholics had the prestige, the Court contacts or indeed the access to advice from English

Catholic priests which distinguished Clanricard, and it is likely that this threat of excommunication was a very potent force in encouraging other doubtful Catholics to join the Association. Certainly, throughout the 1640s, secular Catholics evinced great respect for this particular power of the church. From an early stage in the rebellion, the rebels were keen to invoke the church's censures on their own behalf[30] and the first Supreme Council of the Confederates applied directly to Rome for an explicit declaration of excommunication against Catholics who opposed them. At the same time they successfully requested an indulgence for all Catholics who participated in the Confederate War.[31]

Having played a critically important role in the establishment and in the legitimisation of the Confederate Catholic Association, members of the clergy continued to be associated prominently with the new Confederate government in the following years. All bishops sat of right in the quasi-parliamentary Confederate Assembly and between 1642 and 1644 all four archbishops seem to have spent some time as members of the Confederate Supreme Council. They were joined on this body by two of the younger and most vigorous members of the hierarchy, Emer MacMahon, the Bishop of Clogher, and John Bourke, the Bishop of Clonfert.[32] Yet, although the involvement of prominent clergy in the Council clearly helped substantiate its authority with the general population, the clergy do not appear to have played a particularly important role in Confederate government, nor indeed do they appear to have been particularly successful in placing their own special concerns high on the Confederate agenda.

There seem to have been a number of factors at work in limiting the influence of the clergy within the framework of Confederate government. In the first place, as a corporate body, the clergy lacked a real forum among the institutions of the Association. The bishops were heavily outnumbered by secular voices within the Assembly and many seem to have been reluctant to voice their views there openly.[33] Those on the Supreme Council also constituted a minority, albeit a larger one, and they were apparently willing to accept majority decisions.[34] One way in which this marginalisation could be countered was for the clergy to assembly in convocation at the same time as the Confederate General Assemblies, a development which was especially significant in 1645 and one which Rinuccini seems to have put to use to great effect following his arrival in Ireland.[35] In this, as in much else, the Nuncio's contribution seems to have been in the assertiveness of his leadership rather than in the introduction of radical new policies for the clergy.

The supposition that Rinuccini's leadership was of special importance is strengthened when one takes into account the age profile and pastoral experience of the Irish hierarchy prior to the nuncio's arrival. As Donal Cregan has pointed out, in contemporary European terms, the Irish bishops were unprecedented in the degree to which they were selected for their positions according to ecclesiastical criteria. Political influences did have some part to play in the appointment of certain bishops,[36] but in the main the Irish hierarchy represented a body of highly educated pastors. All the Irish bishops of this era, whether Gaelic Irish or Old English, had been trained in seminaries on the continent, and from 1631 effectively all were resident within their dioceses.[37] There they acquired a vast range of pastoral experience. Most of the hierarchy at the time that Rinuccini was created Nuncio were survivors from the pre-1641 era: indeed only four bishops were appointed in the entire period between 1630 and 1645 and three of these already had extensive experience as vicars apostolic in their sees.[38]

During the 1640s, many of these bishops seem to have been unwilling to devote much attention away from their pastoral activity in order to participate very actively in Confederate politics.[39] For some of the more dedicated pastors, indeed, such as Richard O'Connell of Ardfert, simple geographical inaccessibility meant that any meaningful political involvement would have involved extensive absences from his see. Another factor which militated against extensive involvement of the clergy in the decision-making processes of the Association was the age of many of the bishops. By 1642, not one of the fifteen Irish bishops was younger than 50, three were in their seventies, while one was an octogenarian.[40] Sciatica and excessive corpulence seriously hampered the mobility of another two of the hierarchy.[41] Taking this into account, it is perhaps not surprising that it was the younger blood among the bishops, particularly Ferns, Limerick, Clogher, and Clonfert who were to be most politically active in the period of Rinuccini's *nunziatura*.

Given the financial constraints under which the Confederate Association laboured, it might be expected that the wealth of the church would have given the clergy a degree of political leverage. Prior to 1641, of course, the Catholic Church as an institution had been unable to claim ownership of any property in Ireland. The 1641 rebellion, however, changed this situation to a considerable extent. Basically, in most of the country the Catholic clergy occupied the churches and property which had been in the hands of the Church of Ireland prior to 1641, a development which was confirmed by the decrees of the First Confederate Assembly of October 1642.[42] However, two-thirds of the revenue which the clergy acquired in this fashion was devoted to sustaining the Confederate armies. Crucially, the property from which this revenue was drawn was not left in the hands of the clergy but was given to lay assessors and farmers. Consequently, the clergy lost practically all control of this resource. Not surprisingly, Rinuccini objected to this situation on his arrival and his restoration of clerical control of this property in 1646 was to be one of his first significant victories in Ireland and one which operated to increase the influence of the clergy in general.[43]

Another factor which contributed to the relative marginalisation of the clergy was the increasing importance of the Confederate negotiations with Charles I, negotiations in which the clergy initially seem to have had relatively little input. Partly, this can be attributed to the composition of the various Confederate negotiating teams. There were no clergy present in the delegation which was nominated to go to England during the first cessation to put the Confederate viewpoint to the king.[44] Before and after this unsuccessful interlude, the real work of Confederate negotiation was done with James Butler, Marquis of Ormond, who became Lord Lieutenant of Ireland in 1643. Ormond was reluctant to negotiate directly with any member of the Catholic clergy. Against his objections, the Confederates did insist on the right to have clergy in their negotiating team but, while maintaining this position, they did their best to accommodate the Lord Lieutenant by picking individuals whom they believed would be specially acceptable to him. Only one cleric, the mild, Old English, noble and extremely fat Archbishop of Dublin was included among the negotiators and it has been suggested that he may have remained in the background and out of contact with Ormond.[45] In any case, one clergyman among thirteen negotiators was a small recognition of the real weight of the bishops within the Association. The composition of the Confederate delegation thus naturally limited the amount of influence which the clergy could exert on the negotiating process. Moreover, the negotiators themselves came to play an important role within the government of the Association. Such great importance was attached to the talks with Ormond that the negotiators were effectively co-opted onto the Supreme Council, which increased the secular majority of that body and the influence of Ormond's Confederate supporters.[46]

The church leadership may have acquiesced in their marginalisation from the negotiations, not only because of a certain passivity, but also because of the belief that their demands were unlikely to be satisfied by the king's representatives in any case. Certainly the clergy's desire to secure the right of the Catholic bishops to exercise spiritual jurisdiction and to retain possession of the ecclesiastical property which they had gained since 1641 was unlikely to be met in negotiation. It seems probable that members of the clergy realised this and pinned their hopes for the realisation of these objectives on the arrival of substantial assistance from sympathetic Catholic powers, which would allow the Confederates to dictate their own terms with regard to religious concessions. In this respect, one can note the instructions to Father. Hugh Bourke OFM, who was about to undertake a diplomatic mission to Spain, in which it was stated:

> If it be objected that in our proposicions the freedom of
> religion only is desired, you may inculcate the reason
> (which God knows to be true) it was to win tyme, and our
> constructione shall be freedome in splendor, if holpen
> with possibilitye of subsistence.[47]

Two months previously, in a similar vein, the Supreme Council had written to the most important Irish cleric in Rome, Luke Wadding, summarising the situation which the negotiations had reached:

> wee finde that, through all the proceedings, both heere
> and in England, the Kinge may be wonn to give as much as
> is reasonable for us to demand in temporall matters,
> either for the freedome of the nacion or the assurance
> of their estates, and that he may, perhaps be drawne to
> withdrawe those penall laws whereby the Catholicks were
> punished for exercising their religion, though in a
> privat and retyred way; but for enjoying our churches, or
> restoreing the profession of our faith to its ancient
> splendor is a thing soe odious to the King's partie,
> that wee must make it good in the same way that we did
> obtaine it, and therefore we wonder how a nation, that
> cannot now be thought to continue in armes for any other
> end than the advancement of the Catholick religion should
> receive soe little countenance and succor from those who
> are cheefely intrusted in the propagacion of the
> Catholicke religion.[48]

The clergy's expectation of assistance from abroad, stoked by the promises of Scarampi,[49] may thus have been a factor in disposing them to defer tabling their demands in negotiations.

By mid-1644 however, the reversion of the conduct of negotiations to Ormond in Ireland, and the non-arrival of substantial assistance for the Confederates from abroad, helped ensure that the demands of the clergy would also begin to be raised in negotiations. It is in this period that one can trace the beginnings of a more assertive demeanour on the part of the clergy, which ultimately precipitated an internal crisis within the Association. Despite the limited presence of clergy on the Confederate delegation, one can note that the bishops did succeed in having their claim to jurisdiction voiced in the negotiations. Ormond, to his horror, found that the Confederates wanted the repeal, not just of the Acts of Supremacy, Uniformity, and Faculties, but also the Act of Appeals, parts of the Act of Marriages and several fourteenth-century statutes which ordained the impeachment of clergy appointed without royal consent.[50] During negotiations the Confederates pointed out in defence of these demands that they could not have 'the free use, profession and exercise of their religion and functions without prelates'[51] and that these must have the power to 'instruct, correct and governe, with impunity'.[52] Ormond was staggered by the implications and the extent of the Confederate demand for jurisdiction and he was deeply unwilling to entertain it.[53]

The determination of the Confederates to secure this point was probably partly rooted in the experiences of the Irish bishops during the 1620s and 1630s. Little attention has previously been paid to the fact that in the twenty years prior to the 1641 rebellion, several bishops, most notably the Archbishop of Armagh, were accused of *lèse-majesté* before the state courts and imprisoned on the crime of having exercised a jurisdiction derived from Rome. In practically every case, the bishops seem to have been the victims of Catholic priests from their own dioceses who resented the bishops' attempts to enforce new standards of behaviour and clerical education.[54] This development, which seems to have owed something to the example of an English priest, Paul Harris,[55] represented a considerable threat to the Roman attempt to make the episcopacy the focal point of tridentine style reform in Ireland. Indeed, it was a more serious threat to this process than the insubordination of the regular clergy or of the collegiate church of St Nicholas which have received attention in the past.[56]

The basis of the problem lay in the state's differentiation between the ordinary ecclesiastical activity of a Catholic priest, which was largely tolerated, and the exercise of a Rome-derived jurisdiction.[57] Thus Catholic priests, although themselves engaged in illegal activity, were not afraid to use the state courts to persecute their bishops because the state was prepared to ignore the lesser crime. This problem was clearly at its worst in Ulster but affected the other provinces of Ireland as well. While it was in Ulster that bishops were actually imprisoned, the Bishop of Kildare, Ross MacGeoghegan, and the Vicar

Apostolic of Clonfert, John Bourke, were also severely harassed for this reason.[58] In 1636, fear of state hostility to the Catholic bishops caused the clergy of Ferns to petition *Propaganda Fide* in Rome not to appoint a replacement bishop to the see.[59] One can note, also, that no National Synod of the Irish church was held in the period between 1618 and 1642, despite the revival of the episcopate and the perceived need to ratify the full implementation of tridentine decrees in Ireland. The reason for this seems to have been the level of hostility which the state authorities showed to any exercise of jurisdiction by the Catholic hierarchy. It was not surprising therefore that both the Irish bishops and the Roman authorities considered the legal right to exercise a jurisdiction derived from Rome a point of cardinal importance in the peace negotiations, although Ormond became aware of it only in 1644.

An even more important issue, for both the Catholic church and Ormond, was the question of ecclesiastical property, which the clergy were determined to retain in their possession, while Ormond was determined to force its return to the Church of Ireland. This issue developed explosive importance in May and June of 1645[60] when it threatened either to split the Confederate Association or to wreck the negotiations with Ormond. The development of this crisis is particularly informative in terms of the determination of the Irish clergy not to accept a peace which did not grant their principal demands, a determination which, it must be emphasised, predated Rinuccini's arrival. It also demonstrates, nevertheless, the consistent conciliatory inclination of the çlergy and the manner in which this could be manipulated by the Confederate negotiators, many of whom had come to believe that events in England necessitated the abandonment of the more extreme clerical demands.

Once again, the experiences of the 1630s seem to have influenced the clergy's stance on the issue of church property. The period before 1641 has, with some reason, generally been considered an era of rapid development for the Catholic church in Ireland with the diffusion of tridentine reforms under the leadership of a pastoral episcopacy of a high calibre.[61] What is largely ignored, however, is the manner in which many of the Irish hierarchy of the pre-Confederate era saw lack of finance as a major impediment to the proper functioning of bishops in Ireland.

During the 1630s, the Irish bishops directed a litany of complaints to Rome concerning their poverty and that of their priests and the difficulty of maintaining themselves. This problem was particularly acute in Ulster. In 1637, two days after a provincial synod, the Archbishop of Armagh wrote to the cardinals of *Propaganda Fide*. He informed the congregation that none of the dioceses in the province was able to sustain even the most moderate conception of a bishop's dignity. Not a single diocese was worth more to its bishop than 600 Belgian florins (about £60 pounds) per annum. But what was worse was the steady detrimental effect of continued Scots and English immigration into the province and the simultaneous impoverishment of the indigenous population. Consequently, the value of each diocese was declining inexorably.[62] O'Reilly's testimony is corroborated by that of his episcopal colleagues, John O'Cullenan in Raphoe,[63] and Bonaventure Magennis in Down and Connor.[64] The problems in Ulster were clearly graver than anywhere else but episcopal poverty was by no means confined to the north. Sometime between 1636 and 1640, the four archbishops of Ireland wrote to Rome outlining the poverty of the Irish prelates. Of sixteen resident bishops, hardly eight had more than 100 scudi (20–25 pounds sterling) per annum, in all their emoluments, and no bishop had more than 200 scudi per annum. The archbishops insisted that these were simply inadequate sums, since a bishop needed to journey in his diocese five or six times a year to visit and observe the priests, to preach, to confirm, and to compose controversies between the Catholic clergy and laity. A bishop, they pointed out, in order to accomplish this programme, was forced to maintain at least three horses and several servants. Further proof of the bishops' poverty was their inability to pay their agent in Rome, Edward O'Dwyer (later Bishop of Limerick), who had been there for six years at his own expense.[65] Lack of resources was evidently one of the principal reasons why Rome largely froze further appointments to the Irish hierarchy after 1630 and adopted the expedient of twinning dioceses under one bishop's care.[66] In addition, all further appointments were carefully scrutinized to see if the candidates had the private resources as well the necessary education to enable them to discharge their duties.

As noted above, this situation changed to some considerable extent in the aftermath of 1641 when the Catholic clergy acquired the property of the Church of Ireland. Understandably, the clergy were most unwilling to relinquish these gains in any settlement.[67] Ormond's position had been made clear, however, in July 1644[68] and by May 1645 the Confederate negotiators were reasonably sure that he could not be forced to alter his position on this point. On the other hand, they were also aware of the determination of many of the Catholic clergy not to yield the churches.[69]

A new assertiveness on the part of the clergy in terms of this issue was probably inspired by dissatisfaction with the Supreme Council and the negotiators, and a growing distrust of the dominant clique in Confederate affairs. As the matters of chief concern to lay Catholics were slowly addressed in negotiations with Ormond, the clergy became increasingly and justifiably worried that many influential Confederates would be willing to make peace without securing the jurisdiction of the bishops and the retention of church property.

The military failures of 1644 in Ulster sharpened the suspicion that the chief focus of many in the Supreme Council was now the negotiation of peace rather than the strengthening of the Association. Reluctance to trust O'Neill with the command of the 1644 expedition was seen to have been compounded by massive administrative inefficiency and corruption.[70] Far more ominously, the suspicion was beginning to develop that what was emerging as a Confederate peace party would not be above conspiring to cause the failure of confederate military campaigns. This suspicion was fuelled by the conviction that some of the most important councillors and negotiators such as Muskery, Bellings, Fennell, Talbot, Browne, Martin, and Darcy had a personal interest in reaching peace with Ormond because they expected to benefit from his patronage and that of Clanricard after the peace was finalised.[71]

Matters moved towards a crisis at the General Assembly of May 1645 in Kilkenny during which time the Catholic clergy also gathered in convocation in the same city, thus giving themselves a powerful forum from which to present a unified position. It is possible that news of Rinuccini's appointment encouraged the clergy to adopt a more decisive position at this time but this was clearly not the only factor and Rinuccini, then in France, certainly had no hand in orchestrating the clerical position.[72]

By the opening of the assembly, the Confederate negotiators were already aware that Ormond would not only oppose Catholic retention of the churches and church livings in Ireland, but would require an article in the peace explicitly returning them to the Church of Ireland. On 25 May, therefore, a group of lay Confederates demanded of convocation if the Confederates were bound by their oath to obtain an article in the peace expressly stipulating the retention of the churches, even if such a demand was to be the only obstacle to the completion of peace. The clergy's answer on 31 May was that the Oath of Association did bind the Confederates to obtain such an article and that any failure in this regard would make the Confederates transgressors of divine law.[73]

Eleven of the fourteen bishops present in Kilkenny, as well as a variety of other senior clergy, signed this declaration. In the past, a good deal has been made of the division within the ranks of the Irish hierarchy on this issue.[74] Yet while three bishops stood out from the consensus, it must be emphasised that a very large majority of the clergy voted in favour of retention of the churches even at the expense of peace. This majority included the two relatively moderate Old English archbishops, Thomas Walsh of Cashel, and Thomas Fleming of Dublin, as well as the Old English bishops of Clonfert and Waterford. Moreover, among the delegation of clergy which prepared the convocation's statement were three other Old English clerics who were shortly afterwards elevated to the hierarchy.[75] Thus, the argument that the nucleus of the party of Old English clergy which opposed the nuncio in 1648 first raised their heads during this period is very dubious.[76] Three of the bishops who did most to undermine the Nuncio's position in 1648, John Bourke, Oliver Darcy, and Nicholas French were clearly in support of the more extreme clerical position in 1645.[77] One can also note that the majority position of the clergy in 1645 was practically identical to the unanimous decision of the clergy at the legatine synod of 1646. Therefore, while Rinuccini's arrival in Ireland may have strengthened the clergy in their determination not to accept peace unless their concerns were addressed, it is apparent that a clear majority of the clergy were already committed to this position while he was still on the continent.

Where the clerical consensus of 1645 really appears to have differed from that of 1646 when Rinuccini was present was in its reluctance to risk confrontation with the Confederate government in the pursuit of its objectives. In 1646, the clergy ultimately overthrew the Council rather than accept the Ormond Peace: in 1645, while maintaining the principle of no peace without the right to the churches and jurisdiction, in practice the clergy allowed themselves to be browbeaten by the Confederate negotiators and the peace party within the Assembly.

On 9 June, after prolonged debate, the General Assembly finally adopted a position between that of Ormond's demands and those of the clergy, when it refused its commissioners the right to concede the churches but refused also the clerical convocation's demand that the churches be explicitly retained for the Catholic clergy.[78] This presented a challenge to the clergy and opened an avenue for the peace negotiators, who exerted themselves furiously to force the clergy to adopt the position of the General Assembly. The commissioners apparently claimed that Convocation had accused them of perjury or intended perjury.[79] In an effort to mollify their anger, the clergy effectively retracted their previous decree. They declared that if, as the commissioners insisted, an arrangement could be made by which the retention of the churches could be effectively guaranteed by the military strength of the Catholics, then an explicit article in the peace guaranteeing this point was not strictly necessary. Consequently, no-one in the General Assembly was to be considered guilty of perjury for not demanding express retention. Finally, the Convocation, under pressure from the Confederate commissioners, went even further and declared that the decree already made by the General Assembly on this point could not be considered a breach of the oath.[80]

It seems certain that, in an effort to contrive a treaty which neither the clergy nor Ormond would reject, the Confederate commissioners lied to either one or both sides at this point and that this explains the determination with which they hounded the clergy. The manner in which they signed the Ormond Peace the following year suggests that the main victims of this deceit were the clergy. The clerical convocation had clearly been won to avoid insisting on the explicit retention of the churches on the guarantee that an arrangement of equivalent security would be obtained.[81] In other words, they had not dropped their claim to the churches but they had accepted the assurance of the Confederate negotiators that an article to this effect in the peace was not necessary. To Ormond, on the other hand, the suggestion was made, via Clanricard who was at the Assembly, that the lack of an article expressly dealing with the churches would permit them to be returned to the Protestant clergy after all other matters had been settled.[82]

What this sequence of events suggests is that many of the ingredients which were to shape Rinuccini's *nunziatura* were already in place prior to his arrival. The Irish clergy had already made clear their determination to retain the churches and church livings and to secure the right of their bishops to exercise a spiritual jurisdiction.[83] On the other hand, a peace party had evolved within the Association which had more or less accepted the necessity of abandoning the clergy's principal demands and who seem to have been prepared to use deceit in order to keep the clergy acquiescent, a strategy which they were to repeat when they signed the Ormond Peace in breach of their agreement with Rinuccini in March 1646. In 1645, this was a strategy which seemed to work since the clergy were sufficiently fragmented and conciliatory to accept the dubious assurances of the negotiators that their interests would not be abandoned. The bishops then confirmed their conciliatory stance in August and September when, against Scarampi's advice, they voted to depend for the satisfaction of their demands on Glamorgan's doubtful and secret mandate.[84] The subsequent collapse of Glamorgan's credibility, however, gradually returned matters to the position in which they had been in the summer of 1645. In the meantime, Rinuccini had arrived in Ireland and, under his leadership in the synod of 1646, the clergy demonstrated a decisiveness and an appetite for confrontation which had been lacking the previous year.

Conclusion

It is clear that the dominant role which Rinuccini was to play within Confederate politics had been foreshadowed and prepared prior to his arrival in Ireland. The clergy were integral to the stability of Confederate Catholics from the outset and it was this which was to be the foundation stone of Rinuccini's influence. Moreover, the objectives which he pursued were substantially similar to those which the native Irish clergy had been seeking before he came to Ireland. Among other factors, the Irish bishops' memory of the 1630s meant that there was broad support within the hierarchy for the Vatican's determination to acquire jurisdiction and property for the Catholic clergy. Rinuccini was appointed to the Irish mission at a time when the stance of the Irish clergy within the Confederate Association was already beginning to change. Prior to 1644, the clergy had been unassertive in seeking to utilise their political importance within the Association: they had not enjoyed particular influence within Confederate government and they had been largely and, to some extent voluntarily, marginalised from the negotiations with Ormond. From the middle of 1644, however, the clergy were gradually exerting more pressure on the negotiations and demanding that their interests be maintained. Rinuccini, in a sense, completed a process already in gestation by bringing a previously absent quality of clear-headed and consistent leadership to the clerical party.

NOTES

1. See S Kavanagh (ed), *Commentarius Rinuccianus, de sedis apostolicae legatione ad foederatos Hiberniae catholicos per annos 1645–9* (six volumes, Dublin, 1932–49), i, 320–6.

2. See P Corish, 'Ormond, Rinuccini and the Confederates, 1645–9' in T W Moody, F X Martin, and F J Byrne (eds.), *A New History of Ireland, III, Early Modern Ireland 1534–1691* (Oxford, 1978), 316–335.

3. See D Cregan, 'The confederation of Kilkenny; its organisation, personnel and history' (National University of Ireland, PhD thesis, 1947) 230–235; see also *Commentarius Rinuccianus*, ii, 324–346.

4. Bishop French is one of the few members of the hierarchy to have been studied in any depth: see P Corish, 'Bishop Nicholas French and the second Ormond peace, 1648–9' in *Irish Historical Studies*, 6 (1948), 83–100.

5. *Commentarius Rinuccianus*, i, 591–601.

6. See *Commentarius Rinuccianus*, ii, 318–390; iii, 284–288, 327, 335, 342, 491, 500.

7. D Cregan, 'The Social and Cultural Background of a Counter–Reformation Episcopate, 1618–60' in A Cosgrove and D MacCartney (eds) *Studies in Irish History presented to R Dudley Edwards* (Dublin, 1979), 85–117; P Corish, *The Catholic Community in the Seventeenth and Eighteenth Centuries* (Dublin, 1981), 17–42; H Kearney, 'Ecclesiastical Politics and the Counter-Reformation in Ireland, 1618–48', in *Journal of Ecclesiastical History*, xi (1960), 202–212.

8. J Casway, *Owen Roe O'Neill and the Struggle for Catholic Ireland* (Philadelphia, 1984), 48.

9. *Commentarius Rinuccianus*, i, 314–320; Cregan, 'The confederation of Kilkenny', 42.

10. H O'Sullivan, 'The Franciscans in Dundalk' in *Seanchas Ardmhacha The Journal of the Armagh Diocesan Historical Society*, 4 (1960–1), 47.

11. See the Bellings narrative in J T Gilbert, (ed), *History of the Irish confederation and the war in Ireland*, (seven volumes, Dublin, 1882–91), i, 65; J T Gilbert (ed) *A contemporary history of affairs in Ireland (1641–52)* (three volumes, Dublin, 1879) i, 52.

12. N Canny, *From Reformation to Restoration: Ireland 1534–1660* (Dublin, 1987), 209.

13. *Commentarius Rinuccianus*, i, 311.

14. R Gillespie, 'Mayo and the 1641 Rising' in *Cathair na Mart*, v (1985), 38–44.

15. Bellings narrative (*Irish Confederation*, i, 104).

16. Ibid, 65.

17. *Commentarius Rinuccianus*, i. 314–326.

18. Ibid, 314–315.

19. Ibid, 320–325.

20. Ibid, 430–431; Supreme Council's instructions to Luke Wadding (*Irish Confederation*, ii, 119–120).

21. *Commentarius Rinuccianus*, i, 431–432, 503, 537; *Irish Confederation* iv, 274; Biblioteca Apostolica Vaticana, Barberini Latini, 6483, f 77r.

22. See J C Beckett, 'The confederation of Kilkenny reviewed', in *Historical Studies*, ii, 29–41 and P Corish, 'The rising of 1641 and the catholic confederacy, 1641–5', in *New History of Ireland*, iii, 299. In terms of the obvious parallels with the Scottish National Covenant one can note the interesting reference to the 'confederate calvinists in Scotland' in 'The War and Rebellion in Ireland begun in 1641' (NLI MS 345 (Plunkett-Dunne MS), 946.

23. *The memoirs and letters of Ulick, marquiss of Clanricarde* (London, 1757), 325.

24. *Commentarius Rinuccianus*, i, 351–352.

25. See, for example, the accounts of the rejection of the peace in *Irish Confederation*, vi, 110–131.

26. Bellings narrative (*Irish Confede*ration, i, 115).

27. Ibid, 153.

28. *Commentarius Rinuccianus*, i, 429.

29. *Commentarius Rinuccianus*, i, 323.

30. BAV, Barberini Latini, 6483, f 36r.

31. By the time this last arrived, it may well have caused the Council some embarrassment as it alarmed many of the Protestants with whom they were then busy negotiating a peace. See 'Instructions to Luke Wadding' (*Irish Confederation*, ii, 118); and *Commentarius Rinuccianus*, i, 503–507.

32. See *Irish Confederation*, ii, 85–86; *Commentarius Rinuccianus*, i, 429.

33. There were evidently never more than fifteen bishops in the assembly among more than two hundred secular delegates. See the clerical convocation's response to the Council, 22 August 1646 (*Commentarius Rinuccianus*, ii, 331). It has been suggested that the Assembly was designed as a unicameral institution for precisely this reason; see Kearney, 'Ecclesiastical politics', 209.

34. See 'Multae Sunt', an unnamed and undated memorial to Rinuccini (*Commentarius Rinuccianus*, ii, 44–45).

35. *Commentarius Rinuccianus*, iii, 42.

36. Kearney, 'Ecclesiastical politics', 203–206.

37. Cregan, 'Social and cultural background', 117.

38. Ibid.

39. The chief exception to this rule was Emer Macmahon, whom Rinuccini, himself a dedicated pastor, later criticised as an essentially political animal: see 'Relazione del Regno d'Irlanda', 1 March, 1646 (G Aiazzi, *Nunziatura in Irlanda di Monsignor Gio Baptista Rinuccini Arcivescovo di Fermo negli anni 1645 à 1649* (Firenze, 1844), 111).

40. Cregan, 'Social and cultural background', 87.

41. Aiazzi, *Nunziatura*, 84–85.

42. See acts of the General Assembly, October 1642 (*Irish Confederation*, ii, 82).

43. Aiazzi, *Nunziatura*, 100.

44. *Commentarius Rinuccianus*, i, 467.

45. See 'Viaggio in Irlanda di Dionysio Massari' (Archivio della Sacra Congregazione di Propaganda Fide, Miscellaneae Varie, ix, 81); *Irish Confederation*, iii, 253; *Commentarius. Rinuccianus*, i, 523; Corish, *New History of Ireland*, iii, 313.

46. Aiazzi, *Nunziatura*, 104–105.

47. Instructions to Hugh Bourke, 12 December 1644 (*Irish Confederation*, iv, 93).

48. *Irish Confederation*, iv, 35–36.

49. *Irish Confederation*, iii, 258.

50. *Irish Confederation*, iv, 332.

51. Ibid, 336.

52. Ibid, 339–40.

53. See Ormond to Confederate Commissioners, 28 July, 1644 (*Irish Confederation*, iv, 346).

54. See, for example, P F Moran (ed), *Spicilegium Ossoriense: being a collection of original letters and papers illustrative of the history of the Irish church* (three volumes, Dublin, 1874–84), i, 180–184, 209, 228–231; C. Giblin, 'The *Processus Datariae* and the appointment of Irish bishops in the seventeenth century' in Franciscan Fathers, *Father Luke Wadding: Commemorative Volume* (Dublin, 1957, 578.

55. APF, 'Scritture originale riferite nei Congressi Generali', 140, ff 333r–335v; *Spicilegium Ossoriense*, i, 198.

56. In both these cases, the conflict remained internal to the Catholic Church and ultimately depended for resolution on the consistency of the Roman authorities; see Corish, *Catholic Community*, 26–28.

57. See *Irish Confederation*, iv, 326.

58. APF, 'Scritture originale riferite nei Congressi Generali', 140, ff 308r–309r; Giblin, 'Processus Datariae', 578.

59. APF, 'Scritture originale riferite nei Congressi Generali', 140, f 230rv.

60. *Irish Confederation*, iv, 278.

61. See Cregan, 'Social and cultural background'.

62. *Spicilegium Ossoriense*, i, 220–221.

63. APF, 'S.O.C.G.', 140, 162r, 169rv, 170rv, 173rv, 185rv.

64. Ibid, f 342rv.

65. Ibid, ff 34r–35v.

66. Ibid.

67. The Vatican was also absolutely determined to secure an adequate financial basis for the labour of the Catholic clergy, see Rinuccini's instructions (Aiazzi, *Nunziatura*, xlvi).

68. See *Irish Confederation*, iv, 319.

69. There had been warnings of this since the middle of the previous year. On 20 August, 1644, for instance, the Duchess of Buckingham wrote to Ormond

that she found 'it impossible to make the clergie or those that run that way to be satisfyed without their churches'; see *Irish Confederation*, iii, 258.

70. In this context see Gilbert, *Contemporary History*, i, 82–88. See also the anonymous memorial 'Multae sunt' presented to Rinuccini on his arrival in Ireland (*Commentarius Rinuccianus*, ii, 44–45).

71. Rinuccini certainly developed this conviction from an early stage in his *nunziatura*: see Relazione del Regno d'Irlanda, 1 March 1646 (Aiazzi, *Nunziatura*, 108). Prior to the Nuncio's arrival the Confederates' Jesuit agent in Paris voiced similar suspicions; see Matthew O'Hartigan to Supreme Council, 16 November 1644 (*Irish Confederation*, iv, 62). The same point was voiced in the memorial 'Multae sunt' presented to Rinuccini on his arrival (*Commentarius Rinuccianus*, ii, 43–45).

72. This point is made clear in Rinuccini's letters; see Aiazzi, *Nunziatura*, 6–22.

73. *Commentarius Rinuccianus*, i, 527–529.

74. Kearney, 'Ecclesiastical politics', 208–10.

75. See *Commentarius Rinuccianus*, i, 524–529.

76. Kearney, 'Ecclesiastical politics', 209–212.

77. *Commentarius Rinuccianus*, i, 524–525.

78. Ibid. 529.

79. Ibid, 532.

80. Ibid, 529–536.

81. Ibid, 532.

82. Clanricard to Ormond, 26 May 1645 (*Irish Confederation*, iv, 261–262).

83. In June, the clerical convocation stated unambiguously that no peace which did not guarantee the spiritual jurisdiction of the Catholic clergy over the Catholic population could be tolerated. The point was then taken even further when, in August, the General Assembly unanimously declared that the Protestant clergy could not be allowed to retain any jurisdiction over Catholics in Ireland; see *Commentarius Rinuccianus*, i, 536, 567.

84. For details of Glamorgan's mission see J Lowe, 'The Glamorgan Mission to Ireland" in *Studia Hibernica*, 4 (1964), 155–196.

CHAPTER 7

'Celtic' Warfare in the 1640s

Pádraig Lenihan

An Emergent State

'The state made war and war made the state'.[1] The first part of Charles Tilly's aphorism refers to the remorseless growth of European armies during the early modern period (with a tenfold increase between 1530 and 1700). Whereas in 'peacetime' governments in the later 1500s seldom spent less than 50% of their total revenue on their armies and navies, in times of war this figure could escalate to 90%.[2] In other words, *the* job of the state was to make war. In the second part of the aphorism, Tilly contends that it was these unprecedented fiscal demands which called into being the coercive and fiscal apparatus of the modern state.

If control of a standing army was a crucial determinant of seventeenth-century statehood, then by this reckoning, the Irish Catholic Confederation (1642–49) was an emergent state because it maintained quite large standing armies relative to its limited wealth base. The standing armies of the Confederation reached a peak strength of 20–25,000 men in the summer of 1646.[3] The Confederation possessed other attributes of a contemporary state. It governed through a multi-tiered network of county councils, provincial councils, 'General Assemblies' (national Parliaments by another name) and a standing executive, the Supreme Council. The Supreme Council normally sat at Kilkenny and, at its title implies, exercised effective sovereignty. The boundaries of this proto-state shifted, as would be expected in wartime, but we can see from the map of Confederate Ireland (page 117) that the Council controlled about two-thirds of the island including the wealthy and populous south-eastern quarter.

However, in 1649 the Confederates abandoned their experiment in self-government and were subsumed within a new pan-Royalist alliance. This alliance proved quite unable to resist the Cromwellian reconquest of 1649–52, not least because of its heterogenous character, with disastrous consequences for Irish Catholics. The tantalising possibility (or what appeared to have been so) that a Confederate state might have repelled the Cromwellians gave a special urgency to the question; why

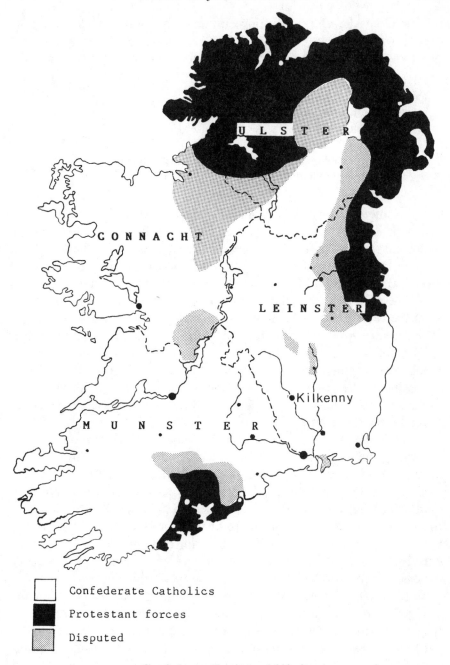

	Confederate Catholics
	Protestant forces
	Disputed

Confederate Territory 1642–9

did the Confederation fall? Irish emigres writing in the 1650s had no doubts what had gone wrong as they surveyed the wreckage of the previous decade. A poet, citing one such historian, put it succinctly:

Tógaim fínne Ristrid Beiling
nach díth daoine, bia no éadaigh
na neart namhaid do bhain díobh Éire
ach iad féin do chaill ar a chéile[4]
[I cite Richard Bellings as my authority
that it was not lack of manpower, provisions, equipment
or enemy strength which took Ireland from them,
but they themselves lost it for each other]

Subsequent historians have mainly taken their cue from partisans of the 'Clericalist' or 'Ormondist' parties so that it has become an historical truism that the Confederation collapsed under the weight of internal factionalism. It is not possible here to explain why the factional model was so appropriate to contemporary Irish Catholic commentators of whatever hue. Rather, the significant point to emphasise is that there is, at the very least, a case to answer that the 'neart namhaid' (strength of the enemy) argument which crushed the Confederates. It has already been noted that, in terms of numbers, the Confederate standing armies reached an all time peak of about 20–25,000 men in 1646/47. Yet at no stage during the 1640s did the number of English and Scottish troops in Ireland (including locally raised Protestants of British descent) fall much below that figure, if at all.[5]

Confederate factionalism only became especially debilitating in 1648, following the heavy defeats of the Leinster and Munster Confederate armies at Knocknanuss and Dungan's Hill in 1647. The Supreme Council was by now controlled by the Ormondist party and the Council cited these battlefield reverses as the main reason for the defeatist mood which led to the winding up of the Confederation. In short, the Confederation did not fall. The question of Confederate battlefield performance must, therefore, be central to explaining why the Confederate experiment in state-building was such a calamitous failure.

When was a battle not a skirmish? One giveaway is when the opposing sides are described as putting their armies into 'battalia' or battle formations; the skirmish was a scrappier, formless affair. But even when the opposing sides did form 'battalia', I would tend to define a 'battle' as set pieces involving more than 8,000 men on each side. Battles, then, were infrequent events, but they were potentially decisive, unlike any single skirmish or siege, because the participants risked the annihilation of an entire field army. Of the half dozen or so real battles which the Confederates fought (Kilrush, Liscaroll, Ballinvegga, Benburb, Dungan's Hill, and Knockanuss), their only victory was at Benburb against Monroe's Scottish army. Why, then, were the Confederates consistently beaten in battle by English armies?

A typical catch-all explanation (of Dungan's Hill in this instance) is that the Confederate army comprised 'Gaelic levies'; an assumption that brings us, finally, to the question of 'Celtic' warfare.[6] The notion of an archetypical and, above all, immutable Celtic style of warfare is implied by Cyril Falls, for example, in the way he painted a composite picture of Irish sixteenth-century tactics which is not really true of any one time and place.[7] More recently, James Michael Hill's analysis of sixteenth and seventeenth century warfare in Scotland and Ireland resuscitated the Celtic warfare motif.[8] According to Hill, Celtic warfare was 'primitive' (a frequently recurring word) and the 'Highland Scots and Irish were averse to adopting the latest military technology'.[9] 'The first and foremost element of continuity in Celtic warfare was the tactical offensive'[10] and Hill went on to cite an account of the 'Highland charge' written shortly before Culloden and suggested that 'it could be applied (excluding the reference to firearms, of course) across time and space to any Celtic army'. But can one generalise so freely across 'time and space'?[11]

'Celtic' Warfare

The following account of a skirmish dates from 1642 and certainly evokes comparisons with Hugh O'Neill's running fights at the Moyry Pass and the Yellow Ford over forty years before, as well as with the warfare practised by the medieval Gaelic lordships.[12]

> We [the English] marched from Newcastle [in county
> Wicklow] loaded with the pillage of our enemies, who
> showed themselves to our fronts making ready to fight,
> and, when we had marched about two miles they came down
> towards Sir Charles [Coote] and his men, as they were
> in a narrow lane, a bog being on one side of them and a
> little wood of the other. Thinking there to have got
> the advantage of that place which is called Kilcoole,
> Sir Charles and his men being in some little disorder
> at the first, the enemy came on boldly and swiftly,
> with a great shout after their barbarous manner; but by
> the time that two or three volleys of shot were given
> on both sides, Sir Charles and his men recovered the
> hill where they found good ground both for horse and
> foot, from which place our musketeers played on them

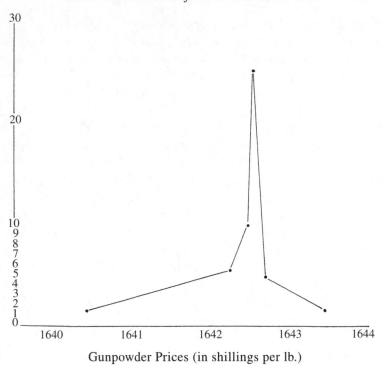

Gunpowder Prices (in shillings per lb.)

very fiercely and both slew some and hurt a great many,
so that they suddenly dispersed themselves, and fled
towards the bog and woods...[13]

The similarities between the 1642 account and accounts of previous encounters were briefly as follows: The O' Tooles disputed the return march of Sir Charles Coote, rather than his outward journey. Initially, they hovered at some distance to his front before congregating at a pass; then, suddenly, they launched an opportunistic assault when they saw Coote's men 'in some little disorder'. After the O' Tooles had sustained about twenty fatalities and it was apparent that the English were able to deploy their firepower effectively, they retreated just as suddenly as they had attacked. The subsequent follow-up charge by Coote's cavalry was hindered by impassible country and the Irish escaped by virtue of their famous 'footmanship'.

However striking they may be, such similarities do not prove that Irish warfare was irredeemably old-fashioned. Hill stresses that the sword was the favourite 'Celtic' weapon[14], but the O' Tooles carried a bewildering variety of weapons; fowling pieces, pikes, pitchforks, halberds, and darts. Moreover, the strategy and tactics of the O' Tooles were a rational response to the localism and political fragmentation which bedevilled the first eighteen months of the insurgency. These problems replicated the conditions of medieval lordships so it is hardly surprising that they should evoke a similar response. The salient effect of political fragmentation and localism was that the O' Tooles were forced to fight without outside assistance and they did not have the capacity to keep soldiers mobilised. It took time to mobilise their 'gairm slua' or hosting of part-timers. Inevitably, they could not counter enemy incursions and the best they could hope to do was to intercept the enemy on its return journey, laden down with plunder and cattle preys. The same phenomenon can also be detected at the provincial level where it took up to ten days to assemble the local militia companies from all over Leinster.[15]

Far from finding this a desirable state of affairs, the Irish eventually countered the threat of incursions by siting fortified outposts abutting the enemy (a sconce was erected at Bray, for example, astride the route from Dublin into Wicklow) and by raising a standing army. In other words, the O' Tooles were not reverting in pavlovian fashion to some Gaelic archetype, but were arriving independently at a similar, if temporary, response to old problems.

At a tactical level it is clear that the sudden charge and retreat must have been carefully choreographed. Throughout the summer and autumn of 1642, the Confederates were critically short of firearms and, above all, gunpowder (refer to graph of gunpowder prices).[16] In these circumstances it would have been suicidal to oblige Coote to a stand up fight. We are not privy to the deliberations of the O' Tooles, but they were doubtless similar to those of the Munster horsemen at Liscarroll;

> ...they did suppose that the English were better
> experienced and armed with guns...than themselves, they
> put on a resolution pell mell and with such sudden
> [illegible] to fall in amongst us that they [the
> English] should have little time to discharge, none to
> recharge and by that means to make their swords and
> numbers to be [decisive].[17]

The stark tactical alternatives facing the insurgents were to hover outside the killing zone marked by the effective range of small arms fire or else to cross that zone as quickly as man or horse could run. Insufficient firepower, not Celtic antecedents, explains Irish tactics during the first years of the Confederate wars.

Above all, there is nothing uniquely 'Celtic' about the sort of irregular tactics described in these accounts;

> They are active, hardy and skilled marksmen, adept in
> all the arts of individual warfare, always seeking and
> seldom missing an opportunity...They lack the
> organisation of a regular army, but they are capable of
> offering stubborn resistance to an advancing column.
> Their mobility enables them to concentrate rapidly for
> a fight. In following up a force withdrawing, harassing
> a column in country suited to their tactics, or
> attacking a detachment isolated beyond reach of support
> they are most formidable foes. Though their favourite
> weapon is the rifle, they are capable of showing
> reckless gallantry in attacking with swords and
> knives...[18]

The reference to the rifle may have given the game away; this is not Ulster in 1598 or 1642 but the north-west frontier of India in the 1920s! The writer's reassurance about the localism of Pathean society strikes another familiar note; 'the extent to which these [tribes] will co-operate against a common enemy is always uncertain'.[19] In other words, one would expect to see broad similarities in the sort of warfare practised by any fragmented and poor society against intrusive and more centralised neighbours.

The fact that the Irish insurgents were described as 'O 'Tooles' seems to show that the old pre-1603 Gaelic clan or sept structure was being resurrected. But while the sept retained its wider economic and political functions in Gaelic Scotland until 1745 this was not the case in the Ireland of the 1640s.

The core of the sept was the 'dearbh fine' [true kin], a group who, by virtue of a shared close descent through the male line, controlled most of the sept's territory and provided the chieftain. That this core group could be quite extensive is evidenced by the fact that the third last 'O' Neills' was succeeded, respectively, by a cousin once removed and by a nephew. The remainder of the sept radiated outwards in more distant degrees of cognatic and affinal kinship to embrace those who were not kin but were clients of the dominant sept. Fosterage, the custom whereby persons of importance committed the rearing of their children to persons of lower status, created an especially close bond of relationship. Customary exactions and duties were the more usual indices of clientship.[20]

By 1640 we cannot meaningfully speak of Irish clans or septs. The 'dearbh fine' of many septs (especially those in the planted counties of Ulster) had been thoroughly culled by dispossession and dispersal while the nexus of dependancy or clientship between the surviving rump of the 'dearbh fine' and their former followers had been drastically attenuated. Insofar as the sept facilitated recruitment, it did so only in an abbreviated form through cognatic kinship, affinity, and fosterage. For example, Sir Phelim O' Neill (the leader of the Ulster insurgents of 1641–42) drew his immediate subordinates and bodyguard from amongst his brothers, first cousins, and his foster family, the O' Haugheys.[21] He tried to assert a wider authority by proclaiming martial law and by assiduously cultivating popular propaganda; most notably by spreading reports of his crown-shaped birthmark and identifying himself with 'that little light from Ulidia [Ulster] prophesied by St Patrick'.[22]

These efforts to assert authority were symptomatic of just how little O' Neill, and other insurgent leaders, could rely on 'traditional' sept loyalty to secure a mass following. The result is epitomised by an account of a Scottish assault on O' Neill's headquarters at Charlemont in north Armagh.[23] Of 100 musketeers lining a defensive breastworks, all but 20 fled at the first charge, and these '...the best men and *all of them gentlemen*, defended it gallantly...'[24] This, and many similar references, indicates that declassé members of the 'dearbh fine' supplied the backbone of many insurgent companies. As a way of mobilising a mass following, however, the clan was redundant.

While the O' Toole's running battle seems, at first glance, to fit some archaic and timeless Celtic archetype, it really represents a temporary response to adverse local circumstances. After 1642 running battles became rarer as the Confederate armies developed along conventional lines and it becomes increasingly difficult to sustain the 'Celtic' warfare hypothesis, except (as we shall see) in the case of the 'Redshanks'. They provide a convincing argument against the notion (implicit in the idea of Celtic primitivism) that modern battle techniques were necessarily better than older ones. .

The Countermarch: Newer as Better?

The Confederates enthusiastically embraced the contemporaneous military revolution insofar as it related to siegecraft and fortifications. To take just one example, an eye-witness pictorial map of the Confederate siege of Duncannon (January–March 1645) in south-east Leinster telescopes the various stages of a precociously modern operation (page 124).[25] The 'saps' (made up of 'gabions', or wickerwork baskets filled with sand and earth) zig zag towards the fortress in the normal manner. But, significantly, we can see a network of gabions and trenches running from one sap to another sap in order to facilitate mutual support and co-ordination of the final assault. In retrospect, this seems

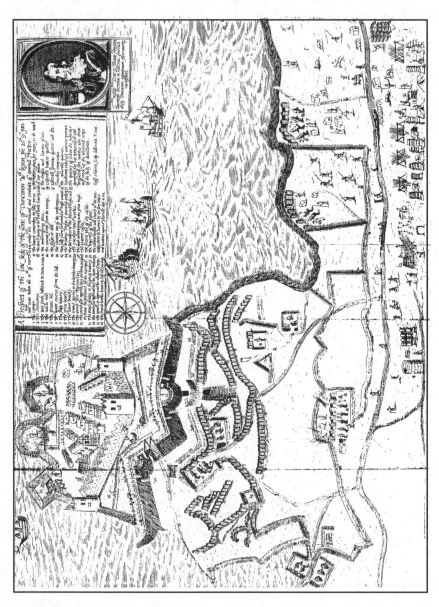

The Siege of Duncannon

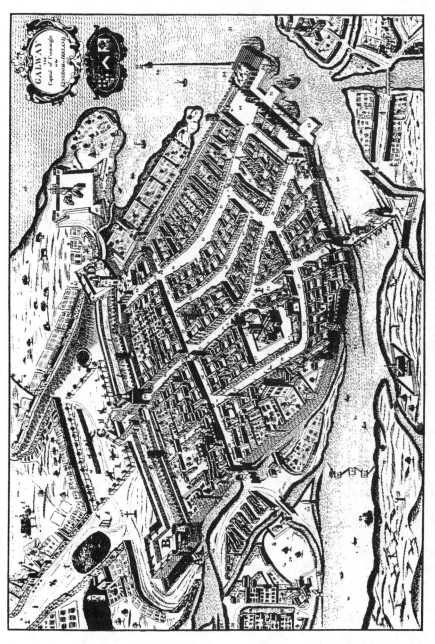

Map of Galway, 1651

like a fairly obvious step in the evolution of siege warfare but it had only just been tried for the first time ever at Gravelines (in Flanders) the year before in 1644.[26] The final assault itself was a three dimensional affair with mortars lobbing in incendiary bombs into the fort, flat trajectory guns sweeping the walls, and sally ports and sappers springing a mine under the ramparts.

Another pictorial map, this time of Galway, shows the series of modern bastions (marked 'a', 'b', 'c' and 'd') which the Confederates built to render the city virtually impregnable by direct assault (page 125).[27] The scale of these works is conveyed by a photograph (page 127) of the foundations of the largest bastion, 'd', which shows the 'clúid an gharraí' [garden angle] (Celtic nomenclature was, evidently, compatible with modern developments). At any rate, in the case of siegework and fortifications, newer was indeed better. The Galway fortifications were unusually elaborate but even a botched earthworks built according to half-understood modern principles could withstand artillery better than an unmodified medieval towerhouse.

The same cannot be said for battlefield tactics. One line of development is clear and that is the increasing dominance of firearms. By the 1640s most continental infantrymen carried a firearm (the arquebus or the heavier musket) rather than the pike, the erstwhile 'Reyna de las Armas', which had itself largely displaced blade weapons some 200 years before. Matchlocks were proverbially liable to misfire (whence terms like 'a flash in the pan' or 'going off at half cock') and the rate of misfire with a seventeenth-century arquebus could be as high as 50%.[28] Taking into account the limitations of human error, defective gunpowder, and visibility (typically, an entire line of infantry would be obscured by the smoke generated by its own volley), it has been estimated that 'not more than fifteen per cent of the rounds *that could have been fired* (my emphasis) were likely to have been effective'.[29] In other words, for every hundred soldiers firing a volley, about seven or eight might actually hit the enemy with lethal force.

Therefore, in order to produce an effective weight of fire, a commander firstly required a large body of musketeers (or harquebusiers). He would then align them six ranks deep (we know that this was the favoured depth of all the contending parties in Ireland) and then order the 'countermarch'.[30] This involved the front rank of musketeers firing and then filing round to the rear to take up position as the sixth men. The other five ranks stepped forward one pace and the second (now the first) rank fired another volley. By the time the original first rank had shuffled up to the front they should, in theory, have reloaded, but

South-eastern face of Shoemaker's Bastion

to achieve this they had to be superbly well-drilled in order to pare reloading time (with over thirty separate movements) down to a minimum of two minutes or so.[31]

The fate of one group of Protestant refugees who were sent to relieve Drogheda in 1642 provides a vivid example of what could happen to new recruits who tried to execute the countermarch. The refugees saw a mass of armed men emerging from the riverside mist in the area near Julianstown bridge (about four miles from Drogheda):

> the rebels forces who now furiously approached with a
> great shout; and a Lieutenant giving out the unhappy
> word of countermarch, all the men, possessed as it were
> of a panic fear, began somewhat confusedly to march
> back; but they were so much amazed with a second shout
> given by the rebels, who, seeing them in disorder
> followed close on, as notwithstanding that they had
> gotten into a ground of great advantage, they could not
> be persuaded to stand a charge, but betook themselves
> to their heels, and so the rebels fell sharply on, as
> their manner is, upon the execution.[32]

Evidently, the government soldiers had only the vaguest idea of what the order 'countermarch' meant. Not that the Irish were any wiser because they, apparently, thought that the Lieutenant had shouted 'contúirt bhaís!' [danger of death].[33] The English commander might have been better advised to let the soldiers fire at will or wield their musket butts like clubs in the manner of a fairground fight. The lesson of Julianstown was clear; half-trained soldiers were worse than untrained ones and it was preferable not to modernise at all than to do so by halves.

Even with better trained soldiers the countermarch was by no means infallible. The Scottish 'Highland charge' evolved to exploit the inherent limitations of volley fire. 'If the fire is given at a distance', observed General Hawley shortly before his defeat at Falkirk in 1746, 'you probably will be broke, for you may never get time to load a second cartridge…'[34] But, as another general defeated by the Highland charge observed,

> The Highlanders are of such quick motion, that if a
> battalion keep up his fire till they be near to make sure
> of them, they are upon it….[35]

Both Hill and Stevenson credit Alasdair MacColla MacDonald with refining the Irish charge to what would become the 'Highland charge'.[36] MacColla had sided with the Ulster insurgents in 1642 and executed the charge successfully at the Battle of the Laney in February of that year. Later, in 1644, MacColla led an expeditionary force to Scotland (under the aegis of the Confederates and the Earl of Antrim) against the Campbells and their Covenanter allies. At this point the Redshanks (as MacColla's men were called) were demonstrably distinct from other Confederate soldiers in that the latter increasingly adopted conventional pike/musket battle tactics.

The Redshanks, on the other hand, relied on the sword and targe just like, as Hill points out, sixteenth-century Irish 'Kern'.[37] However, such continuity by no means implies immutable Celtic archetypes. The sword and target (or buckler as it was more often called) was the main armament of infantry before the pike era and contemporary military theorists like Maurice of Nassau, Montecuccoli, and Orrery were at one in recommending that a small proportion of sword and targe men be kept for close quarter fighting.[38] As late as the Battle of Ravenna in 1512, there were battalions of Spanish swordsmen

> making good use of their bucklers, [who] with great
> agility thrust their way between and under the German
> pikes, and attacked with impunity.[39]

In practice, swordsmen survived only in an attentuated form. By the early seventeenth century a Spanish infantry company of 100 men would typically comprise 60 musketeers, 30 pikemen, and just 10 men wielding a sword and buckler.[40] The point to note is that infantry swordsmanship was not a Celtic archaicism and its demise elsewhere in Europe was relatively recent and by no means universally welcomed. Moreover, this demise reflected the relative ease of training pikemen for the new mass armies. By contrast, skilled swordsmen could not be churned out in a matter of weeks. The point is best illustrated by looking at Ireland. By and large, the 'idle swordsman', that blot on the planter's landscape, had either been rounded up or had fled abroad by the 1620s. During the forty years of peace from 1603 to 1641, a 'hands on' education in swordsmanship would have been available only in Gaelic Scotland and the adjacent MacDonnell territories in Antrim. The former area remained chronically unsettled, a point illustrated by the career as a pirate of Coll Ciotach, Alastair's father. But the thousands of men with military training loose in Ireland in 1640–41 were not swordsmen, but were graduates of the pike and musket school of Flanders or Carrickfergus (the mustering point in 1640 for Wentworth's new army).

Time and again in 1644–45 Covenanter armies were overwhelmed by Redshank weapons and tactics which, except for the opening volley of firearms, were similar to those of sixteenth-century Irish Kern. But the latter did not perform especially well against conventional infantry. Why, then, did the Redshanks perform so well? Hill concluded that the Covenanters lost, rather than the Redshanks won, because the former assembled half-trained armies which were caught in the process of transition between old and new tactics.[41] This gave the Redshanks an opportunity to exploit the inherent limitations of volley fire and the countermarch. Yet this understates what was singular and innovative about MacColla's Redshanks. They were far better disciplined than their Kern predecessors or Irish irregulars in 1641–42. Their discipline can be especially evidenced by their ability to regroup repeatedly after unsuccessful charges (such as at Auldearn and Dungan's Hill) and to coolly deal with enemy cavalrymen by allowing them to penetrate their ranks and then closing up and annihilating them (such as at Tippermuir). Moreover, the Redshanks did not suffer from 'an inability to stand patiently on the defensive' so far as one can judge from the way Manus O' Cahan (MacColla's second-in-command) patiently kept his Irish and Highlander troops motionless until the closing stages of Alford.[42]

In summary, despite superficial similarities there is no real continuity between the strategy and tactics practiced by the Irish during the early years of the Confederate insurgency and 'Celtic' antecedents (except, possibly, in the case of MacColla's Redshanks). This apparent conservatism reflected a universal response to certain conditions, specifically political fragmentation, and critical shortages of firearms and gunpowder, which were temporary in Ireland but chronic in Gaelic Scotland. These conditions, together with the clan's continuing socio-economic relevance and the surviving tradition of swordmanship, favoured the flowering of Redshank tactics in Scotland rather than Ireland.

In the final analysis, the case for the Redshanks as Celtic warriors rests on the fact that they, like their Kern predecessors, fought with sword and targe. Admittedly, this method of fighting was obsolescent, but this does not imply innate Celtic conservatism or primitivism. It was by no means the case that identifiably modern tactics were better unless (and these are crucial reservations) the soldiers were well-trained in the countermarch and could deploy an adequate weight of firepower.

Therefore, the existence of 'Celtic' warfare can be questioned and it can be asserted that the irregular tactics practiced by Irish and Highland Scots' armies were a dynamic and viable response to local conditions. In any event, the Confederates suffered their heaviest battle defeats *after* they had switched to conventional pike and musket tactics. The key to understanding the Confederates' poor battlefield performance is to be found in the fact that they modernised, and specifically, in the way they modernised.

Spanish Warfare

Was the Confederates' modernisation flawed because it followed a relatively old-fashioned Spanish model rather than the Swedish model which was adopted, for example, by the Covenanters?[43] The panorama of the Battle of Lutzen, fought in 1632 between the Imperialists and Gustavus Adolphus (page 131), purportedly illustrates the difference between Spanish and Swedish practice.[44] The Imperialist infantry (at the bottom of the illustration) were formed up in compact regimental sized masses with the stands of pike in the middle. The bastion-like appendages of musketeers at each corner clearly show that these formations were designed for all round defence. By contrast, Gustavus disposed his infantry in a thinner, more linear formation oriented only to the front which would have resembled something like this:

```
M M M M M M P P P P P P M M M M M M
M M M M M M P P P P P P M M M M M M
M M M M M M P P P P P P M M M M M M
M M M M M M P P P P P P M M M M M M
M M M M M M P P P P P P M M M M M M
M M M M M M P P P P P P M M M M M M
```

A Swedish Infantry Battalion[45]

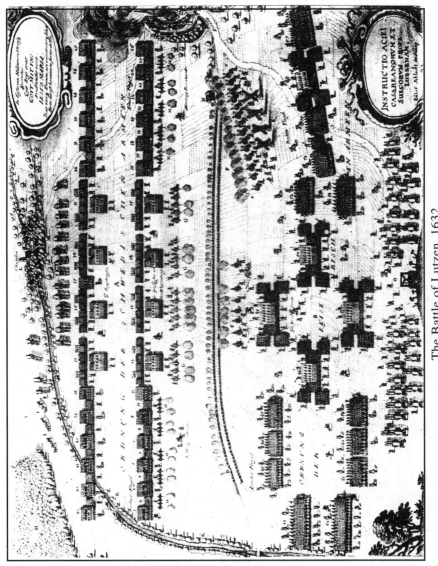

The Battle of Lutzen, 1632

In this case there are six files of pikemen flanked on each side by six files of musketeers, but this could vary according to the strength of the battalion and the relative proportion of pike to muskets. There are three salient points to note about the Swedish formation compared to its Spanish counterpart. Firstly, the Swedish formation consisted of smaller company sized units (102 rank and file in this case). Secondly, firepower predominated over pike; the Covenanter army in Ulster, for example, had a ratio of three musketeers for every two pikemen.[46] Thirdly, the Swedish linear formation made more effective use of its greater firepower towards the front, although this was at the cost of being more vulnerable to a falnk or rear attack.

However, the plan of Lutzen may overstate the differences between the Spanish and Swedish systems. A textbook written in 1634 by Garret Barry, an Irish officer then serving in the Spanish army, shows that infantry formations in Spanish Flanders were evolving on broadly parallel lines to those of the Swedes.[47] The massive battle squares are still there (though without the 'sleeves' of the musketeers) but most of his sample formation represent smaller battle squares of about 300–500 men. Barry starts with the standard square which was a third ('tercio', whence the generic name for the Spanish square) wider than deeper, but he concentrates on progressively more linear examples finishing with a 'square' which is five times as wide as it is deep. The fact that the formations recommended by Barry were not all that different from the Swedish model is important because he later served as general of the Munster Confederate army. We can tentatively infer from Barry's text what battle formations were used in Ireland by veterans of Flanders, such as Barry himself, Preston and O' Neill. Indeed there is evidence of Confederate tactics becoming even more 'Swedish' during the 1640s with the recommended pike/musket ratio changing from 1:1 in 1642 to 1:2 in 1646.[48] Moreover, in an apparent reference to the Battle of Knocknanuss (in 1647), a parliamentary officer explained how the Confederate infantry formations were six deep and 'over winged' his own formations.[49] In other words, by the late 1640s Confederate infantry battle deployments were linear and almost indistinguishable from the Swedish model.

Despite the fact that the recommended pike/musket ratio was shifting in favour of the latter, the only remaining distinctions were that in practice pikemen continued to predominate in the Confederate infantry with the possible exception of the latter part of 1646 and early 1647.[50] However, the relative deficiency of the Confederates in firepower does not seem to have been a significant factor in battle. More significant, perhaps, was the fact that the Confederate pike was different from that of its English and Scottish opponents.

The latter used a sturdy pikehead which was etoilated for better penetration and was fastened by metal plates to the shaft.[51] The Confederate pikehead seems to have been of a very different type condemned by Orrery as 'four square and small...the worst in the world'.[52] These pikeheads were fitted onto the staff by simple socket without a protecting metal strap and Orrery describes how his men were able to cut them off with their swords during the sack of Cashel in 1647. On inspection, it is striking just how tiny these pikeheads are, with a shallow plug socket which was so thin that the staff, towards its point, can only have been half the thickness of a brush handle. Presumably, this old-fashioned and flimsy pikehead commended itself to the Confederates because it was cheap. It may even have been part of the large consignment which Rinuccini (Papal Nuncio in Ireland, 1645–49) bought in Paris at a knockdown price equivalent to 3d each.[53]

This is not just abstract theorising; the size of the Confederate pikehead may have been a decisive battle-winning factor. G A Hayes-McCoy dismissed a contemporary explanation that the Irish beat Monroe's Scottish army at Benburb (1646) because their pikes were longer:

> Pikemen were certainly tempted to lessen the great
> weight of their weapons by cutting a foot or two from
> the shafts and thus reducing their extreme length of
> sixteen feet, but there is no reason to believe that
> such short-sightedness was confined to the British
> soldiers.[54]

But since the Irish pikehead was notably lighter (we are told that the Ulster army pikeheads were 'four square and small') there is every reason to assume that O'Neill's men would be less inclined to shorten their pikes. Therefore, the length of the Irish pike probably was the decisive factor in winning the battle after all. O'Neill, we are told, harangued his men, 'let your manhood be seen in the push of your pike'. We can imagine that it was this steady prodding, rather than cut and thrust, which herded the Covenanters into a crowded killing zone within a loop in the Blackwater where the final execution was carried out at swordpoint.[55]

Thus far, we have established that Confederate battlefield failures cannot be explained by strategic or tactical conservatism, whether of a 'Celtic' or 'Spanish' variety. Of course, it is easier to reject explanations rather than construct a credible alternative.

A clue to an alternative explanation is to be found at Benburb.

Benburb was a singular battle for two related reasons. Firstly, it was an Irish victory. Secondly, the battle was an infantry versus infantry encounter (neither side was stong in cavalry). Confederate battles against English forces fall into an almost invariable pattern (Ballinvagga was a partial exception) with the Confederate cavalry being first driven off and the infantry then subjected to a cavalry attack. Why was the Confederate cavalry so weak? The answer, in a nutshell, is that the Confederates did not maintain anything approaching the desired English 1:2 ratio of horse to foot. For example, as the Leinster army expanded the relative proportion of cavalry fell (refer to graph of the composition of the Leinster Standing Army). The reasons for this phenomenon were, in the first place, a shortage of good quality riding horses, and perhaps, false economy since it cost twice as much to maintain a trooper as it did an infantry private.[56] However, answers in a nutshell seldom tell the whole story and English armies in Ireland also fell far short of the optimum cavalry/infantry ratio.

A supplementary explanation may be that the experience which generals like Preston, Barry and O' Neill absorbed in Flanders did not equip them for cavalry command. Ireland in the 1640s was cavalry country. Admittedly, there were more woods and bogs than nowadays but these alternated with wide stretches of campaign country not yet broken up by *bocage*. Flanders, with its patchwork of canals, towns, and cultivated fields, on the other hand, was an infantry theatre of war. Preston, the general of the Leinster army, provides the clearest example of a general who had no idea how to use cavalry. Not once, but twice, Preston contrived to canalise the opening charge of his horsemen along a covered 'boreen'. On the first such occasion at Ballinvagga, the laneway was covered off by masked cannon which fired into the packed ranks of Irish horsemen with predictably unpleasant results.[57] On other occasions Preston reined in his cavalry when they had an excellent chance of riding down a beaten enemy. His most crucial lapse was at Naas where he missed the chance to follow up on a victory over Michael Jones, the parliamentary general who would annihilate Preston's army just over one month later at Dungan's Hill.[58] A shortage of cavalry and ineptitude in employing what cavalry they did have, does not by any means explain completely why the Confederates' battlefield performance was so dismal. Yet it was an important factor, albeit a definitive assessment of Confederate battle tactics is outside the scope of this discussion.

With reference to the Battle of Dungan's Hill, Nicholas Perry argued that 'once the Irish horse had fled...the infantry were doomed'. In fact, the Confederate infantry at Dungan's Hill still had the chance of

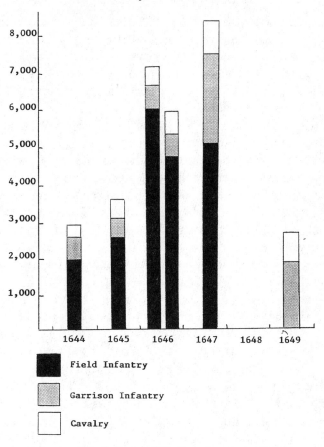

Field Infantry

Garrison Infantry

Cavalry

The Leinster Standing Army

escaping in a body, but they had absolutely no chance of actually winning the battle against enemy cavalry. The reason was that musketeers were totally vulnerable in the intervals between firing and they relied on the sheltering hedgehog of pikemen. But the latter could not move without disordering their formation. This was not a problem in the hurly-burly of an infantry fight, yet enemy cavalry could exploit this disorder. In his description of one of the last battles of the civil wars of the three kingdoms, Orrery related how a body of 1,200 Irish pikemen stood their ground after the cavalry (as usual) and musketeers had run off. Then, unexpectedly, the pikemen charged:

> so that had they guarded their angles when they charged
> them round they would have done us much more mischief,
> if not recovered the day, but by the angles we broke in
> and afterwards the resistance was but small, nor could
> it be otherwise...[59]

'Nor could it be otherwise'[60]; the pike square was weakest at its 'angles', or corners, and it was here that enemy horsemen invariably halted just out of reach of the pikes and fired their pistols to open up a gap. It was difficult enough, while standing still, to clear away the dead and wounded and fill the gaps with fresh pistol fodder; while moving this was next to impossible.[61]

Ironically, at the climactic battles of Knocknanuss and Dungan's Hill the regular Confederate armies were reinforced by two bodies of Redshanks who had been finally driven out of Scotland by the Covenanters. The first, under MacColla's own command, was attached to the Munster army, while a second (which seems to have been mainly Gaelic Scottish) led by Angus MacDonald of Glengarry was attached to the Leinster army. Properly used, the Redshanks could have supplied the mobility and striking power which the pikemen lacked. Instead, the Confederate generals at Dungan's Hill and Knocknanuss failed to follow up the Redshank's initially successful charges.[62]

Knocknanuss was an extreme example of command ineptitude. MacColla caught the Parliamentarians breaking cover and then launched the classic Highland charge; his men having fired and discarded their muskets they then advanced with broadsword and target and cut through the opposing ranks before reaching the baggage train. There, fatally, they dispersed to secure their loot.[63] But by the time they regrouped the Munster cavalry had fled, closely followed by Taaffe, the Confederate general, who threatened to shoot an officer who was pressing him to rescue the Redshanks. As far as each party of Redshanks was concerned, the outcomes of Knocknanuss and Dungan's Hill could not have been more different; MacColla's followers were killed almost to a man, while Glengarry's men escaped relatively unscathed. In both cases, however, the Redshanks fought isolated actions, unsupported by their regular allies.

With the Redshanks, the nearest thing to identifiably 'Celtic' warriors that one could hope to find in the 1640s, we return to our point of departure. Preston and Taaffe lost, not because they were too 'Celtic' or backward, but because they were too rigidly modern and conventional to integrate the Redshanks into their battle tactics.

Conclusion

An assessment of Confederate battlefield performance is essential to understand why the experiment in Confederate state-building failed. No single answer for battlefield failure can be provided, but the Confederates' relative shortage of cavalry (and the often clumsy deployment of the cavalry which they did have) was probably the single most important factor. However, an alternative explanation has been evaluated, namely that Confederate tactics were conservative and backward.

We have seen that Confederate tactics did not conform to any punative 'Celtic' archetype. Accounts of the fighting during the first twelve months of the insurgency indicate superficial similarities with sixteenth-century Irish warfare. Yet this is not sufficient evidence to show that the insurgents consciously reverted to earlier forms of warfare. The opportunistic charge at Kilcoole, Liscarroll, or Julianstown, was a rational response to local conditions at that time and, in particular, to the severe shortage of gunpowder. Nor is there any evidence that residual sept loyalty facilitated Confederate military mobilisation. Insofar as the 'Celtic' tag had any meaning, it can only be applied to the Redshanks who continued to wield swords as well as (rather than instead of) with firearms. But infantry swordsmanship, while obsolescent, was by no means a uniquely Celtic archaicism. The demise of the swordsman elsewhere was relatively recent and by no means universally welcomed.

Finally, Confederate pike and musket tactics were ultimately derived from the relatively old-fashioned Spanish model. However, by the later 1640s there was little difference between the Spanish and Swedish schools as practiced in Ireland, with the significant exception that the Confederates used a smaller pikehead and, consequently, a longer pike. In that respect, all explanations based on Confederate conservatism are unsustainable.

NOTES

1. C Tilly, *The Formation of National States in Western Europe* (Princeton, 1975), 42. See also C Tilly, *Coercion, Capital, and European States, AD 990–1990* (Cambridge, Massachusetts, 1990), chapter three.

2. J R Hale, *War and Society in Renaissance Europe 1450–1620* (London, 1985), 232–234; G Parker, 'The "Military Revolution", 1560–1660 — a myth?' in *Journal of Modern History*, volume 48, (1976), 95; M S Anderson, *War and Society in Europe of the Old Regime 1618–1789* (London, 1988), 83.

3. The Leinster army amounted to 7,200 men; J T Gilbert (ed), *History of the Irish Confederation and the War in Ireland, 1641–49*, seven volumes, (Dublin, 1882–91), vi, 78–81. The Ulster army consisted of 11,500 men; S. Kavanagh (ed), *Commentarius Rinuccinianus...per annos 1645–1649* (Dublin, 1932–49), ii, 240; T O Donnchadha (ed), 'Cin Lae O Meallain', in *Analecta Hibernica*, iii, (1931), 36. The Munster army consisted of circa 7000 men; HMC *Report on the Manuscripts of the earl of Egmont* (London, 1905),

volume I, part I, 300. Although there was a standing army in Connacht, I have no evidence of its size, but I suspect that it was quite small; see J T Gilbert (ed), 'Archives of the town of Galway', in *Historical Manuscripts Commission Report*, (London, 1885), 491–492.

4. S ó Connaill, 'Túireamh na hÉireann', in C O' Rahilly, *Five Seventeenth Century Political Poems* (Dublin, 1952), lines 357–360.

5. Sir John Temple, *The Irish Rebellion* (London, 1646), 43–44; H Hazlett, A History of the military forces operating in Ireland, 1641–49 (Queen's University of Belfast, PhD thesis, 1938), 105; D Stevenson, *Scottish Covenanters and Irish Confederates: Scottish-Irish relations in the mid-seventeenth century* (Belfast, 1981), 194, 237; 'Report on Parliamentary forces in Ireland', in *CSPI* (1633–47), 420.

6. K Myers, 'An Irishman's Diary', *Irish Times*, circa December 1993.

7. C Falls, *Elizabeth's Irish Wars*, (London, 1950).

8. J M Hill, *Celtic Warfare 1595–1763* (Edinburgh, 1986), 1–6, 173–181.

9. Ibid, 176.

10. Ibid, 1.

11. Ibid.

12. G A Hayes-McCoy, 'Strategy and Tactics in Irish Warfare, 1593–1601', *Irish Historical Studies*, 2, (1940–41), 255–279; K Simms, 'Warfare in the medieval Gaelic lordships', in *Irish Sword*, 47, (1975), 98–108.

13. Gilbert (ed), *History of the Irish Confederation and the war in Ireland*, ii, xxxiii.

14. Hill, *Celtic Warfare*, 1.

15. 'Examination of Donogh Murphy', TCD MS 819 (County Wexford), f 139.

16. 1640 prices (Ireland) 16d per 1b. R A Stradling, *The Spanish Monarchy and Irish Mercenaries* 1618–68 (Dublin, 1994), 35. April 1642 (Wexford) 5s per 1b, 'Deposition of Robert Doughtie', TCD MS 815 (Queen's County [Laois]) f 405. June 1645 (Limerick) 'An Impartiall relation of the most memorable transactions of General Owen O' Neill...collected by Henry McTuoll O' Neill', in J T Gilbert (ed), *A Contemporary History of Affairs in Ireland 1641– 1652*, three volumes, (Dublin, 1882–91), iii, 198. Summer 1642 (? Laois) 25s per 1b. 'Deposition of Samuel Frank', TCD MS 815 (Queen's County) f 81. September 1642 (Confederate Ireland) 4–5s. HMC *Report on the Franciscan Manuscripts preserved at the convent, Merchants' Quay*, (Dublin, 1906), 186. Summer 1643 (Confederate Ireland) 14d per 1b. This is from Frank's deposition which implies that the 'normal' price was that charged by the Dunkirk blockade runners of 13–14d per 1b. *Franciscan Manuscripts*, 169.

17. TCD MS 840 number 20, 'A discourse of the battle of Liscarroll'.

18. *Manual of Operations on the North-West Frontier of India* (Calcutta, 1925), 3–4.

19. Ibid.

20. See K Nicholls, *Gaelic and gaelicised Ireland in the later Middle Ages* (Dublin, 1972).

21. 'Examination of William Skelton', TCD MS 814 (County Armagh), f 171; 'Examination of Sir Phelim O' Neale', TCD MS 836 (County Armagh), f 167.

22. 'Deposition of Henry Aeycoffe', TCD MS 814 (King's County [Offaly]), f 62; 'Deposition of Dr Robert Maxwell', TCD MS 839, (County Tyrone), f 43.

23. 'Progress of General Monroe against the rebels in the North', in TCD MS 840, f 34.

24. Ibid.

25. Reproduced in Gilbert (ed), *Irish Confederation*, iv.

26. C Duffy, *Siege Warfare, the Fortress in the Early Modern World 1494–1660* (London, 1979), 138.

27. The detail from the pictorial map of Galway circa 1651 is based on a reproduction from an original in Trinity College Dublin in J. Hardiman, *The History of the town and county of Galway* (Dublin, 1820), 34.

28. F Tallett, *War and Society in Early Modern Europe 1495–1715* (London, 1922), 21.

29. B P Hughes, *Firepower. Weapons effectiveness on the battlefield 1630–1850* (London, 1974), 58–59.

30. Roger Boyle, Earl of Orrery, *A Treatise on the Art of War*, 36; 'Progress of the Rebels in the North from 26 September to the 4 October 1643', in TCD MS 840 number 30.

31. C H Firth, *Cromwell's Army* (London, 1902), 95.

32. Gilbert (ed), *Irish Confederation*, i, 239.

33. E Hogan (ed), *The History of the Warr in Ireland by a British Officer of the Regiment of Sir John Clotworthy* (Dublin, 1857), 15.

34. G Parker, *The Military Revolution Revisited* (Cambridge, 1982), 35.

35. Ibid.

36. D Stevenson, *Alastair MacColla and the Highland Problem in the seventeenth century*, (Glasgow, 1980), 82–85; Hill, *Celtic Warfare*, 5.

37. Hill, *Celtic Warfare*, 24.

38. Boyle, *Art of War*, 26; R Montecuccoli, *Sulle Battaglie*, (Albany, 1975), 100.

39. G Bull (ed), Niccolo Machiavelli, *The Prince* (London, 1981), 137.

40. J X Evans (ed), *The Works of Roger Williams* (Oxford, 1972), 20.

41. Hill, *Celtic Warfare*, 47.

42. Ibid, 57.

43. E M Furgol, 'Scotland turned Sweden: The Scottish Covenanters and the Military Revolution, 1638–1651', in J Morrill (ed), *The Scottish National Covenant in its British Context, 1638–51*, (Edinburgh, 1990), 134–154.

44. Reproduced in H Langer, *The Thirty Years War* (English translation, New York, 1980), plate 107.

45. In the diagram P = pikemen and M = musketeers.

46. Furgol, 'Scotland turned Sweden', 143.

47. Garret Barry, *A Discourse on Military Discipline* (Brussels, 1634), 68–104, 129–138.

48. 'Instructions for the Army of Leinster', dated 13 July 1642, in State Papers Ireland (Charles I) 63/260, 234.

49. Orrery, *Art of War*, 36.

50. *HMC report on Ormonde Mss, i,* (London, 1895), 200–208. In early 1649, at the time of the Confederate dissolution, six regiments of the Munster and Leinster armies mustered 609 musketeers and 872 pikemen. Musketeers predominated in Walter Butler's newly raised regiment, but the regiments which had survived Dungan's Hill and Knockanuss had obviously lost a great deal of their equipment.

51. Orrery recommended this kind of pikehead, *Art of War*, 24. See also D Blackmore, *Arms and Armour of the English Civil War* (London, 1990).

52. Orrery, *Art of War*, 24.

53. O' Farrell and O' Connell, *Commentarius Rinuccianus...per annos 1645–49*, S. Kavanagh (ed), six volumes, (Dublin, 1932–49), ii, 40.

54. G A Hayes-McCoy, *Irish Battles*, (Dublin, 1980), 194. See also G A Hayes McCoy, 'The Irish Pike', in *Journal of the Galway Archaeological and Historical Society,* xx, number two, (1943).

55. Hogan, *A British Officer*, 48.

56. 'Leinster Army Pay', State Papers Ireland (Charles I) 63/264, 64–66.

57. A C Miller, 'The battle of Ross, a controversial military event', in *The Irish Sword*, number 39, (winter 1971), 141–158.

58. Gilbert (ed), *Irish Confederation*, vi, 30.

59. Orrery, *Art of War*, 25.

60. Ibid.

61. There is a vivid description of how an Irish pike formation was systematically broken near Ballintobber (County Roscommon) in 1642 in Edmund Borlase, *The History of the execrable Irish rebellion* (London, 1680), 81.

62. P Lenihan, 'The Leinster Army and the battle of Dungan's Hill', in *Irish Sword*, number 71 (summer, 1991), 139–153.

63. B O' Brien, *Munster at War* (Dublin, 1971), 141–148.

CHAPTER 8

Tories and Moss-troopers in Scotland and Ireland in the Interregnum: a Political Dimension

Éamonn ó Ciardha

The bandit occupies a central position in the popular history of Scotland and Ireland. Historians, however, have often found it difficult to trace these elusive figures through the battlefields, bogs, and highlands. This is not made any easier by the transformation of the bandit in Irish historiography. The popular historians of the nineteenth century portrayed him as a noble robber and Robin Hood-like figure while their early twentieth-century successors often viewed him as a proto-type nationalist figure.[1] J C Beckett, however, began the recent reappraisal of these Irish nationalist icons, dismissing them as outlaws with a 'natural taste for robbery which was strengthened by resentment against the new settlers'.[2] L M Cullen followed suit, viewing Toryism as a late flowering of medieval lawlessness which degenerated to 'mere banditry'.[3] S J Connolly felt it was impossible to reconcile political or religious motives with the acivities of some Tories.[4] While the aforementioned characteristics can be attributed to Toryism throughout the seventeenth century, inadequate attention has been given to the political and religious aspects of the phenomenon in the Civil War and Interregnum periods.

Another characteristic of contemporary historiography has been an over-emphasis on official source-material. This imbalance has recently been identified as disfiguring the historiography of Latin American banditry, much of which attempted to revise E J Hobsbawm's enduring model.[5] Yet Hobsbawm's prototype remains an attractive mould for the study of the bandit throughout the world. As it has been criticised by revisionist historians, it has also been found wanting as a model for the Irish Tory.[6]

This paper will explore the evolution of Toryism in Interregnum Ireland with reference to Moss-troopers and banditry in Scotland. It will investigate the development of these terms as derogatory badges against Irish Confederates and Royalists and their Scottish counterparts.[7] This will provide a platform for a reappraisal of the role of the bandit in the history of the Celtic realms throughout the seventeenth century.

The evolution of Toryism in seventeenth-century Irelandpar

Sir John Derricke described the woodkerne of Elizabethan Ireland, the forerunners of seventeenth-century Tories, in his *Images of Ireland or a discovery of woodkerne* (circa 1580s). He perceived them as nothing more than common robbers who pilfered indiscriminately from English and Irish alike.[8] While woodkerne were initially viewed as disruptive elements in society, the term acquired a political significance in the late sixteenth and early seventeenth century. In addition to being used to describe common thieves, disbanded Gaelic kerne and swordsmen, as well as enemies of the state, it became attached to those who sabotaged the Ulster plantation. This did not escape the attention of the poet Aonghus Mac Dáighre ó Dálaigh who, in his poem 'Dia libh a laochraidh Gaoidhiol' [God be with you heroes of the Gael], lamented the criminalisation of the Gaelic nobility:

> It is a torment to me that in the very tribal gathering
> Foreigners proscribe those that are Ireland's royal chiefs
> Giving them nothing but the lowly woodkerne's name.[9]

The 'Aphorismical discovery of the treasonable faction', (a manuscript history of the Confederate War written in the 1650s), represented the extent to which this type of terminology became a feature of the civil war period. A group of English Cavaliers captured by the Cavanaghs expressed surprise at the civil and courteous manner of these Tories who were portrayed as savage men or beasts.[10] It is obvious that these Tories were not ordinary robbers but commissioned officers and members of the Confederate forces.

It is evident, however, that these Confederates and Tory partisans existed alongside those who manipulated the turmoil of the war for personal gain. An excommunication issued by the Catholic clergy in December 1649 differentiated between Confederate stealths and that of 'tories and such plunderers not in colours'.[11] This differentiation was ignored by the Parliamentarians and has not been sufficiently investigated by historians.

The Transformation of the War

The Tory phemonenon in the Interregnum period must be examined with reference to the gradual disintegration of the conventional Confederate forces in provincial theatres of war. Guerilla warfare emerged as the main tactic of the beleaguered Confederates in the aftermath of Cromwell's campaigns in the late 1640s and Coote's final victory over the Confederate army at Scarrifhollis in June 1651.[12] By mid-July of the same year, Wicklow had emerged as the last haven for rebels and Tories in Leinster. General Ludlow retraced the scorched-earth footsteps of General Hewson who had waged economic warfare on elusive Tory groups by cutting down corn and lifting cattle.[13] The destructive Colonel Cooke employed similar tactics, but none of the trio managed to neutralize the irritant of Toryism. Cooke's destruction of Tory supplies did not go unnoticed and he paid the ultimate price. He lost his life giving battle to one of their parties.[14] The fact that this encounter reputedly lasted for twenty hours was indicative of a stubborn resistance of these Tories.[15]

General Reynolds also fell upon these Tory groups. He pursued the Confederate General, Dungan, and Clanricard's residual Leinster army through the great fastness of Glenmailer, into the King's County and then drove them over the river Barrow into Wicklow.[16] The parliamentary forces also engaged these Leinster 'Tories' on 2 May 1652, particularly Captain Skurlock who had perpetrated the preying and destruction about Wexford in October 1651. Although castigated as a bloody Tory in official sources, he was undoubtedly a member of the residual Confederate forces.[17] Dungan and Skurlock had marched into Wexford intent on its destruction only to be routed with two hundred fatalities, resulting in hundred casualties on the parliamentary side.[18]

In Connaught a retreat into the bogs and fastnesses also occurred. In July 1651 the commissioners of Parliament portrayed the Tories as partisan free-booters, a description befitting the rapparees of the Williamite wars in the late 1680s and early 1690s:

> insomuch as they are being joined with the Tories (who are
> very numerous) and are able to draw together on a sudden,
> parties of considerable strength upon our forces.[19]

In the fashion of the 'war of the flea', however, self-preservation was of the essence:

> when any forces draw towards them to engage, they disperse
> at an instant again and embody again in some remote
> bog.[20]

According to the commissioners, their military potential remained such that

> you can not safely travel two miles from any of the said
> garrisons without a convoy, which proceeds from the
> general dissatisfaction of the Irish'.[21]

This again suggested that the Tories were indeed a popular-based Confederate group. One commentator believed that the local population

pretended they were forced to comply with the Tories.[22] The reduction
of Confederate forts represented another vital mechanism for a transformation from conventional warfare to Toryism:

> for the enemy being driven out of all forts had nothing to
> do but be in the field when they please and as they saw
> advantage to retire to bogs and fastnesses…in the
> meantime committing stealths and plunderings to the walls
> and gates of our garrisons.[23]

The Ulster theatre provides further evidence of this disintegration
of the Confederate armies.[24] Among their ranks were men who were
unwilling or unable to avail of the favourable peace and transportation
terms. These included individuals such as Sir Phelim O'Neill, the 'arch
Tory', and most of his senior officers, 'guilty of blood in the first
rebellion'.[25] Subsequently islands, bogs, and loughs were put outside
the protection of Parliament.[26]

In reference to the prospective armistice, one contemporary commentator
feared that the confederates,

> will try our patience a little longer or else make what
> terms they can, which, once being done our next sport may
> be at hide and seek a tory-hunting for which there is a
> great need'.[27]

Another commentator dismissed the guerrilla activities of the Tories:

> for that the business of the field and garrison to the
> enemy is now quite over so all that we have to deal with
> now are only boys in trousers while some of the more
> desperate sort lie skulking and will not be reclaimed but
> by extremity.[28]

The Plantation

Even after the dispersal of the Confederate forces and the conclusion of
mopping-up operations against residual guerilla forces, Toryism remained
a major preoccupation of the Cromwellian government in the latter part
of the 1650s. Often considered a possible focus of Royalist unrest and
external intrigue in Ireland, their activities became increasingly linked to
the Commonwealth post-war policies of transportation and transplantation.[29]

The close links between these policies received graphic description
in Seán ó Conaill's poem *Tuireamh na h-Éireann* [The Dirge of Ireland]
(circa 1654–59). The importation of such English words as *transport*
and *transplant* into contemporary Irish poetry tell their own story while
the allusion to the decapitation of O'Connor became the fate of many
Tories throughout the seventeenth and eighteenth centuries:

Ceann Uí Chonchubhair ar an Spéice
Transport, Transplant go Jamaica
D'éis ar cuireadh tar Sionainn fá dhaorbhruid
S'an mheid a fuair Pilib gan fille le sgéala.[30]

The head of O' Connor on the spike
Transport, transplant go to Jamaica
After being banished across the Shannon in bondage
And those whom Philip has received have not returned with news.

Irish soldiers could expect generous inducements to transport themselves into the armies of the kings of France and Spain, also a characteristic of post-war Scotland.[31] The first to be lured was Colonel John Fitzpatrick, who surrendered on condition of being transported to Spain.[32] He incurred the wrath of his temporal and spiritual lords in the Irish Confederacy which may explain the unfavourable reaction of some Tories, and Fitzpatrick's subsequent plea to have 'a troop to defend himself against tories and other malefactors'.[33]

Although many Confederate soldiers were transported in this fashion, others defied the directives of the Parliament.[34] These are represented in the Gaelic literary and folk traditions by Éamonn an Chnoic [Ned of the Hill], the solitary Tory on the mountainside whose shadow hung across his native patrimony:

Cé hé sin amuigh ar mhaoilinn an chnoic
ag síor chur mo choladh amú orm?
Ta Éamonn an Chnoic, an pearla breá fir,
is é ag iarradh dul ina dhúiche.[35]

Who is that on the brow of the hill
Always keeping me from my sleep
'Tis Ned of the Hill, that fine pearl of a man
attempting to go into his country.

Another poem celebrated Éamonn an Chnoic's contemporary 'Seán ó Duibhir an Ghleanna' [John O' Dwyre of the Glen], a dispossessed member of the ó Duibhir family of Kilnamanagh, County Tipperary.[36] Like Éamonn, he chose Toryism instead of exile. The poem displays a benevolence towards this unfortunate Irish nobleman, dismay at the destruction of forests, woodlands, and game in the Cromwellian era, and offers a cameo of the dispossessed aristocrat on the periphery of Cromwellian society:

Anois tá an choill á gearradh,
triallaimíd thar caladh,
is a Sheáin — Duibhir an Ghleanna,
tá tú gan géim.

Anois táim ruaigthe om fhearann
in uaigneas fuar óm charaid
i mo luí go duairc faoi scairtibh
is i gcuaisibh an tsléibhe.[37]

Now the woods are being felled
We will cross the sea
Oh Seán ó Duibhir of the Glen
You are without game.

Now I am driven from my lands
in cold lonliness from my friends
Lying depressed beneath under hedges
and mountain hollows.

The contemporary description of the Tory Donogh O'Derrike from official sources also fits into this context. He frequently struck at the political establishment, making himself 'the dread of Leinster and the talk of Ireland'.[38] His adaptation of the Royalist title of 'General of His Majesty's small forces' gave credence to the political motivation of Toryism. His capacity for retribution against Cromwellian settlers characterised contemporary reports. Described as 'a bloody fellow who has murdered many people and discouraged plantation', the parliamentary government held him directly responsible for assassination of seven of William Petty's Down surveyors.[39]

The portrayal of Tories in Gaelic source-material, and the political dimensions attached to the activities of Donogh O' Derricke, has implications for the emergence of the Tory in popular tradition in the late-seventeenth and eighteenth centuries, and his rapid elevation into the Irish nationalist pantheon.

Transplantation: The Gookin-Lawrence Debate

While Toryism in Cromwellian Ireland reacted to the policies of transportation and transplantation, its evolution can also be examined with reference to the conflicting ideas of the contemporary pamphleteers Vincent Gookin and Richard Lawrence.

Gookin attempted to excuse the greater Catholic populace for their participation in rebellion, citing ignorance of design and clerical coercion.[40] He showed an awareness of the coercive capacity of the Tories and the impossible situation of the Irish populace; executed by Parliament for not discovering Tories and killed by the Tories if they did.[41] Having illuminated the plight of the populace, he unfolded his argument against transplantation. A renewal of war in its most hateful possible form threatened the Commonwealth:

inhabitants unable to subsist in their travelling to
Connaught when they came thither would rather choose the
hazards of torying.[42]

Alluding to the custom of dispossessed aristocrats coshering [*cóisir* =
party/feast] and hosting on their former tenants, Gookin accounted for
the aristocratic element within Tory ranks.[43] He predicted that

the Irish masters will disburden themselves on their
adherents and servants and finding themselves excluded
from this will turn to toryism.[44]

The consequences of the transplantation policy were reflected by Sir
John Perceval in October 1658:

I cannot conclude until I mention unto you one grievance
which this country labours under and that is by the
frequent returning of the great dons of the transplanted
persons who commonly once a quarter flock thither attended
with a crew of rogues which monthly passes and receives
their contributions from former followers, those who at
present inhabit on that which was once their estates, by
means whereof great stealths are committed.[45]

Lawrence described the resilience of Tories and accounted for their
survival by their intimate knowledge of the local terrain. He believed
that 'the English soldiers are more afraid of tories than armies and of
woods and bogs than camps', the hardness and boldness of the Irish
making them skilful protaganists in the Tory war.[46] To deal with the
problem he prescribed a drastic change in the settlement pattern, an
isolation of the Irish, 'by bringing them into a body, confining them in
small circuits [so that] if they may be torying they may be torying on
one another'.[47]

Gookin, on the other hand, adopted the attitude that 'transplantation
can not hinder those that would be tories but non-transplantation
cannot further those that would not', an opinion borne out in the mid-
1650s.[48] Moreover his astute observations regarding Toryism were
constantly reiterated by a whole series of political observers in the
Restoration period including Ormond, Essex, Arran, Oliver Plunkett,
and Sir William Petty.[49]

Transplantation and reactionary agrarian Toryism

Having considered the contrasting attitudes of Gookin and Lawrence
regarding the Connaught plantation, it is necessary to examine the
effects of the plantation scheme on Toryism. At the onset of the imposition
of the Cromwellian policies of transportation and transplantation in

early 1654, the omens were not good for tacit Irish acceptance of a further erosion of their tenuous economic position.[50] Coercive measures, including the notorious 'Hell or Connaught' ultimatum, had to be introduced.[51] While reports for the month of March 1654 appeared favourable, Toryism remained a fly in the ointment.[52] In April and May 1654, however, it returned to the forefront of the Irish political scene:

> although the letters from Ireland certify that all things
> are very quiet, yet the tories continue their old trade of
> filching and stealing as ever according to their
> power...all the benefit we have is that their number is
> much less than it once was.[53]

An undercurrent of opposition lurked menacingly in the background.[54] By July 1654, the transplantation moved 'very slowly', with 'not above six score from all other provinces yet moved into Connaught'.[55] A freeze on the transportation of Irish Confederates to Spain accentuated the problem,

> the flood-gates being shut for transportation to Spain,
> the Irish break out into torying and the waters rise upon
> us.[56]

By the end of August, the transplantation dream had turned sour: 'the work is at a stand-still...tories fly out and increase'.[57] Although the author excused this as being 'in the nature of these rebellious people', he blamed this particular rejuvenation of Tory activity on their being 'highly exasperated at the transplantation work'.[58]

By September 1654, however, according to the testimony of Sir Charles Fleetwood, 'we are through mercy in a very quiet condition'.[59] The Tories managed to retain a lurking presence, taking revenge 'against two persons in Wicklow who were active against the rebels'.[60] Colonel Hewson's proposed transportation of the inhabitants of the adjacent town undoubtedly failed to endear him to the populace.[61] Toryism again culminated in a crescendo of activity between April and August 1655, with no less than three proclamations dealing exclusively with the phenomenon.[62]

In August 1656, 'with the publication of acts, ordinances and instructions of parliament concerning transplantation to Connaught and Clare', the obedience of some was matched by the insubordination of others. Some chose

> out of desperate and malicious designs to run out into
> woods and bogs and other fast and desert places to commit
> murder, rapine and spoils on the well affected.[63]

If a tendency existed to dismiss Toryism and equate it with ordinary criminal activity in the latter years of the 1650s, it remained a governmental preoccupation as late as August 1659.[64] With the Commonwealth in its death-throes it further increased as the Restoration approached.[65]

A copy of a despatch from the commissioners of Parliament on the eve of the Restoration, showed the two ways which Toryism affected the plantation:

> their numerousness and insolence in that country of
> late…their robberies and afrightments they put on those
> of our nation not only proving their ruin but such a
> terror is put on them withal as to discourage the late
> hopeful plantation of the country.[66]

Toryism represented a vital characteristic of Irish political life in the Interregnum period. While Gookin and Lawrence disagreed on many aspects of the war and post-war settlement, they were both mindful of the disruptive potential of Toryism to the survival of the embryonic Cromwellian plantation. These fears were realised in the latter part of the 1650s.

Scottish parallels: Moss-troopers and Toryism.

Spenser's 'A View of Ireland' contains the following exchange:

> *Eudox*: I wonder (Irenaeus) whither you runne so farre
> astraie, for whylest wee talk of Ireland, me thinkes you
> ripp up the originall of Scotlande but what is that to
> this?
> *Irenaeus*: Surelye very much for Scotlande and Irelande are
> all one and the same.[67]

Such comparisons between Gaelic Scotland and Ireland remained a preoccupation with Spenser's contemporaries and immediate successors, and has been a recurring feature of early modern Irish and Scottish historiography. Like its Celtic counterpart, violence remained a feature of Scottish society in the early modern period. Protectionism, racketeering, feuding, cattle-raiding, and murder were integrated in the economy of the Highlands and often spilled into Lowland areas.[68] This endemic violence was further fuelled by the political convulsions of the civil war period, its harnessed potential being funnelled into the war effort.[69] As Scottish forces succumbed to the military might of Parliament, they successfully reverted to a type of guerrilla warfare which had successfully pinned down the Parliament's forces in Ireland.[70]

In analysing the military disintegration in Ireland and Scotland in the Civil War period, a notable comparison is that between the dwindling military fortunes of the Scottish Cavalier Middleton and his Confederate counterpart Sir Phelim O'Neill. Moreover, the wording of proclamations and coercive legislation in Scotland was often similar to those in Ireland, with no verbal niceties employed to distinguish between either Tory, Highlander, or Moss-trooper and the common thief or highwaymen.

A recourse to guerilla warfare and sporadic attacks on isolated military detatchments and English civilians became a feature of the war in Scotland in the late 1640s and early 1650s. One reporter warned

> that unless some speedy action is taken, either by
> securing the roads or causing the country to make
> satisfaction, there will be no travelling in these
> parts.[71]

Another report represented the extent to which the Scots and Moss-troopers revived their old customs of robbing and murdering the English (whether soldiers or others) upon all opportunities.[72]

If available evidence suggested comparisons between the Irish and Scottish situation, Tories and Moss-troopers received similar treatment from the Commonwealth. This is evident in a letter from the commissioners of the Parliament in Ireland to their counterparts in Scotland in August 1652:

> your employment in Scotland and that wherein we are
> instructed being of the like nature and tending to the
> same end, the welfare of the Commonwealth.[73]

The fear of the Parliament regarding Tories and Moss-troopers in both kingdoms was not only the threat to law and order but also to English military authority.[74] In Scotland, proclamations encouraged more care in keeping track of movements within set borders:

> nothing to this time has effectively been done but on the
> contrary divers rebels...are suffered to pass, march
> through or abide in any burgh or parish...and take
> opportunity to get intelligence but also to induce many
> loose persons to join them in rebellion and commit
> frequent robberies and barbarous murders.[75]

The Glencairn Rebellion provided a further demonstration of the perceived links between 'lawlessness' and political dissent. This rebellion emerged out of political intrigue between the Royalist clans and the exiled Court, cultured on the immediate post-war restlessness of the Highlands. The Highlanders sought to make optimum use of the fastnesses and avoided direct confrontation with the superior forces of the Commonwealth.[76] However, by September 1654, the forces of the

Earl of Middleton, sent by Charles II to lead the Royalist insurgents, had effectively disintegrated. According to one report they were

> reduced in the Northern highlands to a very quiet pass and
> there is little chance of any contrivances amidst their
> depleted ranks... most of the principal lords, leaders and
> gentry are come in.[77]

In November 1654 five hundred Irish landed on the Isle of Skye to join with Middleton. One reporter dismissively asserted that 'all the prejudice they can do this winter is to rob and plunder'.[78] One can only speculate as to the extent of actual collusion between both parties, but Fleetwood brought the concerted rise in Scottish and Irish expectations to the attention of Thurloe. They were

> in great expectations of some change in England,
> reinforced by a shared belief that Ormond, Inchiquin or
> some of that gang will be here suddenly.[79]

Reports of intrigue between the two parties also sharpened parliamentary paronia. Thus a strict order of 20 October 1654 concerned the

> illegal transportation of several Irish tories by the
> unfaithfulness of such as traffick to Scotland, being
> secretly transported to the prejudice of the
> Commonwealth.[80]

Francis Cromwell underlined the synonymous use of 'Moss-troopers' and 'Tories' in 1655. In a despatch to the Navy Commissioners, he made reference to arms and equipment which he took from 'tories and highlanders'.[81] Moreover, rewards were offered for 'discoveries of robbers and burglars and also moss-troopers on the borders and tories in Ireland'.[82] The synonymous proclamation of Scottish Moss-troopers and Tories coincided with rumours of a possible Royalist descent on Scotland and evidence of a reaction of their Torying counterparts in Ireland. According to a contemporary Royalist report, Charles II intended 'to get all Ireland abroad with him in the highlands', with 'small succours to be sent to the tories in Ireland'.[83] Tory activity in Ireland also reacted to news of the Leveller rebellions in England. According to Fleetwood,

> the very poor tories were very much lifted by hopes of
> enemy successes, there were some of late run out into
> rebellion but through mercy not very considerable.[84]

Allan Macinnes has suggested that the endemic lawlessness of Highland Scotland in the Restoration period represented the machinations of scheming Scottish politicians, a feature of the scare-mongering of such political opportunists as the Earls of Orrery and Conway in Ireland.[85] Similarly, the breakdown of the social constraints of clanship, the growth of the market economy, and the proliferation of masterless men, landless labourers, and disinherited younger sons added to the ranks of those who engaged in banditry in both areas.[86] However, while the Moss-trooper effectively disappeared in Restoration Scotland, the distinctive religious and political nature of Irish society ensured that the Tory survived as a form of social and political revolt.[87] Similarly, when the relative tranquillity of Scottish society was disturbed by the clouds of approaching war in 1685, the Irish rapparee, as a Jacobite partisan, usurped the role which the Tory previously enjoyed.[88]

The legislative struggle against Toryism

A comparison of the various endeavours of the Commonwealth government to eradicate both Tories and Moss-troopers sheds light on the two phenomena. A proclamation of November 1649 ordered that

> all robberies committed by the tories and rebels on those
> adhering to the Protestant party be answered by the
> kindred of those who commit them.[89]

The impossibility of identifying kindred willing to admit to the misdemeanours of their relatives explained the need for the proclamation of 25 February 1649, whereby the pound of flesh was to be taken from 'all inhabitants of the said barony that suffers rebels to go without the hue and cry'.[90]

The Irish poet Éamonn Mac Donnchada an Dúna offered a vivid portrayal of the above legislation:

> *Tories* ghuirid d'fhuirinn an tsléibhe,
> 's an fear astig gan choir gan chéim air
> caithfidh a íoc gach ní dá ndéineann
> an tory amuith má bhíonn a ghaol ris.
> muna bhfuil gaol dá thaobh re féachain
> nó an costas do shoichfeadh an t-éileamh,
> is dá mbiaid gan fios cia rinn an t-éireach,
> caithfidh an tír an díol so 'dhéanamh'.[91]

> Short tories of the team of the mountain
> And the man inside with no rights or status
> or authority over them, must pay for
> everything they do, If he is related to
> the tory outside, or if no other of his
> kindred can be found, or if no
> one knows who should pay the levy,
> then the whole country must pay.

Moreover, Mac Donnchadha suggested that the prosecution of Tories characterised a surrogate parliamentary policy of persecution and liquidation against the Irish. This has repercussions for the place of the bandit in Interregnum politics and Irish nationalist hagiography. His importation of English words add to the intensity of feeling:

Transport transplant mo mheabhair ar Bhearla [my meaning of English]
Shoot him, *kill* him, *strip* him, *tear* him.
A *tory*, hack him, hang him, *rebel*,
A *rogue*, a *thief*, a *priest*, a *papist*.[92]

A progression of proclamations penalised the kindred of Tories, the inhabitants of the respective baronies where crimes were perpetrated and the papists as a whole. The proclamation of 17–25 May 1655 threw caution to the winds, with a direct attack on the Irish Catholic populace in a vain attempt to sever the tap-root of Toryism. The Cromwellian government, exasperated at the limited success against the Tories, recognised the extent to which they depended on their fellow country-men who were living under the protection of the English government.[93] They subsequently placed on the Irish and Scottish populace then to betray the Tories and daily observe the hue and cry. In Ireland, the punishment for non-participation and co-operation was incarceration and transportation to America:

if murderers be not taken…[you are] required to
apprehend four persons of the Irish nation, residing in or
near the place who did not assist the persons
murdered…to some jail or custody for 21 days to be sent
away to some colony in America.[94]

Another proclamation of 19 April 1655 threatened transportation to those who colluded with the Tories or showed an unwillingness to help their victims.[95] Éamonn an Dúna represented the effects of such legislation;

Bíd na mílte dinn i n-aontacht,
iad 'na mbanna dá dtarrang na gcéadaibh
chum gach cuain ar fuaid na hÉireann,
dá gcur don Spáinn ar áis nó ar éigin
A ngoid san úiche dó níd na méirlig
gan fios a n-íde a gcríoch ná a sgéala
gabháil is priosáil gach lae ortha,
is tiomáin go hoileánaibh Statesy.[96]

There are thousands of them together
bands of them bringing in hundreds
to every harbour throughout the country
Banished to Spain with or without their consent

Abducted at night is what these villians do
Not knowing their abuse, end or fate
They are taken and pressed everyday
and driven to the island of Statesy [in the West Indies].

This punishment of transportation was also imposed on the revocation of the death penalty. A the same time merchants petitioned Cromwell for licences to transport Tories to the Carribean Islands.[97] A dehumanisation process followed the depoliticisation of Tory elements and the general persecution of the Irish polity. Tories became increasingly regarded 'not as enemies but like wilde beasts...who come out of their woods at midnight to seek their prey'. This dehumanisation reflected contemporary attitudes towards the 'wild people' of the Highlands.[98] Tories were relentlessly hunted like wild animals and their heads displayed on spikes to strike terror into their comrades.[99]

The government also utilised more devious policies in their efforts to combat Tory and Moss-trooper activity.[100] The cultivation of internal divisions among Tory bands in Ireland often paid more dividends in the fight than the more coercive methods. Whilst the general persecution of Catholics existed in times of necessity, the peripheralisation of Tories and their abettors became the major weapon in the parliamentary arsenal, continously employed with much success in the Restoration and Williamite periods.

1657 also saw a new departure in the fight against Toryism, with an amendment of the political structure at the highest level, amounting to fragmentary martial law:

a course which the wisdom of our predecessors had
experienced as the readiest and most effectual to suppress
the leaderless and wicked generation called tories and
idlers.[101]

Subsequently provincial officers and subordinates were appointed 'with powers which in almost any other case would be considered large and arbitrary' which underlined the serious nature of the problem.[102] The permission given to Francis Rowleston to treat with certain Tories facilitated their discovery and speedy reduction, and became a popular weapon in the Restoration period.[103]

The question of Toryism and the law returned to the foreground of Irish political debate among those Protestant and Catholic interest groups who vied for the affections of the fickle Charles Stuart in the early 1660s.[104] Justification of Tory activity between the arrival of Cromwell and the departure of Clanricard provided the corner-stone of 'The case of the Roman Catholics of Ireland' (circa 1660):

Many who lived under the king's authority were so
unmercifully stripped of their fortunes and some to their
very shirts by the victorious enemies, those who had not a
morsel of bread left of their own and had no access to the
king's quarters, taking sanctuary in the woods and
catching whatever they could from the parliamentarians to
keep alive when the very hull of government was ship-
wrecked, were put into the same class as rebels because
they endeavoured to supply the exigencies of nature by
taking part of their own or the like spoils from arch-
rebels or traitors or rather because they had been
woodkerne against the Cromwellians.[105]

Another Catholic apoplogist (circa 1660) excused stealths and pilfering
in the Interregnum:

whereas by the *law of nations*, more especially the Common
Law of England grounded upon the *law of nature*, a man may
take so much of his neighbours goods by stealth or
otherwise as may preserve him from starving.[106]

These apologies for thievery in the Interregnum provided justification
for the dispossessed aristocracy and their sub-tenantry to turn to Toryism
in the Restoration.[107]

The Protestant answer to these Catholic discourses, provided by
'The House of Common's answer to the objections…', confirmed these
inexorable links between crime, Toryism, and politics:

To which we answer we only understand woodkerne and
tories, men, without *authority* who rob, kill and destroy
and satisfy their own appetites without any regard for the
common good undergoing a bestial employment, living like a
beast of prey.[108]

Similar attitudes towards the tories were expressed by Séamus Dall
Mac Cuarta and Aodh Mac Oireachtaigh in their *agallamh filíochta* [poetic
dialogue] composed in the aftermath of the Williamite wars, that is,
whether Tories were political bandits *buachaillí an tsléibhe* [mountain
boys] or ordinary criminals *bodaigh gan chéille* [senseless churls'].[109]

In his examination of violence and order in eighteenth-century
Ireland, Connolly stressed the extension to Ireland of 'a new and more
rigorous definition of what type of behaviour put a man outside the
law'.[110] Specific types of Tories were offsprings of the turbulent seventeenth
century when the *law*, *law of nations*, *law of nature*, and *common good*
were not easily defined and meant different things to different groups.
The line between the law of nature and the law of nations appeared

very porus in Ireland, especially to men who were, as late as 1671, perceived to be 'sunk in their past misfortunes'.[111]

If historians have shown an inclination to the official view of crime, crime justification in the Cromwellian period died hard among the outlaws of eighteenth-century Ulster. In Cathal Buí Mac Giolla Gunna's [Yellow Charlie Gunn's] eighteenth-century lament for his dead cousin, the petty thief showed some characteristics of the noble robber, particularly in his eagerness to steal from government officials and rich foreigners:

> Is iomdha cró lena thóin a bhris sé
> Is manga mór d'eorna a ghoid sé
> Níorbh fhearr leis stóras *Milord* no *Justice*
> No cuid an deoraí is mó san cruinne.[112]

> Many a byre he broke with his arse
> And bag of corn he stole
> He always preferred the stores of Milord or Justice
> Or the goods of the largest foreigner in the locality.

His outlaw contemporary Cathal Mac Aodh [Charlie Mc Hugh], having boasted his aristocratic forebearers, excused his theft from the English-speakers:

> Thug siad a mbréag ní gadaíthe mé féin
> ar son mé a bheith éadrom, earraideach, baoth
> 's dá mbainfinn luach eadaigh do bhodaigh an bhéarla
> Cé bheadh 'na dheidh ar Chathal Mhac Aodh.[113]

> The tell their lies, I am no thief
> Because I am light-hearted, roving and reckless
> And if I steal the price of clothes from the English-
> speaking churls who will come after Cathal MacAodh

Conclusion

Banditry in Ireland and Scotland in the Interregnum had its antecedents in traditional Gaelic society. It became institutionalised in Scotland in the early seventeenth century when groups of broken men and Highland thugs engaged in protection racketeering, blackmail, terrorisation, raiding, and murder. In Ireland the common thieving woodkerne acquired an additional political dimension in the early modern period. They were perceived to react to the rebellion of Cahir O' Docherty in 1610, became implicated in rumours of a possible descent by the exiled Earl of Tyrone, and constantly associated with the sabotage of the Ulster plantation. These groups of outlaws became much more numerous in both Ireland and Scotland as a consequence of the socio-economic and political dislocation of the 1640s. With the onslaught of the Cromwellian conquest on the Celtic realms, those residual guerilla bands of Confederates and Royalists who continued a defensive struggle became affiliated with ordinary criminals who availed of the turmoil for private gains. If the Moss-trooper disappeared in Restoration Scotland and the lawlessness of the Highlands was exaggerated for political expediency, Toryism retained a disruptive influence in Restoration Ireland and had roots in the Interregnum period. With the onset of the Monmouth and Argyll rebellions, lawlessness, Toryism and banditry re-emerged at the forefront of political life in both kingdoms.

NOTES

1. (Note: all newspapers and pamphlets cited are in the Thomason Tracts). J P Prendergast, *The Cromwellian settlement of Ireland* (London, 1865); T O' Hanlon, *The highwayman in Irish history* (Dublin, 1932); M Davitt, *The fall of feudalism in Ireland* (London, 1904), 14.

2. J C Beckett, *The making of modern Ireland* (London, 1966), 105.

3. L M Cullen, *The economic history of Ireland since 1660* (London, 1972), 20.

4. S Connolly, 'Violence and order in eighteenth-century Ireland', in P O' Flanagan, P Ferguson, and K Whelan (eds), *Rural Ireland 1600–1800* (Cork, 1987), 45. For his recent reappraisal of Toryism, see S Connolly, *Religion, Law, and Power: The Making of Protestant Ireland, 1659–1760* (Oxford, 1992), 205–233.

5. G M Joseph, 'On the trail of Latin American Bandits: A Re-examination of Peasant Resistance', in J E Rodríguez O (ed), *Patterns of contention in Mexican history* (Delaware, 1992), 293, 295, 296, 305–6, 310, 315–4, 318, 319, 320, 332.

6. E J Hobsbawm, *Primitive Rebels* (Manchester, 1959), 3, 16, 21, 23–4, 28; E.J. Hobsbawm, *Bandits* (Harmondsworth, 1972), 21, 22–23, 33; Joseph, 'Bandits',*passim;* S Connolly, *Religion, Law and Power: the making of Protestant Ireland* (Oxford, 1993), 207.

7. Examination of Paul Congan, 22 Jan. 1645–46, HMC, *Calendar of the manuscripts of the Marquis of Ormonde*, ns volumes i–viii, (London, 1902–20), i, 105; T W Moody and F X Martin (eds), *A New History of Ireland*, III, *Early Modern Ireland 1534–1691*, (Oxford, 1978), 375; A I MacInnes, 'The Impact of the Civil Wars and Interregnum: Political Disruption and Social Change within Scottish Gaeldom', in J Dwyer, R A Mason and P Roebuck (eds), *New Perspectives on the Politics and Culture of Early Modern Scotland* (Edinburgh, 1982), 87–89.

8. J P Meyers (ed), *Elizabethan Ireland: A selection of writings from Elizabethan writers* (Connecticut, 1983), 40, 101.

9. C Maxwell, *Irish history from contemporary sources 1509–1610* (London, 1912), 223, 294. See also *CSPI 1607*, 314, 352–353; *CSPI, 1608*, 530–531; *CSPI, 1610*, 474.

10. 'Aphorismical Discovery' (TCD MS 846, Book 6, ff 107, 202, 227; Edited by J T Gilbert as *A contemporary history of affairs in Ireland from AD 1641–52*, three vols. (Dublin, 1879). See also Gilbert (ed), *A contemporary history, iii*, part 1, 67, 134; C Mc Neill (ed), *The Tanner Letters. Documents of Irish Affairs in the sixteenth and seventeenth centuries extracted from the Thomas Tanner collection in the Bodleian Library, Oxford* (IMC, Dublin, 1943), 339–40; 'Eamonn an Dúna' (circa 1658), in C O Rahilly (ed), *Five seventeenth century political Poems* (Dublin, 1952), 90, line 129–30; R Bagwell, *Ireland under the Stuarts,* three vols (London, 1909–16), ii, 330; D Stevenson, *Alasdair Mac Colla and the Highland Problem in the Seventeenth Century* (Edinburgh, 1980), 273; Joseph, 'Bandits', 316.

11. 'Aphorismical Discovery'; book 4 (590); Gilbert (ed), *A contemporary history*, volume ii, part 1, 62. See also Bagwell, *Ireland under the Stuarts*, ii, 211; Bodleian Library, Oxford, Carte MS 18, f 616; *Several letters from Ireland of the late good successes of the parliament's forces there, 18 March 1649/50* (London, 1650), 5; Mc Neill (ed),*Tanner letters*, 325.

12. See Bodleian Library, Carte MS 18, f 616; Bagwell, *Stuarts*, ii, 211; *Several letters*, 5; Mc Neill (ed), *Tanner letters*, 325, 356–357; Gilbert (ed), *Contemporary History*, ii, part 2, appendix, 431; 'Aphorismical Discovery', f191.

13. Commissioners of Parliament to Parliament, 1 July 1651, in R Dunlop (ed), *Ireland under the commonwealth*, two volumes (Manchester, 1913), i, 5. See also C Firth (ed), *Memoirs of Edmund Ludlow. Lieutenant-general of the horse in the army of the Commonwealth of England, 1625–72*, two volumes, (Oxford, 1894), i, 283, 302.

14. *Great and bloody fight in Ireland,* 12 April 1652, in Gilbert (ed), *Contemporary history, iii*, part 1, 71. See also Bodleian Library, Firth MS, f 25, 13 April 1652.

15. *A Perfect Account of Everyday Intelligence*, 29 June 1652.

16. Ludlow, *Memoirs,* ii, appendix, iv, 490.

17. Ludlow, *Memoirs*, iv, 493. See also Mc Neill (ed), *Tanner Letters*, 342; Gilbert (ed), *Contemporary history, iii*, part 1, app. iii, 164; *The taking of Wexford, a letter from and eminent officer in the army under the command of the lord lieutenant of Ireland* (London, 1649); *Weekly Intelligencer*, 26 January 1651, 27 January–3 February 1651.

18. Ludlow, *Memoirs*, ii, 314.

19. Dunlop (ed), *Ireland Under the Commonwealth* i, 6–7.

20. Ibid; Mc Neill (ed), *Tanner Letters*, 350.

21. Dunlop (ed), *Ireland Under the Commonwealth*, i, 67.

22. Ibid. For Scotland see C H Firth (ed), *Scotland and the Commonwealth, 1651–53*, (SHS, Edinburgh, 1895), 240, 274.

23. Dunlop (ed), *Ireland Under the Commonwealth*, i, 9–10.

24. Ibid, i, 15.

25. Ludlow, *Memoirs,* ii, 330; *The Faithful Scout*, 29 October–5 November 1652. See also *The Moderate Intelligencer*, 15–22 December 1652; *Mercurius Politicus*, 27 December 1655–3 January 1656.

26. Bodleian Library, Firth MS f.199–200. See also É ó Ciardha, 'Woodkerne, Tories and Rapparees in Ulster and north Connaught in seventeenth-century Ireland', (University College Dublin, MA thesis, 1991), chapter 10.

27. *Mercurius Politicus*, 7–14 April 1652.

28. Ibid, 6–13 May 1652; TCD MS 844, f128; *A Perfect Account of Everyday Intelligence*, 13–20 October 1652.

29. T Birch (ed.), *A collection of the state papers of John Thurloe esq.; secretary, first to council of state, and afterward to the two Protectors Oliver and Richard Cromwell,* seven vols (London, 1742), i, 478, 562, 619; ii, 287; iv, 87–88, 160, 348, 373, 376, 402, 447, 629; v, 348, 432; vi, 45, 53, 87, 143, 374, 515, 527. See also P Beresford-Ellis, *Hell or Connaught, the Cromwellian colonisation of Ireland, 1652–1660* (Belfast, 1975), 144.

30. S ó Conaill, 'Tuireamh na h-Éireann', in ó Rahilly (ed), *Five poems*, 79, lines 429–34;'Aiste Dháibhí Cúndún', in ó Rahilly (ed), *Five poems*, 45, lines 215–222. See also Iain Lom's 'Fogradh Raghnaill óig' [the exile of Ragnall óg], in A Mackenzie (ed), *Orain Iain Luim* (Edinburgh, 1964), 2.

31. Firth (ed), *Scotland and the Commonwealth*, xlix; F D Dow, *Cromwellian Scotland, 1651–1660* (Edinburgh, 1979), 132; *CSPD 1652–3*, 433, 588.

32. Ludlow, *Memoirs*, ii, 310; Mc Neill (ed), *Tanner Letters*, 360.

33. NLI Fitzpatrick Papers, MS 8,099, f.9. See also Dunlop (ed), *Ireland Under the Commonwealth*, ii, 360; 'Aphorismical Discovery' f193; Bodleian Library, Firth MS f.43.

34. Prendergast, *Cromwellian Settlement*, 163–167, 190; 'The case of the Roman Catholics of Ireland' in *Analecta Hibernica, 1*, (1930), 132.

35. 'Éamonn an Chnoic' (traditional), in P De Brún, T ó Conchaineann and B ó Buachalla (eds), *Nua-Dhuanaire 1,* (Dublin, 1986), 68, lines 10–12.

36. *Nua-Dhuanaire 1*, 127 (traditional). See also E ó Néill, *Gleann an óir* (Dublin, 1985), 43; *The Public Intelligencer*, 17–24; March, 24–31 March 1656.

37. 'Seán ó Dúibhir an Ghleanna' in *Nua-Dhuanaire 1*, 66–67.

38. *Mercurius Politicus*, 27 December–31 January 1655/6.

39. *The Public Intelligencer*, 24–31 March 1656, 28 January–4 February 1655–56. See also J P Prendergast, *The Tory War in Ulster* (private circulation, 1887),

5, (footnote); E Mc Lysaght (ed), 'Commonwealth state Accounts', in *Analecta Hibernica, xv* (1944), 269.

40. V Gookin, *The great case of Transplantation discussed* (London, 1655), 13.

41. Ibid, 13.

42. Ibid, 21.

43. Prendergast, *Cromwellian Settlement*, 166–167.

44. Gookin, *Great Case*.

45. HMC *Report on the manuscripts of the earl of Egmont*, volume I, part I, (London, 1905), 599–600.

46. R Lawerence, *The interest of England in Ireland's trade and wealth stated* (London, 1655), 18; V Gookin, *Author and case. vindicated from the unjust aspersions of colonel Richard Lawrence* (London, 1655).

47. Lawrence, *Interest of England*, 19; Dow, *Cromwellian Scotland*, 18.

48. Gookin, *Author and Case*, 45.

49. ó Ciardha, 'Woodkerne, tories and rapparees', chapters 5–7.

50. *A Perfect Account* of *Everyday Intelligence*, 18–25 January 1654.

51. BL Egerton MS 1762, f.414.

52. Ibid.

53. *A Perfect Account of Everyday Intelligence,* 12–19 April 1654.

54. Ibid.

55. Beresford-Ellis, *Hell or Connaught*, 114.

56. Ibid.

57. *Mercurius Politicus*, 24–31 August 1654.

58. Ibid.

59. Birch (ed), *Thurloe State Papers*, ii, 631.

60. *The Public Intelligencer*, 29 October–5 November 1654.

61. Ibid; *Mercurius Politicus*, 1–8 November 1655; Dunlop (ed), *Ireland Under the Commonwealth*, ii, 514.

62. Dunlop (ed), *Ireland Under the Commonwealth*, ii, 505, 537. See also *A Perfect Proceedings*, 17 May–27 May 1655; *Mercurius Politicus*, 19–26 June 1655, 27 October–3 November 1655.

63. Proclamation, 27 Aug. 1656, in Dunlop, *Ireland Under the Commonwealth*, 619.

64. *Mercurius Politicus*, 9–16 March 1657.

65. Beresford-Ellis, *Hell or Connaught*, 226; Dow, *Cromwellian Scotland*, 244. For political reaction among the woodkerne in 1620s, see J J Marshall, *Irish*

Tories, Rapparees, and Robbers (Dungannon, 1927), 8; ó Ciardha, 'Woodkerne, tories and rapparees', chapters 1, 5 and 6.

66. Commissioners of Parliament to the Council of State, 17 August 1659 (*CSPI 1647–60*, 690). See also Birch (ed) *Thurloe State Papers*, vi, 400; *CSPD 1666–67*, 377–78.

67. Meyers (ed), *Elizabethan Ireland*, 77.

68. See K M Brown, *Bloodfeud in Scotland, 1573–1625. Violence, Justice and Politics in Early Modern Society* (Edinburgh, 1986); K Nicholls, *Gaelic and Gaelicised Ireland in the Middle Ages* (Dublin, 1972).

69. A I Macinnes, 'Repression and conciliation, the Highland dimension, 1660–1800', *SHR*, LXV, 2, No. 180, (1986), 167–195.

70. Dow, *Cromwellian Scotland*, chapters 1–3; Macinnes, 'Repression and conciliation', 172.

71. *A Perfect Account* of *Everyday Intelligence*, 10–17 November. 1652; Firth (ed), *Scotland and the Commonwealth* 337.

72. *A Perfect Account of Everyday Intelligence*, 10–17 November 1652. See also D Stevenson, *Scottish Covenanters and Irish Confederates: Scottish-Irish relations in the mid-seventeenth century* (Belfast, 1981), 109.

73. Dunlop (ed), *Ireland Under the Commonwealth,* i, 256.

74. Dow, *Cromwellian Scotland,* 20, 81, 100, 107.

75. Proclamation by Commander-in-Chief of the Scottish forces, 27 September 1653, in Birch (ed), *Thurloe State Papers*, ii, 57.

76. *The Weekly Intelligencer*, 18–25 October 1653.

77. *Mercurius Politicus*, 25 September–5 October 1653. See also *Mercurius Politicus*, 1 October 1654, 4–11 January 1654–55; Dow, *Cromwellian Scotland*, 139.

78. *Mercurius Politicus*, 23–30 November 1654.

79. Fleetwood to Thurloe, 6 March 1654–55, in Birch (ed), *Thurloe State Papers,* iii, 196. See also Birch (ed), *Thurloe, State Papers*, iv, 376.

80. Proclamation, 20 October 1654, J Mc Caffery (ed), 'Commonwealth Records' in *Archivicum Hibernicum* vi, (1917), 185. See also BL Add MS 43,724, f.9; Dow, *Cromwellian Scotland*, 140.

81. Cromwell to the Navy Commissioners, 27 July 1655 (*CSPD 1655*, 295). See also *Diary of Sir Archibald Johnston of Wariston*, (Edinburgh, 1919), ii, *passim*.

82. Act for the suppression of theft on the borders of England and Scotland, 27 January 1657 (*CSPD, 1657, 15*). For moss trooper activity on the borders, see *The Moderate Intelligencer*, 23–30 Sept. 1647; *Kingdom's Weekly Intelligencer*, 5–12 Oct. 1647; *Perfect Diurnall*, 4–11 Oct. 1647; *Mercurius Anti-Pragmaticus* 12–19 Oct. 1647. I would like to thank D N Farr for bringing these to my attention.

83. *Analecta Hib*ernica, i, (1930), 17. See also Firth (ed), *Scotland and the Commonwealth*, 182, 141; Birch (ed),*Thurloe State Papers*, iii, 305.

84. Birch (ed), in *Thurloe State P*apers, iii, 305.

85. Macinnes, 'Repression and conciliation', 168, 173, 181; ó Ciardha, 'Woodkerne, tories and rapparees', chapters 5 and 6.

86. Macinnes, 'Repression and conciliation', 172. These individuals compare to the 'meathaig uaisle' (degenerate gentry) or 'meathlacháin' in 'Pairlement Chloinne Thomáis', see N Williams (ed), *Pairlement Chloinne Tomáis*, (Dublin, 1981), 30, line 941; G A Hayes-Mc Coy, 'Gaelic society in the late sixteenth century', in N Williams, (ed), *Historical Studies, iv*, (London, 1963), 49.

87. Connolly, *Religion, Law and Power*, 207.

88. Macinnes, 'Repression and conciliation', 172–173, 193; Cullen, *Economic History,* 20; ó Ciardha, 'Woodkerne, tories and rapparees'.

89. Proclamation by the commander in chief of the parliamentary forces in Leinster, 2 November 1649 (TCD MS 844, f 112). See also Dow, *Cromwellian Scotland,* 106–108.

90. Proclamation against Tories, 25 February 1649 (TCD MS 844, f.114). See also Firth (ed), *Scotland and the Commonwealth*, 229, 318.

91. 'Éamonn an Dúna',in ó Rahilly (ed), *Five Poems*, lines 105–113, lines 121–122. See also BL Egerton MS1762 ff 31, 18.

92. 'Éamonn an Dúna', line 128; NLI MS 2411, f.277. See also Iain Lom, 'Cumha Mhontrois' [lament for Montrose], in Mackenzie (ed), *Orain Iain Luim*, 56.

93. *A Perfect Proceedings*, 17–24 March 1655.

94. Ibid; Dunlop (ed), *Ireland Under the Commonwealth*, ii, 514.

95. *A Perfect Account* of *Everyday Intelligence*, 17–24 May 1655.

96. 'Éamonn an Dúna', in ó Rahilly (ed), *Five Poems*, (circa1658), 85–86, 90–91. See also Bodleian Library, Carte MS 65, f 17; T C Barnard, 'Crisis in identity among Irish Protestants, 1641–85', in *Past and Present*, 127 (1990), 72.

97. Dunlop (ed), *Ireland Under the Commonwealth*, ii, 400, 488–91.

98. *Mercurius Politicus*, 12–19 March 1652. See also Firth (ed), *Scotland and the Commonwealth*, 122.

99. Meyers (ed), *Elizabethan Ireland,* 43; Séan ó Conaill, 'Tuireamh na hÉireann', in ó Rahilly (ed), *Five Poems*, 79, line 429; E Mc Lysaght (ed), 'Commonwealth state accounts' 25 March 1656, in *Analecta Hibernica, 15*, 1945), 285; Bodleian Library, Carte MS 35, f 331; NLI MS 2429, f 201; BL Egerton MS 175 f 276; NLI MS 2411, f 57.

100. Prendergast, *Cromwellian Settlement*, 174.

101. *Mercurius Politicus*, 22–29 January 1657.

102. Ibid.

103. Prendergast, *Cromwellian Settlement*, 174; NLI MS 2404, ff 345, 493.

104. Bodleian Library, Carte MS 31 f 249; Carte MS 144 f 36; HMC *Ormond*, iii, 48–49.

105. 'The Case of the Roman Catholics of Ireland', in *Anal. Hib. i* (1930), 32–33. See also the last clause of the Act of Settlement, in R B Mc Dowell and E Curtis (eds), *Historical Documents, 1172–1943* (London, 1943), 169; J Hanly (ed), *The letters of Oliver Plunkett* (Dublin, 1979), 88, 157–161, 198, 325; P F Moran (ed), *Memoirs of Oliver Plunkett* (Dublin, 1861), 56–57; J Perceval (ed), *Montgomery Mss* (Belfast, 1864), 47; O Airy (ed), *Essex Papers*, two volumes, (London, 1890), ii, 305.

106. See also 'The Roman Catholics of Ireland's answers', (Bodleian Library, Carte MS 68, f 17) [my emphasis]; *Analecta Hibernica, i* (1930), 132–133; BL Add MS 28, 938, f.286, Nos. 4–7.

107. Gookin, *Great Case*, 13; Bodleian Library, Carte MS 45, f 478; BL Stowe MS, 215, f 160; ó Ciardha, 'Woodkerne, tories and rapparees', chapter 6.

108. 'The answer of the House of Commons to the objection...' (Bodleian Library, Carte MS 68, f 45–47, (149)[my italics].

109. ó Ciardha, 'Woodkerne, tories and rapparees', chapter 10, 181–182.

110. Connolly, 'Violence and order', 43, 48. See also Connolly, *Religion, Law and Power*, 207; Joseph, 'Bandits', 293, 313–320, 335.

111. A Curtayne, *The trial of Oliver Plunkett* (Dublin, 1953), 71.

112. B ó Buachalla (ed), *Cathal Buí: Amhráin* (Dublin, 1975), 84–85.

113. E ó Muirgheasa (ed), *Amhráin Airt Mhic Chubhthaigh* (Dundalk, 1926), 6–7. See also Meyers (ed), *Elizabethan Ireland*, 40; Bodleian Library, Carte MS 45, f 476.

CHAPTER 9

The Scottish Parliament and the Covenanting Revolution: The Emergence of a Scottish Commons

John R Young

The operation of Scottish political institutions was profoundly affected by the ascendancy of the Covenanting Movement in Scotland. Within the historical parameters of the period 1639 to 1651, the Scottish Parliament underwent an unprecedented degree of political and institutional maturity. In the wider context of the longer seventeenth and early eighteenth centuries, this 'apprenticeship' was only matched by the resurgence of political power and independence from the Crown in the post-Revolution period, 1689–1707, after institutional subordination to Whitehall and the political needs of the Restoration regime of the southern kingdom of the British archipelago. That the Scottish Parliament had increased in stature and had enhanced its power *vis-a-vis* the monarchy in the Covenanting era was reflected in the reactionary Restoration Parliament in Scotland of 1661 which rescinded Scottish parliamentary powers and privileges and fully restored the royal prerogative in Scotland (more so than the English Restoration settlement).[1]

The Covenanting Movement used the forum of the Scottish Parliament not only for the political and constitutional challenge mounted against Charles I, but also as the governing body and administrative unit which oversaw and implemented Scottish military involvement in the conflicts of the British Civil Wars. This phenomenon was not uncommon in continental Europe where representative institutions were often used by opposition movements to challenge monarchical powers.[2]

The Structure of the Scottish Parliament

Unlike the Parliaments of Poland, Hungary, Bohemia, and England which were bicameral (two chamber) institutions, the Scottish Parliament was a unicameral (single chamber) body.[3] Yet in common with other European representative assemblies, the Scottish Parliament was a Parliament of Estates.[4] The Scottish Parliament convened on a regular basis throughout the period 1639–1651. The Second Parliament of

Charles I, 1639–41, consisted of three sessions, the Convention of Estates of 1643–44 consisted of two sessions, whereas the First Triennial Parliament, 1644–47, and the Second Triennial Parliament, 1648–51, were composed of six and eight sessions respectively.[5] The clerical estate had been abolished by the Glasgow Assembly of 1638. In accordance with this, the clerical estate did not attend the 1639 Parliament which convened on 31 August, albeit its abolition did not receive formal constitutional sanction until 2 June 1640. The act 'anent the constitution of the present and all future Parliaments' of that date deemed the Three Estates to consist of the nobility, commissioners of the shires (in effect the gentry), and commissioners of the burghs (burgesses).[6]

This paper contends that within the unicameral structure of Parliament a 'Scottish Commons' emerged, developed, and exerted real parliamentary power, based on the commissioners of the shires and the commissioners of the burghs during the period of Covenanting rule in Scotland. Within the context of the Covenanting Movement as a whole, a 'radical oligarchy/ mainstream' based on the political co-operation and dynamism of the gentry and burgesses operated through what has recently been described as 'oligarchic centralism'.[7] In terms of political labelling, the Covenanting Movement was composed essentially of 'radicals' and 'conservatives'. 'Pragmatic Royalists' have been defined as those Royalists who subscribed Covenanting oaths, most notably the National Covenant of 1638 and the Solemn League and Covenant of 1643, as a prerequisite to participate in the political process, and particularly to secure admission to Parliament.[8]

The 1639 Parliament and the Scottish constitutional settlement of 1640–41

John Scally has clearly articulated the extent to which Charles I was an 'uncounsellable king' throughout 1638 and that the pivotal date which determined the conflict between the Covenanters and the king rested on 20 June 1638. Moreover, Dr Scally has emphasised that:

> in the summer of 1638, the Covenanters were not all
> recalcitrant hard-liners with a set agenda intent on
> abolishing Episcopacy, reforming Parliament, and
> completely re-interpreting the relationship between
> Crown and State, Crown and Church.[9]

Yet prior to the meeting of the 1639 Parliament on 31 August, this situation had changed following the 1638 Glasgow Assembly and the 1639 General Assembly. The organisational opposition of the Covenanters had matured in the form of the Tables, which essentially provided the hierarchical leadership structure to the Covenanting Movement with overall control lying with the Fifth Table (the executive table).[10] A programme of constitutional reform had been drawn up by the Tables with the aim of securing enactment in the 1639 Parliament. Supplications for reform continued to be handed in particularly by gentry and burgess representatives to the Lords of the Articles throughout the autumn and winter of 1639 until the parliamentary session was eventually closed on 14 November. The Lords of the Articles had been the traditional vehicle of parliamentary control for the Crown over the Estates (especially in the reign of James VI and in the Coronation Parliament of Charles I in 1633). The Lords of the Articles represented the main parliamentary institution which the Covenanters demanded be abolished or at least reformed.[11]

A variety of proposals for constitutional reform emanated from the Tables. The most important of these focused on ratification of the clerical estate in Parliament, abolition/reform of the Lords of the Articles, parliamentary control over executive and judicial appointments (Privy Councillors, Officers of State, and Ordinary and Extraordinary Lords of Session), and the convening of Parliament on a regular basis. Demands for greater parliamentary freedom were based on the need for each of the estates to elect its own representatives to the Lords of the Articles (as opposed to being Crown nominees) and the guarantee of parliamentary freedom of speech and voting rights (including the abolition of proxy voting), whilst any member of Parliament was to be allowed to hand in any bill or supplication to the Articles when that body was sitting. Collectively, these demands mark a reaction against the constitutional abuses of the Scottish administration of Charles I, especially that of the Parliament of 1633.

The gentry were particularly to the fore in the demand for constitutional reform, but they also sought recognition of and an increase in their parliamentary power. Clearly, the abolition of the clerical estate created a problem as to the constitution of Parliament. Not only were the Three Estates of the Scottish Parliament to be redefined as nobility, commissioners of the shires, and commissioners of the burghs, but voting rights were to be restricted to members of Parliament only. In addition, the relative voting strength of the nobility was to be decreased by the insistence that nobles who also held high office as Officers of State were to enjoy one vote only and not two votes (as an individual member of the nobility per se and as an Officer of State). Yet this decrease in the relative voting power of the nobility was to be further emphasised by a doubling in the voting strength of the gentry. Each shire had been traditionally been represented in Parliament by two commissioners, but the shire enjoyed only one vote and not two (based on the commissioners). This disadvantage was to be rectified with each individual commissioner receiving an individual vote. Hence the voting power of the parliamentary gentry was to be effectively doubled. The cutting edge of the gentry within the Covenanting Movement and its pivotal role in the Scottish localities was to be matched by an increased parliamentary status.

In reality, the programme of constitutional reform articulated in 1639 and issued to the Lords of the Articles secured legislative enactment in the parliamentary sessions of 2–11 June 1640 and 15 July–17 November 1641, especially in the former session. Commenting on the June 1640 session Sir James Balfour emphasised the dimunition of the royal prerogative in Scotland at the expense of an increase in parliamentary powers. This parliamentary session had been:

> the reall grattest change at ane blow that euer hapned
> to this churche and staite thesse 600 years baypast;
> for in effecte it ouerturned not onlie the ancient
> state gouernment, bot fettered monarchie with chynes
> and sett new limitts and marckes, beyond wich it was
> not legally to proceed.[12]

The act 'anent the constitution of the present and all future Parliaments' of 2 June 1640 fundamentally effected the operation of parliamentary politics by doubling the voting strength of the shires. The gentry had now emerged as a more powerful parliamentary grouping at the expense of both the nobility and burgesses. Each burgh was represented by one commissioner, with the exception of Edinburgh, the capital, which was represented by two commissioners. Scrutiny of the numerical composition of various parliamentary sessions, 1639–51, allows for an assessment of the relative voting strength between the Three Estates. Fifty-six nobles, 50 gentry representing 29 shires, and 57 burgesses representing 56 burghs were present in Parliament on 17 August 1641 (the date when Charles I himself was present for the first time in the Scottish Parliament since 1633). The combined voting strength of the shires and burghs amounted to 157 (50 gentry x2 + 57 burgesses). The Convention of Estates which met on 22 June 1643 was composed of 56 nobles, 44 gentry representing 26 shires, and 54 burgesses representing 53 burghs. Hence the combined voting strength of the shires and burghs amounted to 142 (44 gentry x2 + 54 burgesses).[13] Not only had noble voting power been diminished, but the collective strength of the shires and burghs could now veto any legislation not to their liking. This becomes more pertinent given the fact that the gentry and burgesses provided the backbone behind the Covenanting Movement and that radicalism had a limited base within the noble estate. The bulk of the nobility who chose to take their places in the House were predominantly conservatives or pragmatic Royalists. On the one hand, this ensured that the radical leadership under Argyll could rely on the shires and burghs for the factional strength of their parliamentary base to ensure the enactment of controversial legislation or legislation that was unpopular with conservative and pragmatic Royalist nobles. On the other hand, electoral manipulation of elections for the commissioners of the shires and burghs was required by conservative and pragmatic Royalist nobles to secure factional dominance in the Engagement Parliament of 1648.[14]

Irrespective of faction, the shires and burghs had now become a parliamentary force to be reckoned with. This strength was recognised by Edward Hyde, Earl of Clarendon himself, commenting on political events in Scotland, 1650–51. Faced with the prospect of military conquest by Cromwellian forces, a patriotic accommodation had been initiated to bring together the Scottish political factions with the king (who was crowned on 2 January 1651) to defend the Scottish home-land. The Sixth, Seventh, and Eighth Sessions of the Second Triennial Parliament were largely concerned with this issue, most notably concerning the repeal of the Act of Classes (eventually repealed on 3 June 1651). According to Clarendon:

> The King himself grew very popular, and, by his
> frequent conferences with the knights and burgesses,
> he got any thing passed in the Parliament which he
> desired. He caused many infamous acts to be
> repealed, and provided for the raising of an army,
> whereof himself was general; and no exceptions were
> taken to those officers who had formerly served the
> King [his father].[15]

By 1651 the political dynamic of the shires and burghs had been clearly recognised by Charles II who exploited its potential for Royalist ends. Patriotic zeal and the national interest had infused the ranks of the shires and the burghs as opposed to factionalism. Indeed, such patriotism had been put to good use on 11 March 1651. 'A grate meitting' of the Committee of Estates established on 30 December 1650 (during the Sixth Session of the Second Triennial Parliament, 26 November–30 December 1650) was held to decide whether or not the Seventh Session should convene as per scheduled on 13 March. Balfour asserts that Chancellor Loudoun, Cassillis, and 'ther factione' attempted to prorogue the Seventh Session to a later date. However, the defeat of their motion of Parliament appears to have been due largely to the shire and burgh votes. A total of 16 nobles, 11 gentry, eight burgesses, and three military officials attended the diet of 13 March. In this instance, the votes of the shires and burghs had ensured that national interests outweighed factional ones.[16]

At the opposite end of the historical spectrum, this dynamic as evidenced in 1639–41 was sustained after the close of Parliament on 17 November 1641 and was further tapped to secure the calling of the 1643 Convention of Estates.

The 1643 Convention of Estates

Parliamentary supremacy was maintained after the close of the 1641 Parliament through three parliamentary interval committees; the Committee for the Common Burdens, the Committee for the Brotherly Assistance, and the Committee for the Conservators of the Peace. Although a new Privy Council had also been formed and despite the attempts of James, third Marquis of Hamilton to initiate a Royalist revival through the Privy Council following his return to Scotland in June 1642, the Privy Council was bypassed by the leadership of the radical oligarchy which devoted its resources to the three interval committees. Effective political power in Scotland was transferred from the Scottish Parliament to the three interval committees.[17] Indeed, these three committees were to play a crucial role in determining Scottish military involvement in Ireland (following the Ulster Rebellion) and the English Civil War. With the outbreak of the English conflict, the interaction between the three kingdoms of the British archipelago moved on to a different level, with Charles I as the central figure and catalyst for the three kingdoms. Whilst Charles I had sought the aid of the English Short Parliament to suppress the Scottish Covenanting rebellion, following the outbreak of the English Civil War in 1642 he now looked for Scottish military aid in his struggle with the English Parliament. At the same time, the English Parliament wanted Scottish aid to fight Charles and the Royalists. Scottish Covenanting commitment to an allegiance with the English Parliament (albeit this allegiance was not unconditional) was ultimately determined by events which took place in May 1643.

By May 1643 the radical oligarchy had succeeded in marginalising the Privy Council as a viable political institution for a resurgence in Royalism and as a forum to galvanise a Royalist party. Moreover, the leadership of the radical oligarchy had effectively decided that intervention in the English Civil War on the side of the English Parliament was required. Yet, in constitutional terms, the next plenary session of the

Scottish Parliament was scheduled for June 1644. As early as 10 January 1643 the Conservators of the Peace had thought that the state of affairs warranted the indiction of a Parliament.[18] The constitutional option of a Convention of Estates was the vehicle employed to secure this intervention and the approval of the calling of a Convention of Estates[19] was secured through the parliamentary interval committees in tandem with the Privy Council. The key dates in this process centred on 11 and 12 May 1643. On these dates tripartite meetings of the Committee for the Conservators of the Peace, the Committee for Common Burdens-Brotherly Assistance, and the Privy Council convened. Although the Commission for the Common Burdens and the Commission for the Brotherly Assistance were separate and distinct commissions in constitutional terms, they actually sat as a single commission and enjoyed identical membership.

On 12 May a power struggle took place at the tripartite diet which resulted in a Convention of Estates being called for 22 June 1643. Thirty-eight commissioners were present at the morning session of 12 May. The morning session was crucial as it approved the principle of the necessity of calling a Convention of Estates and it set the date for 22 June. Robert Baillie, a contemporary participant in Covenanting affairs and a future member of the Westminster Assembly, noted that 'of all the three bodies, not 10 were opposit'.[20] Accepting the attendance data of 38 commissioners, then a clear majority of 28 were in favour of the motions discussed. Six of the ten opposition votes consisted primarily of conservative and pragmatic Royalist nobles; Hamilton, Southesk, Callander, Glencairn, Morton, and Dunfermline. The remaining four opposition votes were based on four Officers of State; Sir Thomas Hope of Craighall, Lord Advocate, Sir James Carmichael of that ilk, Treasurer Depute, Sir John Hamilton of Orbiston, Justice Clerk, and Sir Alexander Gibson of Durie, Clerk Register.[21]

The afternoon session of 12 May was devoted to the preparation of correspondence to Charles I informing him of the decision. Six nobles and three Officers of State who had been present at the morning session absented themselves from the afternoon diet. Hamilton, Morton, Glencairn, Lauderdale, Southesk, Dalhousie, Callander, Carmichael of that ilk, Hope of Craighall, and Hamilton of Orbiston formed this grouping. One laird who had been present at the morning session, Sir Patrick Hepburne of Wauchton (Haddington), was absent from the afternoon diet.[22] Therefore the votes of the gentry and burgesses, allied to that of the leading radical nobles such as Argyll, had been crucial in the calling of the 1643 Convention of Estates.

The political importance of the votes of the shires and burghs was further emphasised when the Convention of Estates convened on 22 June. Despite the fact that Charles had agreed by 10 June that the Convention could meet, but should only consider the supply of the Scottish army in Ireland and the more efficient payment of the Brotherly Assistance, debate was still rife concerning the powers of the Convention. Political tension had also increased with the exposure of the king's alleged involvement in the Antrim Plot.[23] Factional strife over the powers of the Convention was focused on a parliamentary session committee appointed to determine the constitution of the Convention and construct appropriate legislation along these lines. On the one hand, was the Convention restricted to the remit by the king as per 10 June (as Hamilton argued)? Or, on the other hand, should the Convention have no restriction of power as it had been called on the authority of the Privy Council, the Conservators of the Peace, and the Common Burdens-Brotherly Assistance Committee (as Argyll argued)?[24]

The Committee anent the Act of Constitution was formed on 24 June and sat until 26 June. It was composed of nine per estate, yielding 27 members in total. In accordance with procedures established in 1640–41, each estate elected its own representatives to the committee. The limited extent of radicalism within the noble estate was reflected in noble representation to the committee. Only two of the noble members, Argyll and Balmerino, were radicals. The remaining seven noble members were either conservatives or pragmatic Royalists; Hamilton, Lanark, Lauderdale, Southesk, Roxburgh, Morton, and Callander.[25] On 26 June the session committee reported its conclusions to the House. It concluded that the Convention was a 'Lawfull free and full Convention' with the power to 'treate Consult and determine in all matters that sall be proposed unto thame als freelie and ampli as any Convention quhilk has beene within this kingdome at any time bygane'.[26] Despite their clear numerical superiority in noble representation, conservative and pragmatic Royalist nobles had been defeated. In turn, Argyll and Balmerino had relied on the votes of the shire and burgh representatives to secure the legality of the Convention. The commitment of the shire and burgh representatives to the cause was likewise stressed by Baillie: 'all the Barrones and Burghs, without exception of one, were for the common weell'.[27] Gentry and burghal representation included noted Covenanting activists such as Sir Archibald Johnston of Wariston (Edinburgh), Sir Thomas Hope of Kerse (Stirling), Robert Barclay (Irvine), John Semple (Dumbarton), Thomas Bruce (Stirling), Patrick Leslie (Aberdeen), and Alexander Douglas (Banff). The geographic and political influence of the House of Argyll was asserted by the inclusion of Sir Duncan Campbell of Auchinbreck (Argyll), Sir William Mure of Rowallan (Ayr), Robert Barclay (Irvine), and John Semple (Dumbarton). In correspondence with Johnston of Wariston on 10 January 1643, Baillie had observed that:

> In all the West I know not one of the Barrons so meet
> as need were; Rowalland is among the best. For
> Burrowes, Mr Robert Barclay farr best: John Semple may
> be thought on.[28]

Certainly Baillie was commenting on his detailed knowledge of the political communities within his own geographic domain, and there are no voting records of the session committee's proceedings between 24 and 26 June. But given Wariston's close relationship with the Marquis of Argyll, Baillie's correspondence with Wariston in January 1643 may well provide an indication of the nature and structure of factional management within the radical oligarchy.

When the Act of Constitution was approved by the Convention, despite the opposition of 19 nobles (including Hamilton and most probably the contingent of conservative and pragmatic Royalist nobles) and one laird, Hamilton and Lanark withdrew from the Convention leaving Argyll and the radical oligarchy in a position of supreme ascendancy. The 1643 Convention then went on to negotiate the Solemn League and Covenant and the Treaty of Military Assistance with diplomatic commissioners of the English Parliament. The Scottish Covenanting Movement would now become fully embroiled in the wars of the British archipelago. Covenanting military commitment was to be traded for the imposition of Presbyterianism on a British basis. The votes of the shires and burghs had therefore been crucial in securing the constitutional legitimacy of the 1643 Convention. The decisions and proceedings of the Committee anent the Act of Constitution, 24–26 June, clearly mark a fundamental historical timepoint in the supremacy of the radical oligarchy within the Covenanting Movement.

The emergence of a Scottish Commons, 1644–46

The political muscle of the shires and the burghs, as evidenced in the 1643 Convention of Estates, was consolidated during the First Session of the First Triennial Parliament (4 June–29 July 1644). This muscle was flexed most notably over the punishment of rebels involved in the uprising of Sir John Gordon of Haddo and other north-eastern Royalists in March–April 1644. The Second Session of the Convention of Estates had convened from 3 January–3 June in four blocks; the third block, stretching from 10–16 April, had met specifically to consider the implications of the rising and construct appropriate policy options.[29] When Parliament met, the issue was dealt with almost immediately with the formation of a specialised session committee, the Committee for Processes, on 5 June. A separate session committee was appointed on 5 June for the examination of witnesses in the process against Lord Banff for participating in the uprising.[30] Two days later on 7 June the House announced that the examination of those rebels who were in custody was to commence. According to Sir James Balfour, this action was due to lobbying and pressure from the commissioners of the shires led by Johnston of Wariston (Edinburgh) as 'speaker for the barrons'.[31] Wariston therefore demanded that action should be taken against 'such of the chief delinquents of the north and south, that has been most active in this late unnatural rebellion, and are now in hold'.[32]

The leading role of the shires in the punishment of malignants continued throughout June 1644. As a result of pressure exerted by the parliamentary gentry, a Committee for Trying of Delinquents was established on 12 June to deal with the case of Gordon of Haddo and seven other local gentry who had been in rebellion. Four per estate supplemented by three additional gentry employed in a legal capacity (Sir John Hamilton of Orbiston, Justice Clerk, and two Justice Deputes) formed its membership. One of the shire representatives, Sir George Dundas of Maner (Linlithgow), emerged as the spokesman for the committee, despite the presence of Linlithgow, Weymes, Barganie, and Elphinstone as the noble members. Dundas of Maner reported that Sir John Gordon of Haddo and Captain John Logie were guilty of high treason and should be punished by loss of life, land, and goods. Conservatives/pragmatic Royalists enjoyed a majority of noble representation on the Committee for Trying of Delinquents and their submission to the shires may simply have been an exercise in realpolitik in attempting to distance themselves from the committee's decision of punishment by death.[33]

The influence of the shires and burghs in the 1644 Parliament was not restricted to the punishment of rebels but also extended to membership of parliamentary committees, especially as a reaction against contrived noble dominance of committees. Shire and burghal membership of parliamentary committees was regulated by legislation enacted on 26 July 1644. Firstly, lists were to be drawn up for the commissioners of shires and burghs from which committee members were to be taken. Secondly, any of the estates could add to the lists, but only with the consent of the relevant estate and that estate was to

be given 24 hours notice to consider the qualification of the person/
persons to be added. Thirdly, any additions to the lists were to be based
solely on members of Parliament or such as were qualified to hold that
office.[34] According to Sir James Balfour, this act was 'giuen in by the
barrons and burrowes' and it secured approval only 'after ane
continuatione and a longe debait betuix some noblemen, the barrons
and burrowes'. In particular, the nobility appeared to have perceived
the act to be 'ane directe violatione of the liberties of parliament'.[35]
This legislation was not of a short-term nature but was to apply 'in all
tymecomeing in ony Commissioun yt shall be granted in parliat or
conventioune of estates ffor qtsomevir bussines or effaires'.[36] It would
appear, at the very least, that the shires and burghs had behaved in a
pro-active manner to control their membership of committees.
Alternatively, it may also have been a reaction against attempts by the
nobility to influence shire and burgh membership of committees.

That the shires and burghs had acted to secure their own interests
through the vehicle of parliamentary enactment was clear. However,
they were not averse to breaking parliamentary regulations when it
suited them. A Committee for Rectifying Valuations was appointed on
1 June 1649 during the Third Session of the Second Triennial
Parliament (23 May–7 August 1649). It was issued with the remit of
deciding on the necessary actions to be taken for rectifying valuations
in the shires. Composed of four per estate, the burghal estate was in
breach of parliamentary regulations. Both John Jaffray (Aberdeen) and
Alexander Jaffray (Aberdeen) were included on the committee, despite
the fact that the burgh of Aberdeen was only entitled to representation
by one commissioner. The committee in question was a session
committee and non-parliamentary membership of session committees,
although not necessarily uncommon, was not usually based on
commissioners from the same burgh.[37] Of more significance was the
breach in parliamentary regulations at the outset of the Sixth Session
of the First Triennial Parliament on 3 November 1646. With the
exception of Edinburgh, burghal representation was based on one
commissioner per burgh. However, seven additional burghs sent two
commissioners (according to the parliamentary rolls); Dundee,
Linlithgow, St Andrews, Haddington, Anstruther Easter, Dunbar, and
Crail. During the same parliamentary session the burghal estate reacted
against what it perceived as a breach of regulations by the shires.
William Grierson of Bargattoun is recorded in the parliamentary rolls
of 3 November 1646 as representing the Stewartry of Kirkcudbright
which is recorded under the shires. Edward Edgar (Edinburgh), for the

burghal estate, protested against the inclusion of the Stewartry as no valid commission had been received. Such evidence also indicates that political tension could exist between the shires and the burghs.[38]

Following the eventual defeat of Montrose at Philiphaugh on 13 September 1645, the punishment of rebels also occupied the attention of the Fifth Session of the First Triennial Parliament (26 November 1645–4 February 1646). This culminated in the enactment of the Act of Classes of 8 January 1646.[39] Four executions had been approved by the House on 16 January and despite the enthusiasm of the Commission of the Kirk to continue with the execution of 'malignants' it was decided instead that fining of malignants should take place on a national basis. In accordance with this, a specialised interval committee, the Committee for Monies, was established on 3 February. The committee was divided into a northern and a southern section, although cross-over between sessions was allowed. The southern section was to be based in Edinburgh and consisted of four per estate, whereas the northern section enjoyed a smaller membership of three per estate.[40] Ninety-five sederunts of the Committee for Monies (South) are recorded between 7 February and 26 October 1646. Cassillis was elected as President of the southern section at the first diet on 7 February and when Cassillis was absent Burleigh presided on nine occasions. However, one of the shire representatives, Sir John Weymes of Bogie (Fife), also presided at five diets. When Weymes of Bogie was President, four nobles were in attendance (Burleigh, Marischal, Coupar, and Arbuthnot), albeit Bogie was present at four diets where Burleigh presided. Therefore a commissioner of the shire was taking precedence over noble representatives. What makes this all the more remarkable is that Weymes of Bogie has the lowest attendance record of any laird on the southern section, attending 49 out of 95 diets (52%).[41] This was not the last occasion when a laird secured the presidency of a committee. At the close of the Sixth Session of the Second Triennial Parliament (26 November–30 December 1650) a new Committee of Estates had been formed, which sat between 2 January and 12 March 1651 (the Seventh Session convened on 13 March). Several subcommittees of this Committee of Estates were established including a Committee for Grievances. This subcommittee appears to have continued to sit throughout the Seventh and Eighth Sessions (13 March–31 March and 23 May–3 June). Two sets of additions were made to the Committee for Grievances during the latter session; eight gentry and one burgess were added on 24 May, whilst three gentry and one burgess were added on 31 May. Sir John Shaw of Greenock (Renfrew) was one of the shire additions of 31 May and he was appointed as convener of the committee. The membership of the original subcommittee had consisted of three nobles, five gentry, three burgesses, and one military official. As a result of the additions of 24 and 31 May, the redefined membership was now overwhelmingly based on 16 gentry. Numerical superiority had been matched with political influence.[42]

Prior to the close of the Fifth Session of the First Triennial Parliament on 4 February 1646, the commissioners of the shires and burghs repelled an attempt to increase the political and parliamentary influence of conservative/pragmatic Royalist nobles. This occurred with the commission to the Committee of Estates on 3 February and was concerned with the renewal of the diplomatic section to negotiate with the English Parliament. Throughout the 1640s diplomatic commissions had been staffed by radical personnel and controlled by the radical oligarchy. This dominance was challenged by Lanark and Glencairn who attempted to have the conservative/pragmatic Royalist Crawford-Lindsay (who was currently President of Parliament) included as supernumerary on the diplomatic commission. This was essentially a ploy to weaken radical influence and provides an indication of the increased profile of parliamentary conservatism which had become apparent throughout 1644 and 1645.[43] The issue was ultimately decided in three key stages. Firstly, a vote was taken to decide whether or not Crawford-Lindsay (President of Parliament) should leave the House while the motion was being discussed. This initial vote decided that Crawford-Lindsay was not obliged to leave. Secondly, a further vote was taken to decide whether or not the issue should be remittted to and decided on by a parliamentary session committee. This option was 'caried be maniest voyces'.[44] The third and final stage rested with the session committee itself. Each estate elected its own representatives; Glencairn, Lanark, and Cassillis for the nobility, Sir Archibald Johnston of Wariston (Edinburgh), James MacDowall of Garthland (Wigtown), and Sir Thomas Ruthven of Frieland (Perth) for the shires, with Sir Alexander Wedderburne (Dundee), George Porterfield (Glasgow), and John Kennedy (Ayr) for the burghs. The session committee concluded that Crawford-Lindsay should *not* be included as a supernumerary on the diplomatic commission. Not only was this a personal snub and humiliation for Crawford-Lindsay, but in de facto political terms it was also a defeat for the noble estate itself. That Glencairn and Lanark, the instigators of the original motion, had been elected by the noble estate, provided a virtual mandate for their actions. The combined voting power of the shires and burghs, aided by Cassillis, had been sufficient to secure victory. Indeed, Johnston of Wariston (Edinburgh), George Porterfield (Glasgow), and John Kennedy (Ayr) were all noted radicals.[45]

What should be noted about this political episode is that the controversy arose *after the full membership* of the Committee of Estates had been named on 3 February. Crawford-Lindsay, in the capacity of President of Parliament, had been named as one of three supernumeraries for the nobility on the commission of 3 February; Leven was included as General of the Armed Forces and Callander as Lieutenant General. The Committee of Estates of 3 February 1646 consisted of four sections; the Committee of Estates (Scotland) which tended to reside in Edinburgh, the Committee of Estates (Ireland) to accompany the Scottish army in Ireland, the Committee of Estates (England) to accompany the Scottish army in England, and a diplomatic section to negotiate with the English Parliament. None of the three noble supernumeraries (nor the two shire and one burghal supernumeraries) were specifically allocated to any of the three sections.[46] The diplomatic section of the previous Committee of Estates of 8 March 1645 was composed of Argyll, Loudoun, Balmerino, and Lauderdale for the nobility, Johnston of Wariston (Edinburgh), George Dundas of Maner (Linlithgow), and Sir Charles Erskine of Cambuskenneth (Clackmannan) for the gentry, with Sir John Smith (Edinburgh), Hugh Kennedy (Ayr), and Robert Barclay (Irvine) for the burgesses. Radical influence prevailed on the diplomatic section, with conservative/pragmatic influence focused on Lauderdale.[47] Within this context, the attempt to have Crawford-Lindsay included as supernumerary on the diplomatic section must be interpreted as a ploy to rectify this situation and dilute radical influence whilst enhancing that of the conservatives/pragmatic Royalists. In constitutional terms, the exclusion of Crawford-Lindsay as supernumerary from the diplomatic section had the effect of also excluding Leven and Callander. The political resources of the radical oligarchy had proved too powerful for Glencairn, Lanark, and Crawford-Lindsay. That radical resources had been deliberately deployed to repel this challenge can be ascertained by consideration of additional pieces of evidence. Shortly before the close of the Fourth Session of the First Triennial Parliament (24 July–7 August 1645), additions had been made on 6 August to the diplomatic contingent of 8 March. No radical nobles were included on these additions, which consisted of *Crawford-Lindsay*, *Lanark*, and Marischal. Sir John Hamilton of Orbiston (Renfrew), Justice Clerk, Sir William Cochrane of Cowdoun (Ayr), and Robert Meldrum of Burghlie (Fife) were added for the shires, with Sir Alexander Wedderburne (Dundee),

William Glendinning (Kirkcudbright), and *John Kennedy (Ayr)* added for the burghs. Yet when the full commission to the Committee of Estates was issued on 3 February, it renewed the acts of commission to the Committees of Estates of 26 July 1644 and 8 March 1645, but made *no mention* of the additions of 6 August 1645. Therefore legislation appears to have been constructed to keep Lanark and Crawford-Lindsay off the diplomatic section. Whilst all three burgess additions of 6 August were included on the full commission of 3 February, there were no places for Marischal or the three shire additions. Therefore the radical leadership had succeeded in excluding Crawford-Lindsay and Lanark from the diplomatic section, despite their addition on 6 August. Moreover, John Kennedy (one of the burghal additions of 6 August) had been a member of the session committee of 3 February which had barred Crawford-Lindsay.[48]

The shires and burghs as the backbone of the Covenanting Movement in terms of parliamentary human resources

The importance of the shires and burghs to the organisation of the Covenanting Movement was reflected in their employment on parliamentary committees. Following the abolition of the Lords of the Articles, an elaborate committee structure developed, based on session and interval committees. Session committees were appointed for the duration of a parliamentary session (although they could also be renewed as interval committees). Interval committees were appointed to sit during parliamentary sessions. The most important interval committee, the Committee of Estates initiated in 1640, was originally descended from the Tables and was established on a regular basis from 1640–1651. In de facto political terms, it acted as a provisional government between parliamentary sessions, albeit it owed its constitutional legitimacy to Parliament itself.

The parliamentary committee structure took on a crucial role in the efficient passage of legislation through the House during a period of unprecedented military and political commitment in England and Ireland, as well as the administration of the kingdom of Scotland itself. The numerous parliamentary sessions highlighted this importance, with the First Triennial Parliament (1644–47) composed of six sessions and the Second Triennial Parliament (1648–51) composed of eight sessions. In general, inclusion on session committees adhered to membership of Parliament, whereas non-parliamentary gentry and burgesses regularly gained membership to interval committees. Given the fact that each shire was represented by two commissioners and each burgh by one commissioner (with the exception of Edinburgh), non-parliamentary membership of gentry and burgesses on interval committees is therefore unsurprising, and was not strictly illegal in constitutional terms. What it does indicate, however, is the commitment for the Covenanting Movement from the Scottish localities. The central role of the shires and burghs to committee membership can be evidenced by recourse to empirical data.

The First Session of the First Triennial Parliament sat from 4 June to 29 July 1644, after the Second Session of the Convention of Estates had ended on 3 June. Eighteen session committees and 11 interval committees have been analysed for the First Session. Twenty-seven nobles, 62 gentry, and 22 burgesses were nominated to the 18 session committees, whilst 50 nobles, 91 gentry, and 56 burgesses were nominated to the 11 interval committees. Only eight of the 62 gentry (13%) and two of the 22 burgesses (9%) included on the 18 session committees were not members of Parliament as per 4 June 1644. Sixty-five of the 91 gentry (71%) and 36 of the 56 burgesses included on the 11 interval committees were not members of Parliament as per 4 June. With regard to the data concerning interval committees, it should be noted that 26 of the 28 gentry and nine of the 15 burgesses included on the interval commission of 19 July 1644, the Committee for the Northern Business, were non-members of Parliament. Discounting these figures still provides a residue of 39 non-parliamentary gentry and 27 non-parliamentary burgesses employed on interval committees.[49] Committee membership of specialised regional committees was often based not only on non-parliamentarians, but also largely on local gentry. Acting on a petition from Sir William Forbes of Craigievar and Arthur Forbes of Echt the commissioners of the shires for Aberdeen during the Fifth Session of the First Triennial Parliament, 26 November 1645–4 February 1646, an interval committee was formed on 3 February to consider the losses suffered by the shire of Aberdeen. The formation of such a committee was in keeping with localised committees formed by previous sessions of the First Triennial Parliament; for example, the Committee for the Burned Lands in Perthshire (interval committee) and the Committee for Trying the Lands in Perthshire possessed, burned, or wasted by the enemy (interval committee) of 7 August 1645. The vast majority of the Committee anent the Losses of the Sheriffdom of Aberdeen were non-members of Parliament (as per 26 November 1645). No nobles were included on the committee and none of the 23 gentry representatives were current members of Parliament. Interestingly, neither Forbes of Craigievar nor Forbes of

Echt secured membership of the committee, despite their central role in its formation. Indeed, their services appear to have been required on interval committees of national importance; Forbes of Craigievar and Forbes of Echt were both included on the Committee for Monies (northern section) (3 February). Craigievar was also included on the Committee for Losses (3 February). Only one of the five burgess members of the Committee anent the Losses of the Sheriffdom of Aberdeen, Robert Farquhar (Aberdeen), was a current member of Parliament, albeit Patrick Leslie, Alexander Jaffray, William More, and Walter Cochrane were all noted north-eastern Covenanting activists. In similar fashion, A Committee for the Revaluation of the Parish of Ayr was formed on 29 June 1649 during the Third Session of the Second Triennial Parliament (23 May–7 August 1649). Its membership consisted solely of three gentry and five burgesses and only Hugh Kennedy (Ayr) was a current member of Parliament (as per 23 May). In these instances, the member of Parliament may well have acted as a co-ordinating link between Parliament and the regional committee in the localities.[50]

Equality per estate was the norm regarding representation on session committees. For example, the Committee for the Irish Business of 28 November 1646 was composed of three per estate.[51] The anti-aristocratic nature of the radical regime established after the defeat of the Engager invasion of England in September 1648 and the Whiggamore Raid on Edinburgh was often exposed in the staffing of committees of the parliamentary radical regime. The limited extent of radicalism within the nobility was reflected by the fact that only 16 nobles were present in the Second Session of the Second Triennial Parliament which convened on 4 January 1649; this represents a reduction of 40 nobles compared to the Engagement Parliament of 2 March 1648.[52] That the human resources of the radical regime were based on the commitment and services of the gentry and burgesses was often reflected in committee representation. The Second Session of the Second Triennial Parliament sat from 4 January until 16 March, although it was based essentially on two subsessions centred on the Proclamation of the Prince of Wales as Charles II King of Great Britain, France, and Ireland on 5 February following the execution of his father. The first subsession is dated from 4 January until 3 February, when the session was adjourned until 6 February. The Estates reconvened on 5 February, however, and the second subsession ran until 16 March. Twenty-four nobles, 42 gentry, and 40 burgesses were employed within the committee structure of the second subsession.

Thirteen of the 42 gentry (31%) and 16 of the 40 burgesses (40%) were not members of Parliament as per 4 January 1649. One of the 13 gentry and three of the 16 burgesses who were not members of Parliament as per 4 January 1649 had sat in the Engagement Parliament commencing on 2 March 1648; Sir Adam Hepburne of Humbie (Haddington), John Short (Stirling), William Glendinning (Kirkcudbright), and Gilbert More (Banff) represented this grouping of personnel who had been part of the radical minority present in the Engagement Parliament.[53]

Conclusion

Until recently, the historiography of the Covenanting Movement tended to underestimate the role of the gentry and burgesses within the movement and the political dynamic and impetus which they gave to the cause. Within the Parliament of Scotland, the commissioners of the shires and burghs enjoyed enhanced parliamentary status and exercised parliamentary power at the expense of the nobility *in relative terms*. In essence this stemmed from the doubling of the vote of the shires as a result of the legislation of 2 June 1640. Moreover, the commissioners of the shires acted as a separate parliamentary estate and were not merely adjuncts of the nobility. Not only had the shires and burghs been to the fore in the articulation of a programme of constitutional reform which secured enactment in 1640–41, but their votes had been crucial in the calling of the 1643 Convention of Estates and securing the constitutional legitimacy of the Convention as per the session committee of 24 June. This momentum was maintained throughout 1644–46 and throughout the period 1639–1651 the shires and burghs provided the pool of human resources for the staffing of parliamentary session and interval committees. Whilst the power and role of the nobility should not be underemphasised, the shires and burghs could not be ignored in terms of factional management by influential nobles such as Argyll and Hamilton. A 'Scottish Commons' had clearly emerged within the single-chamber Scottish Parliament.

NOTES

1. J R Young, *The Scottish Parliament 1639–1661: A Political and Constitutional Analysis* (Edinburgh, 1996), 304–323.

2. H G Koenigsberger, *Estates and Revolutions. Essays in Early Modern European History* (London, 1971), 126, 225; R. Bonney, *The European Dynastic States 1494–1660* (Oxford, 1991), 316.

3. Bonney, *The European Dynastic States*, 317.

4. R S Rait, *The Parliaments of Scotland* (Glasgow, 1924), 165.

5. D Stevenson, *The Government of Scotland Under the Covenanters 1637–1651*, SHS, (Edinburgh, 1982), 174–175.

6. *APS*, v, 260–261; Rait, *The Parliaments of Scotland*, p.168; J Goodare, 'Who was the Scottish Parliament?', *Parliamentary History*, 14, part 2, (1995), 174.

7. A I Macinnes, 'The Scottish Constitution, 1638–1651. The Rise and Fall of Oligarchic Centralism', in J Morrill (ed), *The Scottish National Covenant in its British Context 1638–51* (Edinburgh, 1990), 106–134; A I Macinnes, *Charles I and the Making of the Covenanting Movement 1625–1641* (Edinburgh, 1991), 183–206; A I Macinnes, 'Early Modern Scotland: The Current State of Play', *SHR*, LXXIII (1994), 39, 41–42.

8. Cf Young, *The Scottish Parliament*.

9. See J J Scally, 'Counsel in Crisis: James, third Marquis of Hamilton and the Bishops' Wars, 1638–1640', 21.

10. See Macinnes, *Charles I and the Making of the Covenanting Movement*, 166–172, 186–194.

11. Rait, *The Parliaments of Scotland*, 367–371; C S Terry, *The Scottish Parliament. Its Constitution and Procedure 1603–1707* (Glasgow, 1905), 104, 108–111.

12. Sir James Balfour, *Historical Works*, four volumes, J Haig (ed), (Edinburgh, 1824–25), 379.

13. *APS*, v, 331–332, vi, i, 3–4.

14. See tabular data in Young, *The Scottish Parliament*, 332–333. For the Engagement Parliament, see ibid, 195–196.

15. Edward Hyde, Earl of Clarendon, *The History of the Rebellion and the Civil Wars in England*, W D Macray (ed), six volumes (Oxford, 1888), volume IV, 172.

16. Balfour, *Historical Works*, IV, 253–254; SRO PA 11/10, Register of the Committee of Estates, 2 January–12 March 1651, f 105.

17. SRO PA 14/1, Register of the Committee for Common Burdens and the Commission for Receiving the Brotherly Assistance, 19 November 1641–10 January 1645, ff 1–266; SRO PA 14/2, Proceedings of the Scots Commissioners for Conserving the Articles of the Treaty, 22 September 1642–8 July 1643,

ff 1–72; *RPCS*, P H Brown (ed), 2nd series, volumes i–viii (1625–1660), (Edinburgh, 1899–1906), vii, 142–449; Young, *The Scottish Parliament*, 54–82.

18. SRO PA 14/2, f 21. When this decision was taken by the Conservators of the Peace, four nobles and three gentry declared that 'they were not in thair judgement against the calling' of a Parliament 'bot onelie against the tyme of supplicating for it presentlie' (ibid). Hamilton, Lanark, Glencairn, and Callander formed the grouping of four nobles, whilst Sir William Douglas of Cavers (Roxburgh), Sir Alexander Erskine of Dun (Forfar), and Sir Robert Graham of Morphie (Kincardine) constitute the three gentry in question. Given the developments of May and June 1643, it appears that the actions of Hamilton and his cohorts on 10 January 1643 were merely designed as a stalling device.

19. Conventions of Estates were usually called to discuss and/or legislate on matters of a limited nature, such as taxation (Rait, *The Parliaments of Scotland*, 143–157). However, it is also the case that the 'Convention of 1643–44 marks the complete assimilation of Convention to Parliament in point of membership' (ibid, 156).

20. R Baillie, *Letters and Journals 1637–62*, D. Laing (ed), three volumes (Bannatyne Club, Edinburgh, 1841–42), II, 68.

21. Ibid; SRO PA 14/1, ff 224–225; SRO PA 14/2, f 61; *RPCS*, 2nd series, vii, 93–94.

22. *RPCS*, 2nd series, vii, 93–94.

23. E J Cowan, 'The Solemn League and Covenant', in R A Mason (ed), *Scotland and England, 1286–1815* (Edinburgh, 1987), 189; L Kaplan, 'Steps to War: the Scots and Parliament, 1642–1643', *Journal of British Studies*, IX (2), (1970), 58.

24. SRO Hamilton Papers GD 406/1/1887; Baillie, *Letters and Journals*, II, 72, 76–77, 80; *APS*, vi, i, 3–4, 6; G Burnet, *The Memoirs of the Lives and Actions of James and William, Dukes of Hamilton and Castleherald* (London, 1838), 233–234; *Historical Collections*, J. Rushworth (ed), eight volumes, (London, 1659–1701) volume II (ii), 466.

25. *APS*, vi, i, 6.

26. Ibid.

27. Baillie, *Letters and Journals*, II, 72.

28. Ibid, 42.

29. *APS*, vi, i, 60–95.

30. Ibid, 98.

31. Balfour, *Historical Works*, III, 177.

32. Ibid.

33. *APS*, vi, i, 103–104; Balfour, *Historical Works*, III, 196.

34. *APS*, vi, i, 215.

35. Balfour, *Historical Works*, III, 238.

36. *APS*, vi, i, 215.

37. *APS*, vi, ii, 389–390. One noble, two gentry, and one burgess were later added to the committee on 14 June (Ibid, 414).

38. Ibid, 612–613.

39. *APS*, vi, i, 474–612, 503–505.

40. Ibid, 521–532, 567–570.

41. SRO PA 14/3, Register of the Committee for Monies (South), 3 February–26 October 1646, ff 25–375.

42. *APS*, vi, ii, 631–633, 667, 675; SRO PA 11/10, f 19

43. Lauderdale had been appointed President of the Privy Council on 27 September 1643 (although the Council's proceedings were dominated by a clique of Argyll, Loudoun, Cassillis, and Balmerino) and President of the 1644 Parliament (*RPCS*, 2nd series, viii, 1–22, 63; *APS*, vi, i, 95–97). Lanark's increased prominence was reflected in his nomination to 10 of the 18 session committees of the 1644 Parliament (the highest figure for any noble) and by the parliamentary ratification on 22 July 1644 of his appointment as Sole Secretary of State (*APS*, vi, i, 95–283, 182–183). The parliamentary agenda was still controlled by the radical oligarchy, albeit a working relationship was sought with the leading conservative/pragmatic Royalists primarily to avoid an alignment with Montrose. Lauderdale had been elected as President of Parliament for the Second Session of the First Triennial Parliament (7 January–8 March 1645). Following his death on 17 January, Crawford-Lindsay was appointed the new President; he had previously been appointed Vice-President on 11 January (*APS*, vi, i, 285–286, 288, 296). Crawford-Lindsay also later acted as President of the Committee of Estates, October–November 1645 (Stevenson, *Government Under the Covenanters*, 57).

44. *APS*, vi, i, 579.

45. Ibid; Balfour, *Historical Works*, III, 371.

46. *APS*, vi, i, 570–571.

47. Ibid, 380–383.

48. *APS*, vi, i, 380–383, 457, 570–571, 579.

49. Ibid, vi, i, 95–96, 96–283.

50. Ibid, 203, 277–278, 450, 470, 474–475, 567–570, 572–573, 573–574; *APS*, vi, ii, 450.

51. *APS*, vi, i, 624.

52. *APS*, vi, ii, 3–4, 124–126.

53. Ibid, 3–4, 156, 124–126, 157–376.

CHAPTER 10

Retreat from Revolution: the Scottish Parliament and the Restored Monarchy, 1661–1663

Ronnie Lee

The Covenanting Revolution in Scotland was one of the landmark events in the history of the country, with long-term political and cultural implications. The establishment of a constitutional monarchy and a Presbyterian church on the back of military success by the Covenanters against King Charles I during the years 1638–41 are well known achievements. However, the nature of this revolution remains open to question. Some of the most innovative and thorough recent work has tended to stress the 'radical' nature of the Covenanting leadership, who quite consciously sought the establishment of political and religious checks on the power of the monarchy.[1] The prominent role played by the shire and burgh estates in carrying on the Covenanting cause suggests a social dimension to the conflict, but this is imperfectly understood — perhaps thankfully, no-one has yet postulated the kind of 'long-term social change' explanation of the Scottish conflict which has dogged studies of events in England.[2] Nor does it seem very likely that anybody will. The Scottish Revolution was surely, as far as we understand it at present, an explosive political event. However, perhaps we should be wary of labelling the groups and factions involved in the various events too rigidly. Can we really be certain that the sort of fundamentalist and/or progressive attributes suggested by a term like 'radical' are applicable in this context? Elite groups in mid-seventeenth century Scotland, as elsewhere, were not natural revolutionaries. In addition, our understanding at present is largely confined to events at the 'centre'. There are no local studies for the 1640s — and very few for the previous and subsequent periods. As such, we should perhaps remind ourselves that some of our conclusions about the nature of the revolution can only be tentative. One point, however, is worth stressing. The Covenanting Movement was itself born of reaction — to the arbitrary methods of government employed by Charles I; to religious and economic innovations; perhaps even to what was perceived as a threat to Scottish identity itself. Niels Steensgaard, commenting on R B Merriman's famous *Six Contemporaneous Revolutions*[3], which drew parallels between upheavals in different countries in the 1640s, remarked that the different events "'can only be seen as one if we rechristen them 'the six contemporaneous reactions'".[4] Perhaps we should keep this qualification in mind when we are discussing the course and nature of the events in Scotland.

Moreover, there is surely room for doubt about the numbers of those, throughout the country as a whole, who maintained a consistent and unflinching ideological position. The Covenanters faced outright opponents, but as time passed it seems that many individuals were prone to wobble in their allegiance; for example, over the handing over of the king to the English in 1646, and in the lead up to the Engagement of 1647–48.[5] This is unsurprising, because in some respects the Covenanters had been following policies since 1641 which were in essence reactive, when they had to respond to events unfolding elsewhere in the British Isles. We should not underestimate the effect of confusion, fear, and uncertainty. It has also been noted that by 1651 the country as a whole was exhausted by the demands of war and other hardships, including plague.[6] If we add to this nine years of foreign military occupation after the Battle of Worcester in September 1651, is it any wonder that by 1660 most of the country was more than ready to reject what was perceived to be the cause of the kingdom's woes — the Covenanting revolution itself?. What had seemed necessary to most in 1638 was eschewed after the return of Charles II from exile in May 1660. The Restoration Parliament, meeting in three sessions in each of the years 1661–3, proved consistently and overwhelmingly loyal to the restored monarch. Once again, we should be careful not to equate this sentiment too readily with the country as a whole, but it seems safe to assume that most people welcomed the potential return of stability and independence which the monarchy promised. The underlying problems of the regal union had not been resolved — as subsequent events would demonstrate — but for the moment Scots were clearly determined to consign to history the conflicts they euphemistically referred to as the 'troubles'.

I

In his opening speech to the Scottish Parliament on 1 January 1661, the King's Commissioner, John, Earl of Middleton, exhorted the Parliament to condemn the measures passed by the Covenanters and restore the king's prerogative powers.[7] His words did not fall on deaf ears. Parliament was well attended, but more significant were the attitudes of those present. A recent study has shown that less than half of the 75 peers present had been involved with the Covenanting Parliaments. Even more striking is the fact that somewhat less than one-third of the shire and burgh commissioners had previous parliamentary experience (although some others had served on local committees, or had been active in burgh politics).[8] Thus, a large majority in Parliament can in a sense be regarded as 'new' men, without prominent records or noticeably strong allegiances. There is evidence for management of the elections, but we cannot discount the possibility of a genuine Royalist reaction. Julia Buckroyd has noted the contemporary view that there was a groundswell of antipathy towards ministers, who were, of course, closely associated with the Covenants.[9] What is clear is that Parliament as a whole had no Covenanting axe to grind; its proceedings reveal consistent loyalty to the restored monarch.

Middleton proceeded cautiously during the opening weeks of the Parliament. His instructions make no mention of church government, perhaps highlighting the wariness at Court over this issue. The priority was to secure the prerogative powers of the Crown which had been removed by the Covenanters. The Convention of Estates of 1643 and the Parliament of 1649 were to be annulled, as they had proceeded without royal authority. However, the Parliaments which had been authorized by the king (Charles II) were to retain their legal status. Specific enactments which curtailed the prerogative were to be rescinded. These instructions indicate uncertainty about attitudes in Scotland to Presbyterianism, and, significantly, to the role of Parliament itself. This uncertainty stemmed from insecurity at Court: after all, Charles II had returned to England little more than six months previously. Consequently, in his opening speech, Middleton also urged the Parliament to grant financial provision for the maintenance of a military force to secure the monarchy.[10] This caution should not be overstated, however, because within three months (the Parliament sitting on only 27 days), the Royalist agenda had been achieved. Indeed the king's expectations had been surpassed with the passage of an act which wiped out all the constitutional legislation introduced by the Covenanters, including that relating to the government of the church.

The first step, on 4 January, was the imposition of an Oath of Allegiance containing a strong suggestion of unfettered monarchical authority and hinting at interference in the church. This met with a small, if vocal, opposition led by John Kennedy, 6th Earl of Cassillis, with some (including Cassillis himself) actually leaving the chamber.

More significantly, however, the vast majority of members took the oath without reservation. Thus, Parliament signified its loyalty to the Crown.[11] A few days later the Lords of the Articles were chosen. The revival of the Lords of the Articles signified a renewed determination on the part of the Crown to control the agenda of the Parliament and minimize debate. The attempts by James VI and, more particularly, Charles I to reduce the Estates, through this committee, to little more than a rubber-stamp for royal policies, led the Covenanters in 1640 to make the Articles optional, and subject to the will of Parliament; if utilized, each estate was to elect its own representatives to it. In 1661, this remained the case, but it is clear that the committee was fairly strictly controlled. Crucially, Officers of State were included in the membership of the committee: the Commissioner was taking no chances.[12] Safeguards were enacted for Parliament as a whole; if the Lords of the Articles did not represent an overture to the House, any member was free to present it to the Commissioner and the full Estates, who were to meet twice a week to that end. If this seems to signify institutional development, there is nothing to indicate whether it was utilized. Moreover, the discretionary powers granted to the Commissioner and the political context served as further limitations upon freedom of action for members. The ultimate agenda of the Crown is revealed by the cautionary remark that the current structure of the committee,

> shall be without prejudice of any course the Kings
> Majestie with advice of the estates shall think fitt to
> take hearafter either as to the number or maner of
> election.[13]

It is likely that the safeguards were included to avoid antagonizing the Parliament at this early stage, but their significance should not be exaggerated. The structure utilized by Charles I could not be introduced until the episcopate was resettled: the bishops were in fact added to the committee in the 1662 session.[14]

The control of the parliamentary agenda by the Lords of the Articles makes it more difficult to judge the mood of the 160 or so other members of the House. However, directed by the Articles, Parliament now proceeded to pass legislation reasserting the king's right to choose his own ministers and Privy Councillors and nominate Lords of Session, and his right to call and dissolve Parliament at will without statutory safeguards. This negated two of the most important measures of the constitutional revolution of 1640–41. A few days later, enactments passed during the reign of James VI prohibiting the convocation of subjects or the making of leagues or bands without royal consent were revived.[15] The re-enactment of the 1585 law against private banding without royal consent marks the direction of legislative policy. In 1638 those heading the challenge to Charles I had taken care that the National Covenant did not come within the scope of this particular legislation.[16] The 1661 acts demonstrate awareness of the legal shrewdness and ideological subtlety of the National Covenant whose implications they were out to destroy: obedience to the monarchy was to be unconditional.

A further act reserved to the king the sole right to declare war and make peace, to conclude treaties, and to raise his subjects in arms, reversing further the legislation of the 1640s.[17] These enactments of January 1661 were an explicit rejection of an executive function for the Parliament. In particular, the rescinding of the Triennial Act, which guaranteed the constitutional right of the Parliament to sit regardless of royal wishes, highlighted the strength of reaction. That this was not simply a Crown diktat is apparent from a petition of 1660 to Charles II from the nobles, gentry, and burgesses of Scotland in London, which had stated that 'the sole power of calling and holding of parliaments, and the way and manner thereof, doth reside in your majesty'.[18] However, it was still envisaged that Parliament should perform some role in the government of the country. The act granting to the king the sole right to arm his subjects contained a clause which stated that the kingdom should not be required to pay for any additional military force unless this was agreed in a Parliament or Convention of Estates. This important qualification of the king's powers guaranteed a role for Parliament in the granting of extraordinary taxation — although it was clearly hoped that such grants would not be required.[19]

In general, however, the attitude of the Parliament is unmistakable. Sir Archibald Primrose, Clerk-Register, wrote to Lauderdale that, 'never was there a parliament so frank for the king'.[20] James Sharp, Royal Chaplain and soon to become Archbishop of St Andrews, remarked that the Parliament had simply made amends for its previous actions and had vindicated the honour of the kingdom, a sentiment echoed by Sir John Hamilton, Lord Belhaven, in February.[21] If Middleton set the agenda, the majority followed his lead; at the very least, they were willing to acquiesce in the demands of the restored king. This precipitous desire to demonstrate the loyalty of the Parliament, perhaps more than anything else, helps to explain the Restoration settlement in Scotland.[22]

It is clear that the initiative lay with the Royalists, and gradually the uncertainty which existed prior to the meeting of Parliament was dissipated. At the end of February, it was enacted that all those in public office had to display their commitment to, or acquiescence in, the civil settlement imposed by statute. All office-holders, from Privy Councillors to clerks in the lowest courts, had to take the Oath of Allegiance and sign an 'Acknowledgement of his Majesties Prerogative'; otherwise, they would lose their places, and 'be lookt upon as persones disaffected to his Majesties Authority and Government'.[23] The acknowledgement basically affirmed the legislation passed in January, while explicitly rejecting the legitimacy of the Covenants. In June, the policy was extended to the ecclesiastical sphere when it was ordained that ministers had to take the Oath of Allegiance before they could be presented to benefices; if a patron did not comply, the right of presentation would fall to the king. Thus, in the long term, it was hoped to secure a loyal ministry.[24] More importantly, with the passing of the Oath of Allegiance, it would be fair to say that the tables had been well and truly turned on the Covenanters.

Moreover, it is in this context that the restoration of Episcopacy in Scotland should be regarded. For the Royalists the agenda was straightforward, the rhetoric basic, even fundamentalist; Presbyterianism was inherently rebellious, and incompatible with the security of the monarchy; it was the 'pretence of religion' which disguised and justified the treasonable designs of the Covenanters.[25] The Act Recissory, which passed on 28 March 1661, paved the way for the return of Episcopacy. This act, which annulled the Parliaments of 1640 to 1648 (but not that of 1649, which had already been declared unlawful), removed the statutory basis of the Presbyterian system introduced by the Covenanters. The accompanying 'Act Concerning Religion and Church Government' stipulated that any ecclesiastical settlement would rest on compatibility with monarchical government, the final decision being referred to Charles.[26] The passing of the Act Recissory represented something of a gamble for Middleton; precociously, he decided to press ahead without waiting for royal approval.[27] Such a sweeping measure can perhaps be viewed as unwise, especially after the earlier systematic and careful unpicking of the Covenanters' legislation. Yet it can be argued, as the Commissioner's confidence suggests, that it was precisely the success of the Royalists during January and February which prompted Middleton to take the initiative, regardless of conservative opinion, and in spite of vociferous criticism from the kirk, which was simply brushed aside. Middleton wanted to enhance his Royalist credentials, presenting an image of the arch-Cavalier in total control of the Scottish Parliament, where so much humiliation had been inflicted upon the king's father. In this the Commissioner was at least partly successful, at any rate among Royalists elsewhere in the British Isles; he was said to have been popular in the House of Commons, where there was actually a proposal — after the passage of the act in Scotland — that the legislation of the English Long Parliament be repealed in its entirety — a proposal blocked by the king.[28]

The Act Recissory stirred some within the Scottish Parliament to express their doubts about its implications. William Douglas, third Duke of Hamilton, and John Lindsay, Earl of Crawford-Lindsay — a member of the government — headed the relatively small group (perhaps 40 out of more than 200) who expressed criticism of the act. Hamilton argued that the 1648 Parliament had acted in the interests of Charles I, and had received the latter's approbation. Furthermore, the 1641 Parliament should be regarded as legal because Charles I had in fact been present. A Parliament warranted by the King could not be disregarded in such a manner.[29] This argument highlights unease about the implications for Parliament contained in such a measure, demonstrating the obvious point that positive memories of the 1640s had not completely vanished. However, Hamilton's view also provides an expression of the mood of the Parliament in 1661, and a reason for the relative ease with which Middleton carried his agenda. The emphasis was on the *loyalty* of the Engagement Parliament of 1648. The 1641 meeting was legal *because* it had received royal approbation; the military victories of the Covenanters were conveniently forgotten. A Parliament meeting without royal permission was illegal; implicit was the rejection of the right to resist the Crown, the essence of the National Covenant. Thus, the criticism of the Act Recissory within Parliament could achieve nothing in practical terms, and it passed easily enough.

Towards the end of May, the reaction against the Covenants was expressed visibly with the executions of Archibald Campbell, Marquis of Argyll, and James Guthrie, a prominent minister associated with the 'Protester' faction. The story is well enough known.[30] Here, it is simply worth remarking that the execution of Argyll symbolically marked the end of Scotland's Covenanting experiment. Nobody was more closely associated with the revolution than the Marquis. In his remarkably stolid scaffold speech, he claimed God remained on his side; to most observers this must have seemed unlikely.[31] The actions of the Parliament were surely evidence that the Lord had deserted his chosen people.

II

Episcopacy was formally restored in the 1662 session of Parliament, which opened in May, although the episcopate had been selected during the previous winter. This completed the revival of pre-1638 institutions. It is probable that the reintroduction of the bishops was exclusively a government initiative, unlike the restoration of the king's civil powers, which enjoyed support in Parliament. If some areas of Scotland were more amenable than others to the return of the bishops, it can hardly be said that there was an upsurge in popular support similar to that which occurred in England.[32] For the government, Episcopacy was a way of enhancing royal power: bishops were to act as a controlling influence in the kirk, and were to sit as the first estate in Parliament. This had been the reason for their revival under James VI and their prominence under Charles I. The initial reluctance of Charles II to countenance the necessary legislation stemmed from practical concerns about the timing of the move, rather than scruples about the desirability of it. After Middleton had presented him with the choice, he did not require much persuasion.

The Parliament itself seems to have exhibited greater docility than in the previous year — or, at least, there is no record of any debates or opposition. The vast majority of the peers and shire commissioners who attended in 1661 did so again. It should be noted, however, that Hamilton and Crawford, who had both criticized the Act Recissory, were absent in 1662, although the former reappeared the following year. A small group of 'radical' peers stayed away, but noble attendance remained at more or less the same level, due to the appearance of men who were not present in 1661 — some of whom had Royalist backgrounds.[33] Another point to note is that the burgh estate was badly depleted, with 19 of the 60 burghs who sent commissioners in 1661 unrepresented in the following two sessions. This prompted the passing of an act specifying fines for non-attendance (for all estates). There is no obvious reason for the absence of so many burgh commissioners, but indifference or hostility to the settlement are the most likely candidates. In 1663 the King's Secretary, John Maitland, Earl of Lauderdale, was certainly concerned about disaffection in western burghs, but most of the absentees were from elsewhere. Whatever the reason, the combination of a lower turnout and the presence of the bishops served only to benefit the government.[34]

The act which passed on 27 May returned to the bishops the rights they had enjoyed in 1637 in relation to their position within the church, their jurisdictions, and their properties. The act also explicitly acknowledged the royal prerogative in matters concerning the 'externall government & policie of the church'.[35] A couple of weeks later, more provocative measures were enacted. In 1661, Parliament had ordered that services were to be held throughout the kingdom on 29 May to commemorate Charles II's return from exile (it was also his birthday). This profane gesture was contemptuously ignored by many ministers. Consequently, an act of 11 June 1662 condemned such perverse ingratitude for the country's deliverance from oppression; the culprits were to lose their benefices, unless they acknowledged their wrongdoing to the Archbishop or Bishop. They were then to take the Oath of Allegiance, and inform their congregations of their actions. On the same day, it was enacted that ministers admitted since 1649 were to receive presentation from the relevant patron and collation from the bishop.[36] This reflects concern with forms and legitimacy, and the rights of property owners; at the same time, the view that 'this was the work of Middleton and designed simply to rub the noses of the ministers in the fact of episcopal government', is probably also valid.[37] Yet such an act was not inconsistent with the tenor of the legislation passed since 1661.

The 1662 session also saw the passage of an equally important, and underestimated, act, which continued the ideological attack on the Covenants. The 'Act for Preservation of his Majesty's Person, Authority and Government', passed on 24 June, defined explicitly the constitutional order: the conditional nature of obedience to the monarchy, which was the main feature of the National Covenant, was rejected, and Episcopal church government was upheld.[38] In addition, office-holders throughout the country were subjected to the imposition of yet another oath — the 'Declaration to be signed by all persons in public trust', which was based on the text of part of the act of 24 June; it was also to be taken by those who attended Parliament.[39] This built upon the oaths imposed in the previous session. The imposition of proscriptive oaths represented an attempt to inject new dynamism into the traditional structures of power in the kingdom by binding all in office, at any level — effectively the political nation — to the person of the king. It also demonstrated a willingness on the part of the government to utilize the coercive tools for exclusion of political opponents introduced by the Covenanters, despite the attempt to eradicate other traces of revolutionary change. Subscription of the National Covenant had been the prerequisite for exercise of civil power during the 1640s; by 1662, this policy had been reversed, with the imposition of oaths demonstrating commitment to the royal prerogative.[40]

By September 1662 government objectives in terms of civil authority and the church had been achieved. Therefore the promised indemnity could finally be passed.[41] Traditionally, the possibility of reprisals for previous actions has been regarded as a stick wielded above the heads of members to ensure loyalty.[42] However, too much can be made of this. It is certainly true that the delay in the passage in the act was in marked contrast to England, where an indemnity was passed as early as August 1660.[43] However, Parliament itself was to conduct trials and name exceptions; as such, most could feel reasonably secure.[44] Moreover, it is possible that the delay in the passage of this act stemmed from government inertia rather than deliberation. Middleton had received instructions to pass such an act prior to the first session, and in March 1661 he claimed a draft would be sent to Charles, although nothing was achieved at that time. Two months later, James Sharp reported that William Cunningham, Earl of Glencairn, Lord Chancellor, and Lauderdale were in favour of passing it at once, while John Leslie, Earl of Rothes, President of the Privy Council, was worried about the 'inconveniences' which would follow.[45] In January 1662, Middleton had received further instructions which make it clear that the intention was to ensure some financial gain through the imposition of punitive fines; a commission was appointed to decide upon names and amounts, ostensibly because there would not be enough time at the sitting of the Parliament.[46] Another nine months passed before the list of exceptions was presented to the Parliament, forming the basis of a separate act. A total of 896 individuals were named, including only eight nobles, and fined varying amounts.[47] Very few of those fined were sitting in Parliament. The threat of punishment cannot really be held to have influenced more than a small number of individuals. Nor can the settlement of 1661–62 be attributed solely to royal management. Parliament itself displayed its loyalty, in what can be described as a reaction against disorder and rebellion. This was a conservative settlement, but also aggressive; to what extent the attitudes of those sitting in Parliament were representative of the country as a whole is a different matter.

III

The restored monarchy also required practical means to give effect to the absolute authority claimed in legislation. Here again, Parliament was forthcoming. In March 1661, it was enacted that the king should receive £480,000 Scots a year from excise duties.[48] This money, in conjunction with the king's rents and customs, was intended to provide a stable base for the monarchy. Charles was also to benefit from arrears of taxation dating from the Covenanting period, which were to be used largely to pay off his debts.[49] Significantly, the annuity was in part specifically designed to pay for Royalist troops: 'towards the interteanment of any such forces as his Majestie shall think fit to raise and keep up within this Kingdome'.[50] The provision for military security should come as no surprise; monarchical authority had been severely curbed and finally displaced through the utilisation of such violent means by the opponents of Charles I and his son. The Crown intended to crush any future opposition to its authority by force if necessary.

It should be noted, however, that the settlement of the king's finances made no provision for additional grants of direct taxation. These had become more regular under James VI and Charles I, and both the Covenanters and the Cromwellians had operated high taxation regimes.[51] In 1660, the fiscal burden was a major grievance.[52] The act of March 1661 granting the excise actually contained a clause stating that the king would refrain from exacting any more cess (a monthly imposition introduced by the Covenanters).[53] The £480,000 was to be derived mostly from excise duties imposed upon the brewing industry; this represented something of a victory for landowners, because they avoided direct taxation. However, the settlement was also in effect an updated version of the traditional belief about royal finances in Scotland — that the king should 'live off his own'. In recognition of the increased needs of the Crown, the excise, which had been introduced to the country by the Covenanters in 1644, was retained. In return, the king was not to make any new demands for taxation. This hope was to prove to be a chimera.

Of course, Charles II was not the only person to benefit from the proceedings of Parliament in 1661. It was clearly important that there was a minimum of disruption during the transition to monarchical government. However, many Royalists expected scores to be settled with former enemies, or to be rewarded for their loyalty. Charles II had to balance these demands against his own financial limitations and his view that pragmatism was the best way to achieve stability.

An important means of avoiding unnecessary disruption was to secure property rights while altering constitutional arrangements. Legal judgements of the previous two decades were held to be valid, although there were provisions for appeal.[54] In fact there was considerable pressure for the speedy settling of the law courts, and as a result it was enacted that the Court of Session was to sit from 4 June.[55] This represented a desire not only to facilitate the transaction of private business, but also to restore normality to the country; law and order under the monarchy replacing the unnatural impositions of the Cromwellians.

The traditional mesh of heritable jurisdictions was returned (with the exception, until 1662, of Episcopal jurisdiction), signalling the restored power of the nobility in particular throughout the country. In addition, also in this traditionalist vein, all royal burgh charters were ratified.[56] This 'restoration' highlights the conservatism of the Parliament; the settlement was both reactionary and pragmatic.

In addition, there were a large number of measures designed to alleviate the financial distress caused by the 'troubles', and also to reward Royalists. An act of July 1661 allowed debtors six years grace, upon the fulfillment of specified conditions, including provision for interest payments. This was clearly a contentious issue, and Charles II had been keen to ensure a minimum of disruption.[57] The act contained safeguards and specified rights and obligations. In the present context, the significant point is that it represented a compromise, designed to balance a delicate situation. Likewise, a number of individuals who were bound for public debts from 1638–41 and 1645 were granted a breathing space until the following session; in 1662, this suspension was simply re-granted.[58]

The estates of Royalists who had been forfeited during the 1640s were restored. This was both symbolic and practical. James Graham, second Marquis of Montrose, was the most notable of these; in addition, he received the Cowal peninsula from the forfeited Campbell estates as compensation for his family's losses.[59] Moreover, during the 1661–62 sessions, Parliament ordained that numerous nobles and lairds were to receive arrears of taxation dating from the Covenanting period.[60] It is probably fair to say that the desire for financial favour affected the attitudes of many within the Parliament. Two former 'radical' Covenanters, John Campbell, Earl of Loudoun, and William Ker, Earl of Lothian, are good examples of this: both expected Charles to stump up for pensions he had promised. Loudoun explicitly referred in a petition to his support for the measures passed in Parliament in favour of the prerogative.[61] It seems that loyalty could be bought. This aspect of Parliament's work should not be underestimated. It is perhaps impossible to determine with regard to individuals where loyalty and conservatism ended and financial necessity or expectation began. Suffice to say, for many the two were closely related.

IV

The factional struggle which developed between the Earls of Middleton and Lauderdale, Commissioner and Secretary respectively, cannot be fully addressed here. The so-called 'billeting affair', when Middleton and his allies attempted to exclude the Secretary by the innovative means of rigged parliamentary ballot, is one of the better known events of the Restoration period in Scotland.[62] However, its significance should not be exaggerated; the outcome was a change of personnel, not of policy. The episode, which led to Middleton's disgrace, demonstrated that Court intrigue was a dangerous game. Lauderdale's immediate problem was that Middleton had no shortage of backers at Court, while he himself remained unpopular among Cavaliers and faced a barrage of rumours about alleged Presbyterian sympathies.[63] However, the Secretary adopted a shrewd tactical approach, concentrating on Middleton's abuses of the king's trust, and refraining from making direct, personal criticism. He also distanced himself from an attack on the Earl of Clarendon, the English Chancellor, by the Earl of Bristol, in order to show that he was unwilling to condone any such challenge to the king's appointed servants.[64] Lauderdale ensured his political ascendancy by creating an image of himself as the ultimate servant, motivated not by his own interests but by those of his royal master. The legislation passed in the 1663 session proved that he was as capable of serving the king effectively as Middleton had been.

An inquiry ordered by the king into the billeting affair was the excuse for Lauderdale to accompany the Earl of Rothes, who replaced Middleton as Commissioner, to Edinburgh for the Parliament which met in June, leaving one of his friends, Sir Robert Moray, to liaise with Charles in London. In Edinburgh, a committee consisting of Lauderdale and five others was appointed and their report condemned Middleton and his ally, Sir George Mackenzie of Tarbet, for their abuse of the king's authority, despite the delaying tactics of some of their friends. A report was sent to Charles, and the offending acts were repealed.[65] Lauderdale's victory was supreme. Distancing himself from the excesses of Middleton, who had Archibald Campbell, son of the executed Marquis of Argyll, thrown in prison the previous year on a spurious charge of leasing-making, he urged that the former Commissioner and Tarbet simply forfeit their places rather than face indictment for treason.[66]

At the same time Lauderdale, aided by the new Commissioner Rothes, was keen to bolster his Royalist credentials, and once again, Parliament was obliging. On the first day of the session Crown control of the Parliament was tightened with an act which reformed the means by which the Lords of the Articles were appointed. The procedure adopted was more stringent even than that utilized by Charles I. In 1633, all the clergy and nobility together had chosen the gentry and burgesses; by the present act, however, the clergy chose eight noblemen, and the nobility eight bishops, and this group of sixteen selected the representatives of the other two estates. The efficacy of the measure was highlighted by the exclusion of some of Middleton's associates who had been members of the Articles in the previous session.[67] Lauderdale also boosted his standing with Royalists and High Church Anglicans in England, by passing an 'Act against separation & disobedience to Ecclesiastical Authority', which reaffirmed the Episcopal settlement, urged the Privy Council to take action against dissenting ministers, and specified penalties for non-attendance at the parish kirk on a Sunday. Thus, Lauderdale signalled his commitment to the established church and the maintenance of order. In addition, it was ordained that all current office-holders throughout the country were to subscribe the Declaration before 11 November, thus tightening up the previous year's act. At forthcoming burgh elections, anyone who refused to sign the Declaration was not only debarred from office, but was to forfeit their trading privileges.[68]

Therefore, in 1663 Lauderdale was keen to take advantage of Parliament's continuing loyalty. Another act expressed his long-term strategy for security, although at this stage the offer of a national militia of 20,000 foot and 2,000 horse was more rhetorical than practical. Gilbert Burnet, a contemporary chronicler, stated that Lauderdale had outlined his vision of a loyal nation-in-arms as early as 1660; certainly, it seems that the Secretary had identified the Crown's major problem in later seventeenth century Scotland — security.[69] The act listed proportions of soldiers to be supplied by the various shires of the kingdom, which were also to provide arms and 40 days' provisions. The king was to choose the senior officers, while organizational problems were remitted to the Privy Council. Crucially, it was ordained that this militia was,

> to be in readinesse as they shall be called for by his
> Majestie to march to any parte of his dominions of
> Scotland, England or Ireland for suppressing of any
> forraigne invasion, intestine trouble or insurrection or
> for any other service whairin his Majesties honour,
> authority or greatness may be concerned...[70]

This extraordinary clause made the proposed Scottish force — if it could be organized — an exciting prospect for the Crown. Although the Scottish militia was to employ the nobility and gentry throughout the kingdom, there is no indication that the proposal was the result of pressure from the Parliament itself.[71] The idea had been discussed at Court in 1661, and had now been hijacked by Lauderdale and his allies as their own.[72] This was an initiative from above, but once again

Parliament had almost surpassed itself in its willingness to support the Crown's proposal.

Yet it is important to keep in mind that the proceedings of the Parliament were not solely concerned with the powers of the Crown. Lauderdale and Rothes also had to be responsive to private concerns, as Middleton had been. Those bound for public debts were granted yet another breathing space.[73] In addition, there were already many complaints about the collection of tax-arrears dating from the Covenanting period. Lauderdale was the epitome of moderation, stating that, although he did not intend to hinder the collection of the sums ordained by the Parliament, he was keen to stamp out abuses. It should be noted that he did not interfere with the rights of those who were to benefit from the arrears. Furthermore, he later intimated to the Duke of Hamilton that he hoped for some reward himself.[74] Nevertheless, the promise to deal with abuses must surely have been regarded with favour. In August, a proposal urging general subscription of the Declaration was rejected as simply provocative and unnecessary.[75] So the pattern of the previous two sessions was continued; the passage of legislation in favour of the prerogative, and other measures designed to benefit the country as a whole or particular individuals. It must surely be concluded that the Crown got the best deal.

Although Rothes was the Commissioner, it is clear that Lauderdale was the prime mover behind the legislation of 1663. He demonstrated that his own commitment to the exaltation of the prerogative was as great as Middleton's had been and also that he would do exactly as Charles ordered without abusing his position, thus distancing himself from what was characterised as the blatant avarice of the former Commissioner and his allies. The strategy was a total success. The king was overjoyed with the 1663 legislation, and the Secretary even managed to silence his critics at Court. Although Charles allowed Middleton a final chance to make himself heard, by the end of the year the old soldier was finished in Scotland.[76] The power struggle between the two royal servants originated in a shared desire for influence. Lauderdale did not initiate any policy changes in the wake of Middleton's demise; he merely continued in a similar vein, and for the same reason — to protect and enhance his position at Court. Both men exploited the essentially loyal mood of the Parliament for their own benefit, although this is not to absolve the latter body from its own legislation. In 1663 Lauderdale was astonished at the attitude of the Parliament. Upon the repeal of an act passed in the previous session in favour of the Lord Lyon, he remarked,

heir it is observable what interest his Majesties
Commissioner hath in our Parliament, for the last
Commissioner caried this act, and now it was rescinded
without one contrarie vote...[77]

This attitude, bordering on contempt, developed into arrogant expectation when Lauderdale himself became Commissioner from 1669. This partly explains the aggressive policies pursued in Scotland until the end of his career.

Conclusion

The return of Charles II from exile in 1660 was welcomed by most of the elites throughout the British Isles because monarchy appeared to offer stability, in the absence of viable alternatives. The Restoration settlement of 1661–63 in Scotland reflected the essential loyalty of the Parliament; the constitutional revolution of 1640–1 was swept aside in a wholescale attack on Covenanting ideology, while Episcopacy was restored as the form of church government most compatible with monarchical authority. Executive power was personified by the king himself, with a minimal role for the legislature, although the consent of Parliament was still required for additional grants of taxation. The holding of office in Scotland was made conditional upon public testimony of acquiesence in the constitutional and religious order. This settlement can be described as conservative, but also dynamic and aggressive. Provisions for military security indicate that the Crown was not prepared to err on the side of complacency: the country's first peacetime standing army proved ultimately to be the most important innovation of the period, a disruptive, rather than a stabilizing, force.

Parliament also provided for the reinvigoration of the traditional social hierarchy, and the return of the structures of local power which reflected it — in particular, the dominant position of the nobility was restored, along with their heritable jurisdictions. In addition, there were numerous financial provisions designed to benefit groups such as debtors, or individuals. Impoverished landowners petitioned the Crown for assistance: such pecuniary difficulties undoubtedly contributed to the willingness of the Parliament to countenance the demands of the king. The annuity of £480,000 Scots granted to Charles II, to be composed mostly of excise from brewing, highlighted the strength of the landed interest; this did not, however, prevent the government demanding additional taxes a few years later. Political favour — a key way to replenish depleted fortunes — depended upon the ability to serve the interests of the Crown. This is amply demonstrated by the fortunes of the two most prominent politicians during these early years, the Earls of Middleton and Lauderdale. In crude terms, their rivalry developed into a contest to see which of them could best serve their royal master. Indeed, commitment to the maintenance of royal power as the means of preserving his own position remained the underlying principle of Lauderdale's administration for over fifteen years. Yet it is important to realise that Parliament itself had consistently displayed its loyalty to the Crown. There was very little in the way of serious opposition to the trend of legislation. The settlement of 1661–63 represented a conservative reaction to the disorders of the previous two decades — ironically enough, perhaps this was similar to the reaction of the Covenanters to the arbitrary methods of government and innovations of Charles I. The Restoration witnessed a rapprochement between Crown and elites in Scotland. It remained to be seen whether it would last.

NOTES

1. J R Young, 'The Scottish Parliament, 1639–1661: A Political and Constitutional Analysis' (University of Glasgow, PhD thesis, three volumes, 1993), volume one, 526–538; A I Macinnes, 'The Scottish Constitution, 1638–51: The Rise and Fall of Oligarchic Centralism' in J Morrill (ed), *The Scottish National Covenant in its British Context* (Edinburgh, 1990), *passim*.

2. B Coward, *The Stuart Age: a History of England, 1603–1714* (London, 1980), 160–2.

3. R B Merriman, *Six Contemporaneous Revolutions*, (Oxford, 1938).

4. N Steensgaard, 'The Seventeenth-Century Crisis' in G Parker and L Smith (eds), *The General Crisis of the Seventeenth Century* (London, 1978), 44.

5. Young, *The Scottish Parliament*, 534.

6. Macinnes, 'The Scottish Constitution', 128.

7. G Burnet, *The History of my Own Time*, O Airy (ed), two volumes, (Oxford, 1897–1900), volume one, 206–7.

8. Young, 'The Scottish Parliament', 505, 520. Additional biographical material can be obtained from J Balfour-Paul (ed), *The Scots Peerage*, nine vols. (Edinburgh, 1904–14), and M D Young (ed), *The Parliaments of Scotland: Burgh and Shire Commissioners*, two volumes, (Edinburgh, 1992–1993).

9. J Buckroyd, *Church and State in Scotland, 1660–1681* (Edinburgh, 1980), 31–32. See also Young, 'The Scottish Parliament', pp 505–6; G Donaldson, *Scotland: James V–James VII* (Edinburgh, 1965), 365.

10. O Airy (ed), *The Lauderdale Papers*, three volumes, (Camden Society, London, 1884–85), volume one, 39–40; Burnet, *History of My Own Time*, i,

207; Buckroyd, *Church and State*, 26–30; G Davies and P H Hardacre, 'The Restoration of the Scottish Episcopacy', *Journal of British Studies*, 2, 1962, 43.

11. *APS*, vii, 7–8; Burnet, *History of my Own Time*, i, 255–256; Buckroyd, *Church and State*, 28–29.

12. *APS*, vii, 8–9; Young, 'The Scottish Parliament', 507–508.

13. *APS*, vii, 9.

14. Ibid, 371.

15. Ibid, 10–12; W C Dickinson and G Donaldson (eds), *A Source Book of Scottish History*, volume three (Edinburgh, 1961), 241–242, 246–247.

16. Macinnes, 'The Scottish Constitution', 108.

17. *APS*, vii, 13.

18. *A Source Book of Scottish History*, iii, 241–2; *Lauderdale Papers*, i, 32.

19. *APS*, vii, 13; Burnet, *History of my Own Time*, i, 211–212.

20. *Lauderdale Papers*, i, 63.

21. Ibid, 63, 67; BL, Lauderdale Papers, Add Ms 23115/72.

22. Middleton's remarks to Charles II and to Chancellor Hyde in January 1661 support this view, see W D Macray and F J Routledge (eds), *Calendar of the Clarendon State Papers in the Bodleian Library*, volume v (Oxford, 1970), 75.

23. *APS*, vii, 44–45.

24. Ibid, 272–3; SRO, Yule Collection, GD 90/2/260.

25. For examples of this rhetoric, see the preambles to many acts of the 1661–2 sessions.

26. *APS*, vii, 86–88.

27. Buckroyd, *Church and State*, 33–4; R. Hutton, *Charles II: King of England, Scotland and Ireland* (Oxford, 1989), 161–162.

28. *Calendar of the Clarendon State Papers*, v, 85; Buckroyd, *Church and State*, 34; HMC, *Calendar of the Mss of the Marquess of Ormonde preserved at Kilkenny Castle*, vol. iii, (New series, 1904), 52; J R Jones, *Charles II: Royal Politician* (London, 1987), 57.

29. SRO, Hamilton Papers, GD 406/M9/148; Sir G Mackenzie, *Memoirs of the Affairs of Scotland from the Restoration of King Charles II*, T Thomson (ed), (Edinburgh, 1821), 28–29; Burnet, *History of my Own Time*, i, 213–216.

30. J Willock, *The Great Marquess: Life and Times of Archibald 8th Earl, and 1st Marquess, of Argyll* (Edinburgh and London, 1903), 301–334; Burnet, *History of my Own Time*, i, 220–228; Mackenzie, *Memoirs*, pp. 34–39; Hutton, *Charles II*, 141–142, 171–172.

31. Burnet, *History of my Own Time*, i, 226.

32. *APS*, vii, 370–374; Buckroyd, *Church and State*, 41–45; I. B Cowan, *The Scottish Covenanters, 1661–1688* (London, 1976), 53–55; P Seaward, *The Restoration, 1660–1688* (London, 1991), 48–49.

33. *APS*, vii, 3–5, 368–369, 446–447.

34. Ibid, 5, 369–370, 371–372, 447–448; BL, Lauderdale Papers, Add Ms 23119/159.

35. *APS*, vii. 372–374.

36. Ibid, 199–200, 376–377.

37. Buckroyd, *Church and State*, 46.

38. *APS*, vii, 377–379.

39. *APS*, vii, 405–406.

40. Macinnes, 'The Scottish Constitution', 115, 119, 125–127; *A Source Book of Scottish History*, iii, 116–117.

41. *APS*, vii, 415–416.

42. Mackenzie, *Memoirs*, 19; Burnet, *History of my Own Time*, i, 217; Buckroyd, *Church and State*, 40; J Patrick, 'A Union Broken? Restoration Politics in Scotland', in J Wormald (ed), *Scotland Revisited* (London, 1991), 124.

43. Hutton, *Charles II*, 140–141; Jones, *Charles II*, 47.

44. SRO, Yule Collection, GD 90/2/260, Proclamation, October 1660.

45. NLS, Newhailes Papers, MS 25383/97.

46. *Lauderdale Papers*, i, pp. 39–40, 103–105; *Calendar of the Clarendon State Papers*, v, 85.

47. *APS*, vii, 420–429; Mackenzie, *Memoirs*, 65–6; Burnet, *History of my Own Time*, i, 258–259, 262–263.

48. The £ Scots was valued at 1/12 of the £ sterling.

49. *APS*, vii, 32–33, 78, 88–95, 326–327.

50. Ibid, 88.

51. J Goodare 'Parliamentary taxation in Scotland, 1560–1603', *SHR*, LXVIII, (1989), 23, 46–47; K Brown, *Kingdom or Province? Scotland and the regal union, 1603–1715* (London, 1992), 28–29; D Stevenson, 'The King's Scottish revenues and the Covenanters, 1625–51', *HJ*, XVII, i, (1974), 18–20; A I Macinnes, *Charles I and the making of the Covenanting movement, 1625–1641* (Edinburgh, 1991), 104–106, 114–116; D Stevenson, 'The financing of the cause of the Covenants, 1638–1651' *SHR*, LI, ii, (1972), *passim*; D Stevenson, 'Cromwell, Scotland and Ireland', in J Morrill (ed). *Oliver Cromwell and the English Revolution* (London and New York, 1990), 178.

52. NLS Lauderdale Papers, MS 597/50–2.

53. *APS*, vii, 78.

54. Ibid, 31–32, 62–63, 87.

55. BL, Lauderdale Papers, Add MSS 23114/77; 23115/77; *APS*, vii, 189.

56. *APS*, vii, 118.

57. *Lauderdale Papers*, i, 40; BL, Lauderdale Papers, Add MS 23115/100; *APS*, vii, 317–320, 430.

58. *APS*, vii, 313–314, 430.

59. Ibid, 29, 102–103, 163–164, 197–198, 204, 231–233, 367, 391; P Hopkins, *Glencoe and the End of the Highland War* (Edinburgh, 1986), 40.

60. *APS*, vii, 167–168, 299–300, 321–324, 385, 387–388, 389–390, 409–410.

61. BL, Lauderdale Papers, Add MS 23116/27, 105.

62. Mackenzie, *Memoirs*, 73–113; Patrick, 'A Union Broken', 124–128.

63. Mackenzie, *Memoirs*, 69–70; Burnet, *History of my Own Time*, i, 360; *Calendar of the Clarendon State Papers*, v, 275, 374; BL, Lauderdale Papers, Add MSS 23119/84, 86, 89; 23120/57.

64. *Lauderdale Papers*, i, 136, 146–147, 151, 158, 160; Burnet, *History of my Own Time*, i, 350–352; Jones, *Charles II*, 64–65.

65. *APS*, vii, 450–451, 458–461, 471–472; *Lauderdale Papers*, i, 138–141, 144–145, 164–165.

66 *Lauderdale Papers*, i, 166–172; Burnet, *History of my Own Time*, i, 261–262.

67. *APS*, v, 9–10, vii, 449; BL, Lauderdale Papers, Add MS 23119/56, 99–100; *Lauderdale Papers*, i, 137–138.

68. *APS*, vii, 455–456, 462–463; *Lauderdale Papers*, i, 162; BL, Lauderdale Papers, Add MS 23119/159.

69. *APS*, vii, 480–481; Burnet, *History of my Own Time*, i, 195–196.

70. B Lenman, 'Militia, fencible men and home defence, 1660–1797', in N Macdougall (ed), *Scotland and War AD 79–1918* (Edinburgh, 1991), 173–174. Lenman regards the proposal as somehow coming from 'the nobility', without being more specific.

71. Ibid.

72. BL, Lauderdale Papers, Add MSS 23116/41, 43, 69; 23119/174; NLS, Newhailes Papers, Ms 25383/2; SRO, Yule Collection, GD 90/2/260, Instructions and Warrant to Middleton, 10 June 1661.

73. *APS*, vii, 501.

74. *Lauderdale Papers*, i, 159–160; SRO, Hamilton Papers, GD 406/1/2676.

75. NLS, Lauderdale Papers, MS 597/95; *Lauderdale Papers*, i, 175.

76. *Lauderdale Papers*, i, 178–179, 182, 184, 191; NLS, Newhailes Papers, MS 25382/27, 32; Burnet, *History of my Own Time*, i, 368; Hutton, *Charles II*, 205–207.

77. BL, Lauderdale Papers, Add MS 23119/93; *APS*, vii, 458.

CHAPTER 11

The Paradoxical Virtue of the Historical Romance: Sir George Mackenzie's 'Aretina' (1660) and the Civil Wars[1]

Clare Jackson

In 1660 Sir George Mackenzie of Rosehaugh (1636–91) published *Aretina, or the Serious Romance*. As Lord Advocate of Scotland during the notorious 'Killing Times' of the 1670s and 1680s, Mackenzie is usually better known as 'Bluidy Mackenzie' for his part in the forcible suppression of the Covenanters. He was, however, a polymathic intellectual whose prolific and heterogeneous output encompassed works on stoic moral philosophy, Scottish history, witchcraft, and heraldry. Professionally, Mackenzie was also one of the earliest jurists to publish extensively on Scots law, producing the first manual of Scots criminal law, *The Laws and Customs of Scotland in Matters Criminal* (1678), followed by *The Institutions of the Laws of Scotland* (1684). His major work of political theory, *Jus Regium, or the Just and Solid Foundations of Monarchy* (1684) was the only substantial piece of Scottish Royalist writing to appear during the Restoration and represents the apotheosis of Scottish Royalist political sentiment in the twilight years of Stuart absolutism. Perhaps Mackenzie's most lasting achievement was pioneering the foundation of the Advocates' Library in 1682, which became the National Library of Scotland in 1925.[2]

As the youthful author of *Aretina*, Mackenzie is also entitled to separate recognition for this contribution to imaginative literature. As an independent piece of prose fiction, *Aretina* has frequently been acclaimed as the first Scottish novel. Of particular interest is Mackenzie's inclusion of an allegorical interpretation of recent historical events. By this means he accomplished the first native historical account, albeit covert, of the recent Civil Wars in Scotland and England.

Aged only twenty-four when he published *Aretina*,[3] Mackenzie acknowledged in later life that he had abandoned the sphere of *belles lettres* to concentrate on legal writings; 'the Spring of my Age being past, it is fit those blossoms should ripen into Fruit'.[4] Romances provided an especially attractive option for young writers keen to experiment: Samuel Pepys, for instance, wrote a novel while at

Cambridge when he was aged only twenty, although he subsequently tore up the manuscript.[5]

Aretina was first published in Edinburgh by Robert Brown in 1660. Evidently popular, it was reprinted the following year in London by two separate publishers; Ralph Smith and George Sawbridge. Although advertised as 'Part First', no other parts were to follow. It is now a book of extreme rarity 'nearly all the copies published in its three issues having been thumbed out of existence'.[6] Written as four separate books, *Aretina* amounts to approximately 100,000 words. Although regularly cited by literary commentators as the first Scottish novel, scarcely any detailed analysis has been made of its intellectual and historical content. In 1979 the literary scholar, Michael Spiller, examined the work in terms of the romance genre and the role of narrative and discourse.[7]

Increasing attention has recently been paid to the literary component of English political culture during this period.[8] The history of Royalist culture and thought in Restoration Scotland remains, nevertheless, a subject about which very little is known. This paper aims to re-examine Mackenzie's *Aretina* from the viewpoint of an historian of political ideas, rather than that of a literary critic. The first section surveys the nature of prose literature and its relationship to history in this period. The next section considers Mackenzie's own reasons for composing such a romance. A brief outline of the work is provided, together with an identification of various major themes. I will concentrate on the third book in order to illustrate and assess Mackenzie's allegorical history of the Civil Wars, looking first at his interpretation of their origins, before discussing his account of the wars themselves.

I

Orthodoxy has asserted that 'the seventeenth century is the dullest in Scottish literature, since the fourteenth century anyway'.[9] The acme of English literature remained the romance, as exemplified by Sir Philip Sidney's *Arcadia* of 1593.[10] The permanent departure of the monarchy from Scotland after 1603 hindered the emergence of a vibrant literary court culture such as that which flourished in Caroline England. There, Charles I's French bride, Henrietta Maria, sought to espouse the pastoral genre, while Charles personally identified with spiritualised versions of the chivalric romance.[11] The restoration of the monarchy in 1660 did nonetheless offer Scots Royalist writers such an opportunity; prefixed to *Aretina* are two panegyrical poems by Mackenzie, one of which is personally dedicated to the restored Charles II.[12]

With the exception of Sidney's *Defence of Poesie* (1595), most contemporary statements about the perceived role of prose fiction in the sixteenth and seventeenth centuries appear in the prefaces to individual works. During the seventeenth century, prose romances remained an aesthetically marginal genre because, unlike the more accepted formal genres of tragedy, epic and history, they lacked a classical precedent. Aware that romance-writing was often perceived as a somewhat frivolous occupation, Mackenzie's preface to *Aretina* is entitled 'An Apologie for Romances' evincing his primary concern to establish the seriousness of his purpose.[13] The product of a classically humanist education in Scotland, followed by legal training in France, Mackenzie considered himself part of an established Continental literary tradition. With a certain amount of magniloquence and candid name-dropping, he contends, 'who should blush to trace in these paths which the famous *Sidney, Scuderie, Barkley*, and *Broghill* hath beaten for them', as well as 'thousands of Ancients, and Moderns, Ecclesiasticks and Laicks, Spaniards, French and Italians?[14]

On the title page *Aretina* is clearly described as having been 'Written Originally in English', denoting that it is, above all, not a translation from a foreign work. Nevertheless, French influence on English literature was immense. It has been estimated that almost half of all fictional works published in England during the seventeenth century were translations; three-quarters were from French works and the rest were from Spanish and Italian sources.[15] Such Gallican influences moved the Edwardian Walter Raleigh to comment that 'Riding as it does on the crest of the wave of French influence', *Aretina* represents 'the happiest attempt to naturalise that romance in Britain'.[16] Mackenzie published his novel only the year after he returned from France, where much of the work was perhaps composed. Another contemporary romance-writer, Roger Boyle, Lord Broghill, declared that a knowledge of romances was considered essential culture for learned gentlemen in France. As he explained in the preface to his *Parthenissa* of 1655,

> Making some residences in France, I assotiated my selfe
> with Persons of my own Age, where I soone found, that
> he who was ignorant of the Romances of those Times was
> as fitt an object for wonder, as a Phylosopher would
> be, who had never heard of Aristotle.[17]

Mid-seventeenth century distinctions between history and literature were, after all, often indistinct. As the preface to Sir Percy Herbert's allegorical romance, *The Princess Cloria* (1661) claimed, 'the Ground-work for a *Romance* was excellent' for 'by no other way almost, could the multiplicity of strange Actions of the Times be exprest, that exceeded all belief'.[18]

Even for those who preferred to attempt straightforward narrative history, the extreme nature of recent events frequently strained credulity. According to the English Royalist Thomas Dancer, the fall of Richard Cromwell seemed such 'a very Romance', that his own historical account might 'very hardly find belief in future ages'.[19]

II

Mackenzie's intentions were rather different. Didactically defending prose romances, he claimed 'albeit they seem but fables, yet who would unkernel them, would find hudled up in them reall truthes'.[20] He went so far as to consider romances even to be superior to history, contending that

> many would be incited to vertue and generosity, by
> reading in Romances, how much it hath been honoured; So
> contrary wise, many are deterred by historical
> experience from being vertuous, knowing that it hath
> been oftner punished than acknowledged.[21]

In undertaking his project Mackenzie therefore claimed that 'where Romances are written by excellent wits, and perused by intelligent Readers', he was confident 'the judgement may pick out more sound information from them, then from History'.[22]

According to Mackenzie, this was because history 'teacheth us onely what was done, and the other (fiction) what should be done'. Similarly, 'whereas Romances present to us, vertue in its holy-day robes', history presents her 'in these ordinary, and spotted suits which she wears whilst she is busied in her servile, and lucrative imployments'.[23]

A skilled rhetorician himself, Mackenzie was drawing on ancient traditions, aware that classical authors such as Quintillian had deemed fiction to be the safest and most effective means of presenting political literature amid volatile circumstances. Such ideas later influenced Renaissance discussions of historical epistemology. As Sir Philip Sidney asserted, histories themselves

> are no other, then certain kinds of Romances to
> succeeding posterity; since they have no testimony for
> them but mens probable opinions; seing the Historical
> part almost of all countrys is subject to be
> questioned.[24]

Much of the criticism directed against prose fiction during the seventeenth and eighteenth centuries related precisely to this element of the apparently manipulative incorporation of history within fiction. Particularly in absolutist France, it was the perceived potential of romances, and later of novels, to imitate and appropriate established literary forms which many alleged would confound readers, denying them the critical capacity to distinguish fact from fiction.[25] Ecclesiastical and secular critics alike feared the possible corruption of the reader's integrity and the attendant threat this posed to the social and moral fabric of the nation. In his *Dictionaire Historique et Critique* of 1697, Pierre Bayle objected to the difficulties involved in discerning fact from fiction and called for government legislation to 'serve as a hook to separate one from the other, truth from falsehood'.[26]

For Mackenzie, the very appeal of romance-writing lay in its polysemous nature; 'the appetit of mens judgements is become so queasie', he believed 'that it can relllish nothing that is not either vinegared with Satyres, or sugared with Eloquence'.[27]

Moreover, his description of the publication of the unfinished *Aretina*, as 'but an abortive birth, posted to the world before its time, by an unavoidable emergent' confirms that even at this early stage, his concerns were predominantly with exploring the political aspects of the relationship between contemporary history and literature, rather than with the perfection of the romance *per se*.[28]

Aretina appeared in the year of the Restoration when many, as Mackenzie observes, 'did now coin thousands of hopes in the mint-house of their expectation'.[29] In 1660 Mackenzie was one of a rising generation of Royalists whose future was apparently secured by the restoration of the monarchy. Cavalier prose of the Civil War period has been traditionally characterised as the literature of defeat, unlike the political engagement of republican writers such as John Milton and Marchmont Needham. Yet as Paul Salzman has shown, the political or allegorical romance became one of the chief literary forms used by Royalists to construct their own political engagement with contemporary events.[30] By displacing history into romantic fiction, such works imaginatively sought to make sense of the ways in which their worlds were being 'turned upside down'.

Salzman identified five allegorical romances relating directly to the Civil War period. Sir William Sales' *Theophania* (1655) details political events in England from the viewpoint of the Earl of Essex and attributes the outbreak of civil war to a series of royal failures.[31] Richard Braithwait's *Panthalia* (1659) narrates the history of Britain from the Elizabethan era until the death of Cromwell, intertwined with the fictional tale of the heroine, Panthalia.[32] Mackenzie's *Aretina* followed in 1660. Sir Percy Herbert's *The Princess Cloria* (1661) offers a history of the English Revolution from its origins to the Battle of Worcester, including an account of affairs in Myssia (Scotland). Finally, the burlesque anti-romance, *Don Juan Lamberto* (1661) published by John Phillips or Thomas Flatman focuses on the decline of the parliamentary cause after the death of Cromwell.[33]

Although the Civil War provided the historical materials under which the allegorical romance flourished, the genre was not a mid-seventeenth century innovation. In 1621 the Gallicised Scot, John Barclay, had published his enormously successful *Argenis*, which combined an encoded political history of sixteenth-century France with a romantic narrative interspersed with strong moral and political didacticism.[34] James VI and I requested an English translation of this work from the original Latin and translations were also made into French, Spanish, Italian, Dutch, Polish, Hungarian, and Icelandic. In Scotland, copies of *Argenis* were to be found in the libraries of the Marquis of Montrose, Archbishop Robert Leighton, and Bishop Henry Scougal.[35]

The literary question of what essentially distinguishes a novel from earlier forms of prose fiction, such as the romance, remains contentious. Despite the apparently unanimous acceptance of *Aretina* as 'the first Scottish novel', in my opinion it remains essentially a romance with a significant historical component. It is 'romantic' in being primarily a prolonged and episodic story of adventure, set in a remote and exotic location in an idealised and distant past. Moreover, it follows the fate of a set of aristocratic heroes who exist in a world where virtue consistently triumphs. The third book is arguably more 'novelistic', since it takes as its provenance a more recent, unheroic and national setting where Mackenzie provides a detailed account of political machinations where virtue and good are often seen to count for little.

III

In Mackenzie's *Aretina*, the main plot of the 'romance' revolves around the Sidneian theme of the successive fates and fortunes of a quartet of lovers: especially the pursuit of the eponymous Aretina by Philarites, intertwined with the simultaneous wooing of Agapeta by Megistus. However, Book Three is entirely devoted to a retrospective digression by Megistus who recounts then political machinations of two particular nations as observed during his previous travels. In this way, it offers a thinly disguised representation of political events in both Scotland and England from around 1603 to 1660.

By way of an extremely brief outline of *Aretina's* plot: Megistus and Philarites first encounter Aretina and her companion, Agapeta, at Monanthropus' country-house in Egypt. Book Two sees the action shift to the Egyptian city of Alexandria where romantic pursuits continue against a backdrop of internal political disputes in Egypt, further complicated by external military attacks on the Egyptians by Persian forces.[36] The subject matter of the third book is considered in detail below. Although of most contemporary historical interest, the stylistic nature of the book sits incongruously with the rest of the work. Not one of the protagonists, including the reputed heroine, Aretina, is mentioned in this part. The fourth and final book returns to recounting the vicissitudes of fate that continue to plague Mackenzie's heroes. After a dramatic abduction, the romance apparently comes to an abrupt end, only to be continued with a hasty postscript added by Mackenzie. This second conclusion is equally unsatisfactory, resembling the more violent excesses of French romances with the florid narrative describing rapid series of violent events.

Aretina begins in *medias res* with Monanthropus, recently Chancellor of Egypt, having retired to his country house. Descriptions of country residences later became a favourite theme of Augustan poetry, and during the 1660s Mackenzie also drafted *Caelia's Country-House and Closet*, which remains the only country-house poem published in seventeenth-century Scotland.[37] Throughout *Aretina*, the attraction of the Horatian retirement topos is a recurrent leitmotif, echoing English Royalist garden literature of the 1640s and 1650s. The latter had been characterised by a philosophy of virtue in adversity and the maintenance of tranquillity, wisdom, and self-sufficiency amidst political mael-strom.[38] In Book Four of *Aretina*, the merits of this contemplative life are extolled to Philarites by a recluse who declares 'happy he who impales himself within the circuit of a Country cottage', since

a Country-man, may under the shade of some great Oak,
or upon the brink of some murmuring River, tast as much
pleasure, in invisaging or viewing his own contemplated
happiness, as a Courtier can in eying the real objects
of Court delights.[39]

Strongly pastoral, the initial setting of *Aretina* resembles that of Sales' *Theophania* (1655) in which a nobleman, Synesius, withdraws from the confusion of the English Civil War to his country estate. In articulating such themes, Mackenzie was also inspired by continental traditions. In the mid-sixteenth century, neostoics such as Guillaume de Vair and Justus Lipsius had advocated virtuous retirement as the morally superior alternative amid the wholesale destruction of the European Wars of Religion. Such ideas appeared in Barclay's *Argenis* when the reigning monarch, Anaerestus, relinquishes his crown, proclaiming that 'to neglect Riches; to refuse Honours, to free the mind from the disquiet of wordly cares', should be deemed 'indeed an act of perfect virtue'.[40]

Aretina's narrative is frequently interrupted by the interpolation of sundry discourses on various moral paradoxes, apparently original, in a style foreshadowing that of La Rochefoucauld's *Maximes* (1665) and Mandeville's *Fable of the Bees* (1712). Discussions among the characters form interjected essays on polite behaviour and specific moral dilemmas, such as the greater virtue of love or courage. During the 1660s, Mackenzie composed a number of Senecan-style essays on moral philosophy including *A Moral Paradox Maintaining that it is much easier to be Virtuous than Viscious (1667)*. The appearance of an earlier work, *A Moral Essay Preferring Solitude to Publick Employment* (1665), provoked the English diarist, John Evelyn, to counter in 1667 with *Public Employment, and an Active Life, preferred to Solitude...In Reply to a late Ingenious Essay of a Contrary Title*. As the English poet, Abraham Cowley informed Evelyn, his debate with Mackenzie was indeed 'one of the noblest controversies between ancient and modern'.[41] The inherently paradoxical nature of this debate becomes evident on a brief reflection of the subsequently notorious public career adopted by Mackenzie, compared to Evelyn's deliberate retreat from public attention.

Throughout *Aretina*, scattered comic diversions prevent the prevailing tone from becoming too didactic, despite the work's claim to be 'A Serious Romance'. Mackenzie's quick and acerbic wit appears through the continual inclusion of humorous and satirical apophthegms throughout his romance, presaging the terse and often witty style which characterises his Restoration memoirs. Mackenzie's facility to compose in elegant English prose rivals his characteristic eloquence in Latin. The humanist desire to express ideas attractively remained a life-long concern. As he argued in *What Eloquence is Fit for the Bar* (1681), 'where Statesmen endeavour to reclaim a mutinous Multitude; there, Eloquence is not only allowable but necessary'.[42]

The encoded history of the Civil Wars provided in the third book of *Aretina* offers a colourful accompaniment to Mackenzie's own political *Memoirs of the Affairs of Scotland from the Accession of Charles II*, published posthumously in 1822.[43] In both fiction and historical writing, the desire to write of one's own times became a distinguishing characteristic of the seventeenth century, as exemplified by William Camden, the Earl of Clarendon, and Gilbert Burnet.[44] At one juncture in *Aretina*, Mackenzie admires the inspirational military command of 'Oranthus' (the Marquis of Montrose) who confidently assures his troops that 'what we do with our swords, shall be done over again by the pens of learned Historians'.[45]

IV

Book Three of Mackenzie's *Aretina* begins with an account of Lacedemon (England) and Athens (Scotland), described as two countries formerly 'enemies as vindictive as old', but recently brought together by dynastic union.[46] In a similar manner to Gilbert Burnet's later accounts of English and Scottish politics in his *History of His Own Times*, Mackenzie devotes approximately equal attention to considering the complex political history of both 'Lacedemon' and 'Athens'. At the outset, Mackenzie discusses at length the teething problems which Sophus (James VI and I) encounters on acceding to the Lacedemonian throne, thus suggesting that it was collective failure to resolve such tensions that explained the subsequent outbreak of war within both kingdoms. In taking his history back to 1603, Mackenzie's account of the origins of the Scottish Revolution contrasts with that of other contemporaries. Sir James Balfour, for instance, identified the year 1633 as 'the fontaine and spring from quhence all the succiding grate alterations, both of church and stait, did seim to flow'.[47]

According to Mackenzie's analysis, the major reason for the increasing political instability and dissension was the increasingly profligate and parasitic court. In the form of an early 'Court-Country' debate, Mackenzie criticises the misgovernment of rural estates by an absentee *rentier* nobility who were increasingly spending at Court in luxury, rather than at home in hospitality. Consequently, 'the mony which the poor country men buy with their sweat, must be sold for silks and spices', hence 'we must give forreigners things that are necessary, returning nothing but what is superfluous'.[48]

Such attacks on Court luxury were a familiar theme in seventeenth-century Scots literature inspiring, for example, the celebration of provincialism found in William Lithgow's poetry of the 1630s.[49]

Aware that 'nobles are the moths that consume the Nation',[50] the potential problems of absentee monarchy are made explicit to Sophus when he is informed that Athens in particular is 'naturally factious, as being commanded by Nobles, who have the Commons fully at their devotion'. This tendency is exacerbated by the fact that 'your absence feeds this humour in them'.[51]

In Lacedemon, Sophus's expensive habit of indulging personal favourites is severely censured, ensuring that his reign contrats unfavourably with previous Lacedemonian kings whose 'treasuries [have] often grown fatter, whereas yours become daily more lean'.[52] To remedy this situation, Mackenzie's courtiers counsel traditional Spartan moralism observing that

> those Nations flourish best, and conquer most, whose
> subjects are poorest, and whose treasures are fullest,
> the riches of subjects occasioning their luxury, and
> their luxury kindling a war.[53]

A range of specific solutions is promulgated, such as the increasing of Crown rents, the reducing of the number of official 'money-suckers', the payming of regular proportional salaries to tax-collectors and establishing of a state budget to reduce corruption.[54] Despite the otherwise passive tone putatively adopted by Megistus throughout the third book, Mackenzie's own interest is evident when he unintentionally slips into the first person, claiming that 'I prefer either of these wayes, to that which hath been formerly practised by the Lacedemonian Senate': allowing members of Parliament to distribute revenues which usually renders King and Parliament 'implacable enemies'.[55]

Mackenzie never considers ideas of closer union between Lacedemon and Athens when he relates the various political projects entertained by Sophus. Mackenzie himself remained resolutely opposed to such ideas, dismissing as quixotic arguments mooted in the early 1670s that Anglo-Scottish union would yield economic prosperity for Scotland. For 'though we carry our Money to *England*, it is for spices, silks and other Commodities', which Mackenzie contends, 'we may not only want, but likewise we are the worse for having.[56]

In his later *Memoirs*, Mackenzie consistently defended the workings of Stuart multiple monarchy, for, 'whilst the kingdoms stood divided, his Majesty had two Parliaments whereof the one might always be exemplary to the other'.[57] Likewise, in *Aretina* he contrasts their different methods of political representation: the Lacedemonian Senate being described as 'composed ordinarily of the wittiest and turbulentest persons in the Nation', unlike the predominantly aristocratic nature of Athenian politics.[58] To diffuse this situation, Sophus favours reforms ensuring the election of genuinely local representatives, each of whom 'might understand best the necessities of his Town, and would nible lesse at the Royal Prerogative', instead of electing nominated magnates and lawyers who 'dipped too much in what belonged to the King, and too little in what concerned the place represented by them'.[59]

In reading *Aretina*, it is indeed sometimes difficult to remember that Mackenzie later became castigated in popular memory as 'the servile tool of a profilgate court',[60] or as one who exemplified subservience to 'a state which maintained regal union through despotic rule'.[61] Describing debates in the Lacedemonian Senate, Mackenzie champions the rights of representative institutions: as one member proclaims, 'how necessary must Freedom be to Subjects, seing without it they are slaves rather than subjects'. Moreover,

> of all the liberty which subjects can contend for, that
> of debating freely before any Taxation or Law be
> statuted (which is our case) is the most considerable.[62]

Maintaining the distinction between the office of monarchy and the personal conduct of the individual who occupies the post, Mackenzie accepts that a king 'may prove a Tyrant, for goodnesse was never entailed uninterruptedly upon any one succession'.[63] The subjects' safety thus lies in preserving a free Parliament, since if monarchs are allowed to over-rule free debate, political leaders become 'like Wine which cannot rellish well when the spirits are once extracted'.[64]

As an elected shire commissioner in the Scottish Parliament, Mackenzie represented Ross-shire from 1669 to 1674, before his appointment as Lord Advocate in 1677.[65] In Parliament, Mackenzie adhered to the principles noted above; his early opposition to Lauderdale frequently involved issues affecting the welfare of his constituents, such as the calling of free elections in the burghs or opposing the imposition of various taxes.[66] However, the increasingly polarised and dangerous nature of Restoration politics from the mid-1670s was to shift Mackenzie to a more unequivocally absolutist position. By 1684, Mackenzie's attitude towards parliamentary privileges had become strongly dismissive. In Mackenzie's own words, 'why should we oppress our Kings, and raise Civil Wars…if parliaments be such ridiculous things as we cannot trust when they are impowered by us?[67]

Similarly, although he still accepted that 'a mixt Monarchy may seem a plausible thing to Metaphysical Spirits and School-men', yet 'to such as understand Government, and the World, it cannot but appear impracticable'.[68]

Historiographically, religious factors have been consistently perceived as crucial in explaining Scotland's troubles, since religion provided the sole legitimating pretext for political resistance. By contrast, Mackenzie's version of events in *Aretina* is markedly *politique* in its primary concern with the preservation of the commonwealth rather than with the defence of religious purity. In Mackenzie's casuistical opinion, 'such a crime as treason would seem horrid, if it were not palliated by imaginary Religion'. For this reason,

> Religions have been at first hatch't, meerly to tame
> wild humours, which albeit they have been known to
> their first founders to be the product of their own
> brains, yet have thereafter been by their posterity
> imbraced as sacred truths.[69]

Again slipping into the first person, he attacks notions that implicit faith should oblige men 'to believe what Ecclesiasticks say' as well as ministerial claims that 'we ought not to confine Religion within the narrow bounds of Reason'.[70] Church-State controversies, such as the restitution of former church lands, led Mackenzie to contend that 'providence and policy differ only as do two words' and men adopt such pretexts 'pretending Religion, and intending gain'.[71] This interpretation echoes that of the contemporary English prelate, Peter Heylyn, who alleged that in Scotland, 'though *Liturgy* and *Episcopacy* were made the *occasions*, yet they were not the causes of this Warre'. According to Heylyn, religion was instead only the 'vizard to disguise that business, which Covetousness, Sacriledge and Rapine had the greatest hand in'.[72]

Mackenzie's intense hatred of extreme fanaticism engendered a religious scepticism and adiaphorism which he went on to develop in his *Religio Stoici* of 1663.[73] Paradoxically for one later remembered as the bigoted and 'bluidy' Advocate, his *Religio Stoici* denounced scholastic and dogmatic intolerance over external church forms, emphasising instead the importance of personal religion. Such latitudinarian themes subsequently characterised the works of Restoration Scottish Episcopalians such as Robert Leighton and Henry Scougal. Serving a predominantly Presbyterian population, the ecclesiastical moderation of Scottish Episcopalian apologists contrasts with the more aggressively theocratic ideology articulated by their Anglican counterparts south of the border.[74]

The inflated and erroneous political and religious aspirations which consequently arose among the Lacedemonian and Athenian citizens in *Aretina* ensured that 'Loyalty was now accounted slavery, and the meanest act of jurisdiction tyranny'.[75] Politically subversive forces were unleashed by a dissatisfied minority who did 'by the pestiferous breath of their treasonable discourses, infect others'.[76] As Mackenzie ominously observed,

> when anything falls to pieces, it is surely near ruine;
> and when a Nation doth by faction become two, it will
> probably at last become none at all.[77]

Mackenzie's *politique* account of personal weaknesses, factional rivalries and fiscal shortages ultimately differs from Argyll's recorded impression that 'seditions and Civil Wars begin often from light Occasions from which no man would think could come to such an Issue'.[78]

V

As the two countries punge into war, Mackenzie's account of subsequent events becomes a maze of individual vignettes. Although his narrative contains several chronological discrepancies, such as the execution of Oranthus (the Marquis of Montrose) occurring before that of Anaxagius (Charles I), the creative nature of allegory is such that historical accuracy should not perhaps always be taken as the author's prime objective. It is also worth remembering that Mackenzie was only about two years of age when the National Covenant of 1638 was formed and that he was abroad for much of the 1650s. Emanating from the Royalist Mackenzie of Seaforth dynasty, he unsurprisingly focuses his narrative on the fate of the successive monarchs: Sophus, Anaxagius and Theopemptus (Charles II), as well as upon the 'elephantine virtue' of Royalists such as Oranthus.[79] Less attention is consequently paid to explaining the ways in which Scotland became a conquered province of England in 1651, remaining under military occupation until 1660.

In explaining the early successes of the English parliamentary forces, the strength of the Lacedemonian capital is perceived as crucial. Although England had only one-fifth of the inhabitants of France, London was nevertheless the largest city in Europe. Thus for Mackenzie, a 'cardinal error in *Anaxagius* [Charles I] was that...he relinquished the City [London]'.[80] Initial military successes enjoyed by the Lacedemonian Senate were largely due to their having 'the City at their devotion' who 'doted the Army with all privileges imaginable'.[81] Within a European context, Mackenzie relates how the Lacedemonian Senate 'treated with another Commonwealth of *Corinth* [Holland] to send them Arms, promsing they should have liberty of fishing in their Seas, without any toll'.[82] Royalist difficulties were further compounded by the fact that 'it was advantageous for *Egypt* [France] to see *Lacedemon* in such a hubbub',[83] since the Egyptian king (Louis XIII) was the brother of the Lacedemonian Queen (Henrietta Maria), which involved financing the expensive amity of Sophander (Cardinal Mazarin).

In Mackenzie's narrative, the efficient military organisation of the Lacedemonian Senate contrasts strongly with the haphazard nature of affairs in Athens. There, Mackenzie focuses upon the power struggle which evolved between Phanosebus (Marquis of Argyll) and Autophilus

(Duke of Hamilton): 'two twins strugling in the womb of the Common-wealth, [who] tortured vehemently their miserable mother'.[84] Clarendonian in his analysis, Mackenzie explains Athenian political events principally in terms of this internecine factional rivalry. For instance, regarding the compromise 'Engagement' forced between the Autophilist faction and Anaxagius, the opposition of Phanosebus is solely grounded on factional rivalry and the seeming advantage it accorded to Autophilus. No consideration is conceded to the considerable military risks involved.

Interesting historical contingencies as well as unproveable anecdotes can be found within Mackenzie's account. Included in his narrative is a version of the visit to Edinburgh by Autarchus (Oliver Cromwell) in October 1648 after the Royalist annihilation at the Battle of Preston. The nature of the treaty subsequently agreed by Phanosebus and Autarchus was such that '*Autophilus* who was then a prisoner in *Lacedemon*, should be beheaded; and that *Phanosebus*, in requital of this, should destroy all who opposed the Lacedemonian Senate in *Athens*'.[85] The accusation that Argyll's perfidious machinations caused the death of Hamilton by the debarring of the Engagers is unsupported by current historical evidence.[86]

The fragile alliance between Autarchus and Phanosebus is soon shattered by hostile Athenian reaction to the execution of Anaxagius in Lacedemon. Mackenzie elaborately describes events of 30 January 1649: 'that fatall day wherein wickedness was to show to the world its masterpiece'.[87] The lengthy Thucydidean oration that Mackenzie has Anaxagius deliver on the scaffold contains many of the Royalist shibboleths found in Charles I's *Eikon Basilike* (1649). The tone of the condemned monarch is defensive, for the constitutionally dependent nature of the Lacedemonian Senate underscores the illegality of their actions. Those who claimed to judge him 'had either no power; else if they had any, they derived it from me'. Likewise, 'if they condemned me as members of the Lacedemonian Senate', then 'they derived their authority from me: who only did establish it'.[88]

Passionately patriarchal, Anaxagius denies the practical effective-ness of the Senate's actions, for 'how can these love one other mens children who have murdered their own father?' Moreover, 'how can they fear murder who are guilty of parricide?[89]

With a degree of comfortable hindsight on Mackenzie's part, Anaxagius concludes by prophesying that Lacedemon would indeed soon 'judge it expedient to call home its Banished Prince'.[90]

Describing the Interregnum, Mackenzie concentrates on relating how Autarchus 'endeavours to retain by cheats, that power which he had gotten by force', illustrating the illegal means by which 'he who had been in appearance so much an enemy to Arbitrary Government... became an affecter of it in his own'.[91] In describing how Cromwell 'resolved to moddel such an Ecclesiastick Government, as might be wholly subordinate to the Civil,'[92] a degree of covert admiration can perhaps be discerned, considering Mackenzie's subsequent opinion of the Restoration episcopate in Scotland. As he recorded approvingly in his *Memoirs*, following the re-establishment of Episcopacy in 1662, royal power 'was as absolute here as could be desir'd'. Moreover, the royal supremacy was

> ...now equal or greater to that which Henry VIII took
> in England, but [which] was resum'd by the Parliament in
> the reign of Queen Elizabeth, as inconsistent with the
> liberties of England.[93]

In the midst of this state-building Autarchus dies: 'the most hatefull Tyrant who ever lived'.[94] The successful military activities of Monus (General Monck) in Athens are endorsed by the Lacedemonian Senate who confirm the absolute nature of the restored monarchy and jettison all notions of limited monarchy. For, quite possibly, such 'conditions would have been by the next ensuing Senate, declared Treason, and the Treators declared Traitors'.[95] Despite Mackenzie's inclusion of the spontaneous rejoicings which greeted the restoration of Theopemptus (Charles II) across Scotland, memories of the recent revolution render the preservation of peace and tranquillity the chief political priority for the future. Caution, rather than triumphalism, characterises Mackenzie's narrative and Theopemptus is informed in strongly Machiavellian terms that henceforth, 'as to war against neighbouring States, and such like martial imployments; they are not necessary, but [only] as they defend Justice'.[96]

VI

A unique piece of mid-seventeenth century Scottish prose, Mackenzie's *Aretina* colourfully discredits claims that contemporary literary activity was moribund. As the first native account of political events to appear, Mackenzie's romance evinces youthful audacity and imaginative political engagement. Despite its Royalist bias, much of Mackenzie's allegory is nonetheless couched in a powerful 'country' critique of the Stuart court. Although a highly political interpretation, moral pride of place is not given to court affairs, controlled by 'State-mountebanks'.[97] For an author who was presumably seeking legal and political preferment there is surprisingly little 'confected with the sugar of flattery' as Mackenzie puts it.[98] His disdainful contempt for high politics appears in such observations as 'if men took as much pains to gain favour in Heaven, as they do to ingratiat themselves at Court', Mackenzie contends, 'they could not miss to be canonized as the most eminent in the Kalendar of Saints'.[99]

The next two centuries were to see a steady sophistication of all forms of prose fiction. The historical novels of Sir Walter Scott represent examples of perhaps the most self-conscious and deft manipulation of the relationship between fiction and history. It is thus perhaps ironic and fitting that many of the negative popular perceptions of Mackenzie bequeathed to posterity were derived from the vivid portrayals of 'the bluidy Advocate Mackenzie' by both Scott and Robert Louis Stevenson.

The legacy of the Civil War shaped not only the nature of Mackenzie's mature writings, but also his subsequent embrace of an active political career. Paradoxically for one who had extolled the virtues of retirement, Mackenzie became one of the most public and enthusiastic participants in the Restoration period.

He was perhaps also aware of the dictum of another Continental neostoic, Michel Montaigne, that the 'only good histories are those written by such as commanded or were employed in weighty affairs'.[100] Mackenzie's subsequent career enabled him to boast in the preface to his Restoration *Memoirs* that 'no man hath writ an history who knew more intimately the designs, and observ'd more narrowly all the circumstances of those actions he sets down'.[101] By the end of the 1660s, he had self-consciously decided to 'leave off to write, that I may begin to act virtuously',[102] ironically confriming Argyll's belief that ''tis Business and action that strengthens the Brain, while Contemplation weakens it'.[103]

NOTES

1. I would like to thank John Cairns, Mark Goldie, Jonathan Scott, and Margaret Storrie for their comments and suggestions on an earlier draft of this paper. The cited references demonstrate the benefit I have derived from the work of other scholars. As Mackenzie himself wrote in the preface to *Aretina*, 'he who writes now should read what hath been written formerly; not to the intent that he might borrow, but least he should borrow anything that is theirs', (Sir George Mackenzie, 'Preface' to *Aretina, or The Serious Romance*, [London, 1661], 8).

2. The only full-length biography of Mackenzie at present is Andrew Lang's *Sir George Mackenzie of Rosehaugh, King's Advocate (? 1636–91): His Life and Times* (London, 1909). For Mackenzie's works, see F S Ferguson, 'A

Bibliography of the Works of Sir George Mackenzie, Lord Advocate, Founder of the Advocates' Library', *Edinburgh Bibliographical Society Transactions*, I, (1936), 1–60. Also of interest is T I Rae, 'The Origins of the Advocates' Library', in *For the Encouragement of Learning: Scotland's National Library 1689–1989*, P Cadell and A Matheson (eds), (Edinburgh, 1989), 1–22.

3. Mackenzie may have been only twenty-two. See Lang, *Mackenzie*, 22, for the possible confusion over the date of Mackenzie's birth.

4. Mackenzie, Preface to 'Pleadings in Some Remarkable Cases', in *The Works of that Eminent and Noble Lawyer, Sir George Mackenzie of Rosehaugh*, T Ruddiman (ed), two volumes, (Edinburgh, 1718–22), II, 10.

5. J Sutherland, *English Literature of the Later Seventeenth Century* (Oxford, 1969), 205.

6. Ferguson, 'Bibliography', 11. Only eight copies of *Aretina* are now to be found; one each in the National Library of Scotland, Edinburgh Public Library, the Bodleian Library, and the British Library, with four copies in the United States of America. Perhaps because of its unfinished state, *Aretina* was not included in the two volumes of Mackenzie's collected works, edited by the Jacobite antiquary, Thomas Ruddiman, published in 1718 and 1722 (see footnote 4 above). All quotations cited in this paper refer to the Bodleian Library copy of *Aretina* (London, 1661). This is the edition published by Ralph Smith.

7. M R G Spiller, 'The First Scots Novel: Sir George Mackenzie's *Aretina* (1660)', *Scottish Literary Journal*, Supplement, 11, (1979), 1–20. Where *Aretina* is mentioned by other commentators the bibliographical details alone are frequently inaccurate. For instance, Annabel Patterson refers to 'Sir James Mackenzie's *Aretina* of 1668' in *Censorship and Interpretation: The Conditions of Writing in Early Modern England*, (Madison, 1984), 199.

8. See, for example, K Sharpe, *Criticism and Complement: The politics of literature in the England of Charles I*, (Cambridge, 1987) and D Hirst, 'The Politics of Literature in the English Republic', *The Seventeenth Century*, 5, (1990), 133–155.

9. D Reid, *The Party-Coloured Mind* (Edinburgh, 1982), 1. See also D Reid, 'Prose after Knox', in *The History of Scottish Literature Volume 1: Origins to 1660*, R S Jack (ed), (Aberdeen, 1988). 183–197. As Jack commented on page 9 in the Introduction to the above volume, 'Where on earth is Scottish prose fiction? Where, above all, is the Prose Romance?'.

10. Cf P Salzman, *English Prose Fiction 1558–1700: A Critical History* (Oxford, 1985).

11. Cf R Strong, *Van Dyck: Charles I on Horseback* (London, 1972).

12. Mackenzie, 'Great Gloucester's Cipress-bearse, wreathed by a Loyal hand' and 'A poem by the same author, upon His Majesty's royal Return', in *Aretina*, 12–14.

13. The preface to *Aretina* is discussed in C Davies, *Prefaces to Four Seventeenth-Century Romances* (Los Angeles, 1953).

14. Mackenzie, 'Preface' to *Aretina*, 6.

15. E A Baker, *The History of the English Novel*, ten volumes, (New York, 1963), II, chapter two.

16. W Raleigh, *The English Novel* (London, 1904), 96–99.

17. [R Boyle], *Parthenissa*, Part One, (London, 1655), Av.

18. [Sir P Herbert], *The Princess Cloria: or, The Royal Romance* (London, 1661), Av.

19. Quoted by R Macgillivray, *Restoration Historians and the Civil War* (The Hague, 1974), 26.

20. Mackenzie, 'Preface' to *Aretina*, 7.

21. Idem.

22. Idem.

23. Idem.

24. Quoted by Patterson, *Censorship and Interpretation*, 196.

25. Cf T DiPiero, *Dangerous Truths and Criminal Passions: The Evolution of the French Novel 1569–1791* (Stanford, 1992) and M Mueller, *Les Idées Politiques dans les Romans Heroiques de 1630 à 1670* (Harvard, 1984).

26. Quoted by L Davis, *Factual Fictions: The Origins of the English Novel* (New York, 1983), 36–37.

27. Mackenzie, 'Preface' to *Aretina*, 7–8.

28. Mackenzie, *Aretina*, 'Dedication to all the Ladies of the Nation'.

29. Ibid, 34.

30. P Salzman, '*The Princess Cloria* and the Political Romance in the 1650s: Royalist Propaganda in the Interregnum', *Southern Review* (Adelaide), 14, (1981), 236–246.

31. [Sir W. Sales] *Theophania, or severall Modern Histories represented by way of Romance and politckly discours'd upon* (London, 1655); Cf A H Shearer, '*Theophania*: An English Political Romance of the Seventeenth Century', *Modern Language Notes*, XXXI (1916), 65–74.

32. R Braithwait, *Panthaliats, or the Royal Romance* (London, 1659); Cf B Boyce, 'History and Fiction in *Panthalia: Or the Royal Romance*', *Journal of English and Germanic Philology*, 57, (1958), 477–491.

33. Montelion, [pseudonym], *Don Juan Lamberto* (London, 1661). Salzman has argued that more allegorical romances were likely to have been written, quoiting a letter of Dorothy Osburne in which she notes, 'My Lord Saye, I am tolde has writ a Romance…and Mr Waller they say is making one of our Warrs'; Salzman, '*The Princess Cloria*', 237.

34. Cf G Langford, 'John Barclay's *Argenis*: A Seminal Novel', *University of Texas Studies in English*, 1947, 59–76 and J Ijsewijn, 'John Barclay his Argenis: A Scottish Neo-Latin Novelist', *Humanistica Lovaniensa: Journal of Neo-Latin Studies*, 32, (1983), 1–27.

35. M C T Simpson, 'The Library of the Reverend James Nairn 1628–1678: Scholarly Book-Collecting in Restoration Scotland', (University of Edinburgh, PhD thesis, 1987), 248; E J Cowan, *Montrose: For Covenant and King* (London, 1977), 14.

36. Spiller has suggested that parts of Book Two are loosely allegorical, recording events in mid-seventeenth century France ('The First Scots Novel', 18).

37. Mackenzie, *Works*, I, 3–17. Cf M R G Spiller, 'The Country-House Poem in Scotland: Sir George Mackenzie's *Caelia's Country-House and Closet*', *Studies in Scottish Literature*, 11, (1974), 110–130.

38. For Royalist literature, see R A Anselment, *Royalist Resolve: Patient Fortitude in the English Civil War* (London, 1988); M Butler, *Theatre and Crisis 1632–1642* (Cambridge, 1984); T N Corns, *Uncloistered Virtue: English Political Literature 1640–1660* (Oxford, 1992); L Potter, *Secret Rites and Secret Writing: Royalist Literature 1641–1660* (Cambridge, 1989).

39. Mackenzie, *Aretina*, 260.

40. [J Barclay], *John Barclay His Argenis, Translated out of Latine into English, by Sir Robert Le Grys Knight* (London, 1628), p. 454.

41. Quoted by B Vickers, *Public and Private Life in the Seventeenth Century: The Mackenzie-Evelyn Debate* (New York, 1986), xii.

42. Mackenzie, 'What Eloquence is Fit for the Bar', in *Works*, I, 12.

43. Mackenzie, *Memoirs of the Affairs of Scotland from the Accession of Charles II ADMDCLX*, T Thomson (ed), (Edinburgh, 1822).

44. Cf Macgillivray, *Restoration Historians*.

45. Mackenzie, *Aretina*, 260.

46. Ibid, 216.

47. Sir J Balfour, *Historical Works*, four volumes, (Edinburgh, 1825), II, 205. Mackenzie's willingness to attribute part of the blame for the troubles to James VI and I, instead of exclusively on the personal misrule of his son, correlates with recent historiographical opinion: cf K M Brown, 'Aristocratic Finances and the Origins of the Scottish Revolution', *EHR*, (1989), 46–87.

48. Mackenzie, *Aretina*, 224.

49. Cf *The Poetical Remains of William Lithgow 1618–1660*, J Maidment (ed), (Edinburgh, 1863).

50. Mackenzie, *Aretina*, 223.

51. Ibid, 230.

52. Ibid, 223. Mackenzie perhaps makes this reference to 'kings' of England

gender-specific to avoid discussion of the fragile Elizabethan financial inheritance bequeathed to James.

53. Ibid, 238.

54. Ibid, 241.

55. Ibid, 242.

56. Mackenzie, 'A Discourse concerning the Three Unions 'twixt *Scotland* and *England*', in *Works*, II, 648.

57. Mackenzie, *Memoirs*, 138.

58. Mackenzie, *Aretina*, 219.

59. Idem.

60. D Irving, *Lives of Scottish Writers*, two volumes, (Edinburgh, 1834), I, 86.

61. I B Cowan, 'Anglo-Scottish Relations', *HJ*, 32, (1989), 231.

62. Mackenzie, *Aretina*, 249.

63. Ibid, 250.

64. Idem.

65. *The Parliaments of Scotland. Burgh and Shire Commissioners*, M Young (ed), two volumes, (Edinburgh, 1992–93), volume two, 458–459.

66. Lang, *Mackenzie*, 94.

67. Mackenzie, *Jus Regium, or the Just and Solid Foundations of Monarchy*, (Edinburgh, 1684), 8.

68. Ibid, 42.

69. Mackenzie, *Aretina*, 243.

70. Ibid, 244.

71. Ibid, 244–245.

72. Quoted by Macgillivray, *Restoration Historians*, 41.

73. Mackenzie, *Religio Stoici* (Edinburgh, 1663).

74. Cf M Goldie, 'The Theory of Religious Intolerance in Restoration England', in *From Persecution to Toleration*, O Grell, J Israel and N Tyacke (eds), (Oxford, 1991), 331–368.

75. Mackenzie, *Aretina*, 252.

76. Ibid, 248.

77. Ibid, 254.

78. [A Campbell], *Instructions to a Son, by Archibald, late marquis of Argyle* (London, 1661), 124.

79. Mackenzie, Aretina, 258.

80   Ibid, 275.

81. Ibid, 278.

82. Ibid, 277.

83. Idem.

84. Ibid, 255.

85. Ibid, 292–293.

86. Spiller, 'The First Scots Novel', 14–15. Spiller surmises that Mackenzie either had hearsay information or access to a hitherto unknown section of Sir Archibald Johnston of Wariston's diary since Johnston was another participant in the negotiations.

87. Mackenzie, *Aretina*, 294.

88. Ibid, 297.

89. Ibid, 299.

90. Idem.

91. Ibid, 317.

92. Idem.

93. Mackenzie, *Memoirs*, 4.

94. Mackenzie, *Aretina*, 322.

95. Ibid, 330–331.

96. Ibid, 339–340.

97. Ibid, 405.

98. Ibid, 33.

99. Ibid, 402–403.

100. Quoted by D Allan, *Virtue, Learning and the Scottish Enlightenment: Ideas of Scholarship in Early Modern History*, (Edinburgh, 1993), 12.

101. Mackenzie, *Memoirs*, 4.

102. Mackenzie, 'A Moral Paradox Maintaining that it is much easier to be Virtuous than Viscious' in *Works*, I, 135.

103. Argyll, *Instructions*, 139.

Index